TRANSITIONS

Sophie Watson

TRANSITIONS

New Australian feminisms

Edited by
Barbara Caine and Rosemary Pringle

ALLEN & UNWIN

First published 1995
Allen & Unwin Pty Ltd
9 Atchison Street, St Leonards, NSW 2065 Australia

National Library of Australia
Cataloguing-in-Publication entry:

Transitions: new Australian feminisms.

  Includes index.
  ISBN 1 86373 776 6.

  1. Feminism—Australia. I. Caine, Barbara.
  II. Pringle, Rosemary.

305.40994

Set in 10/12 pt Times by DOCUPRO, Sydney
Printed by Kim Hup Lee Printing, Singapore

10 9 8 7 6 5 4 3 2 1

Contents

Contributors

Ien Ang is Senior Lecturer in the School of Humanities at Murdoch University, where she teaches in the Communication Studies program. She was educated at the University of Amsterdam, where she taught until 1990 and was involved in numerous women's studies and feminist theory initiatives. She is the author of *Watching Dallas: Soap Opera and the Melodramatic Imagination* and *Desperately Seeking the Audience*.

Barbara Caine is Associate Professor of History and Director of Women's Studies at the University of Sydney. She will take up a Chair of History at Monash University in mid–1995. Her publications include *Destined to be Wives: The Sisters of Beatrice Webb* and *Victorian Feminists*. She is currently working on a history of English feminism.

Julie Ewington was trained as an art historian and taught in Australian universities and art schools for many years. She is a critic, broadcaster and curator, currently Curator, Museum Education, at the Museum of Contemporary Art, Sydney. In the 1970s and '80s she was involved in the Women's Art Movement, Adelaide, and in campaigns for the equal representation of women artists.

Anna Gibbs teaches writing and textual theory at the University of Western Sydney, Nepean. Her current writing aims to transgress the boundaries between fiction and academic genres.

J. K. Gibson-Graham is the product of two personae, that of Katherine Gibson, who is Director of the Centre for Women's Studies and Senior Lecturer in the Department of Geography and Environmental Science at Monash University, and that of Julie Graham, who is Associate Professor in the Department of Geology and Geography at the University of Massachusetts. These two industrial and feminist geographers have been working with each other for seventeen years since they were graduate students together.

Sally Macarthur was Music Officer with the chamber music organisation Musica Viva Australia from 1990–92, and has lectured at the Sydney Conservatorium and at Sydney University, where she is completing a PhD. In 1994 she was appointed Lecturer in Comparative Musicology at the University of Western Sydney. She is joint editor with Marianne Helm of *New Music Australia* and with Susan Erickson of *Sounds Australian: The Woman's Issue*.

Jill Julius Matthews is Senior Lecturer in the Women's Studies program, Faculty of Arts, at the Australian National University. She is the author of *Good and Mad Women: The Historical Construction of Femininity in Australia*, and of a number of articles dealing primarily with issues of power, sexuality and femininity in Australia. She is currently completing *Melting Moments: Moments of Women's Pleasure in the 1920s and 1930s*, and several books deriving from her convenorship of the 1993 Humanities Research Centre's annual theme, 'Sexualities and culture'.

Rosemary Pringle was Associate Professor of Sociology and Chair of the Women's Studies Committee at Macquarie University while the book was being prepared, but is now Professor of Women's Studies at Griffith University. She is co-author of *Gender at Work* and author of *Secretaries Talk: Sexuality, Power and Work* and numerous papers on gender and sexuality, women and occupations, feminist theory and the state. She is currently working on a book about women in medicine.

Susan Sheridan teaches Women's Studies at Flinders University, and is currently engaged in research projects on the *Australian Women's Weekly* and a history of women's writing in Australia. She is the author of *Christina Stead*, editor of *Grafts: Feminist Cultural Criticism*, and co-editor of *Debutante Nation: Feminism Contests the 1890s*. Her latest book is a study of Australian women writers' uses of the discourses of sex, nation and race in their fiction and journalism.

Zoë Sofia (Sofoulis), formerly of Murdoch University, is a senior lecturer in feminist theory and cultural studies in the School of Humanities and Social Sciences at the University of Western Sydney, Nepean. Her interest in psychoanalytic approaches to technological issues dates from her work as an ecofeminist activist in the 1970s. She has recently begun working on applications of psychoanalysis and the philosophy of technology to gender issues in computer education (*Whose Second*

Self) in collaboration with computer graphics and performance artist Virginia Barratt. She is researching a book on Australian women electronic artists titled *Double Agents*.

Barbara Sullivan is presently a postdoctoral fellow in the Political Science program at the Research School of Social Sciences, Australian National University. She is writing a book about Australian politics and the sex industry.

Catherine Waldby has worked in various areas of feminist research since 1984. She has published in a number of journals and anthologies on questions of sexuality, biomedical representations of HIV/AIDS, and feminist and social theory. She is currently completing a PhD thesis on 'AIDS and the idea of the body politic' in the Women's Studies program at Murdoch University.

Sophie Watson is Professor of Urban and Regional Planning at the University of Sydney and previously taught social policy at the University of Bristol. She is well known for her work on women and housing and has recently, with Catherine Gibson, edited two collections on postmodern cities following on from a conference of that name in 1993. She is also the author of *Playing the State* and *Accommodating Inequality*.

Elizabeth Wilson teaches in the Psychology Department at the University of Sydney. She has recently completed a PhD on cognition, deconstruction and sexual difference.

Anna Yeatman is Professor of Sociology at Macquarie University, having previously been Foundation Professor of Women's Studies at the University of Waikato. She is the author of *Bureaucrats, Technocrats, Femocrats* and *Postmodern Revisionings of the Political*, and co-editor (with Sneja Gunew) of *Feminism and the Politics of Difference*. She is currently co-editing with Margaret Wilson a New Zealand collection, *Justice, Biculturalism and Difference* and preparing *Feminist Theory* for the University of Melbourne Press.

Introduction

Barbara Caine and Rosemary Pringle

Designing a new anthology of Australian feminist essays is an exciting but not a simple task. Feminist theory and women's studies have developed so rapidly in the past decade that while new areas abound, partial coverage and major exclusions are inevitable. This collection offers an introduction to some new directions in current Australian feminist scholarship while in no way pretending to be comprehensive.

The current moment within feminism is very much a reflective one, and many of the pieces presented here involve a rethinking of previous positions and approaches. In the process, almost every category of feminist theory has been problematised or deconstructed. This process of rethinking is not an easy or comfortable one—and indeed, this volume contributes to the sense that the categories we use to understand the world are unstable, constantly shifting under us like a continuous earthquake. In this collection, the meanings of 'feminism', 'oppression' and 'patriarchy'—all central concepts of feminist thought and politics for the last couple of decades—are questioned and even rejected by some writers. Since the category of 'woman' has also been questioned for some time now (Riley 1988) the meaning of 'women's studies' itself has to be reconsidered. We are in the strange position of offering an introductory text to a subject whose very existence is being challenged and redefined.

'Feminism' itself, as Barbara Caine points out, does not have a solid cumulative core, a great tradition on which later generations draw, but rather has been characterised by a series of new starts as each generation redefines its key projects, sometimes in opposition to the definitions of earlier generations. The diversity, and even contradictions, evident in the ideas and politics that have been included under the label feminist serves to demonstrate the shifting and unstable meaning of the term.

The changes in feminist ideas and approaches are taken up by Catherine Waldby, who addresses epistemological and methodological questions, rethinking earlier feminist approaches to knowledge and power. These general methodological essays are counterpointed by those of Sally Macarthur and Elizabeth Wilson, both of whom ask feminist questions of specific disciplines. Macarthur looks at the ways in which the once completely masculine musical canon and the apparently neutral discipline of musicology are slowly beginning to respond to questions not only about gender but about the importance of embodiment in both the composition and the analysis of music. Wilson looks at the problems which have been faced by those seeking to expand psychology to include women, even within a feminist framework, and argues that the feminist project in psychology needs rather to devote itself to deconstructing the discipline.

Questions about power are raised throughout the volume, along with new questions about what constitutes resistance. Some of the new understandings of power are well conveyed by Elizabeth Grosz's suggestion that power can be thought of as running around and through us, like honey, in various degrees of fluidity and sticky congealment.[1] This raises major questions not only about our understanding of feminism but about our political possibilities. The fundamental question is whether it is still meaningful to target particular institutions and practices as major sites of oppression. Barbara Sullivan's reflections on prostitution raise this issue in regard to the sex industry while at the same time problematising feminist stances which have tended to be critical of prostitutes.

The question of rethinking is also pursued here by the social scientists, particularly in terms of the implications of poststructuralist ideas for empirical studies. The need to recognise the problems involved in universal claims is emphasised by Anna Yeatman in her analysis of the category of 'oppression' and its meaning and in her insistence on the importance of context for understanding gender, class and race relationships. J. K. Gibson-Graham reconsiders women in mining communities, long treated as either socialist heroines or failed revolutionaries, and finds that instead of inhabiting a world structured by capitalism and patriarchy, where they are inevitably bound to failure, they live out multiple subjectivities.

The importance of texts, and the implications of recognising that all our organising concepts are discursively constructed, is raised particularly by Rosemary Pringle and Sophie Watson. In a world of texts where even the social is recognised to be discursively constructed, Pringle asks whether it is still useful to invoke the notion of 'patriarchy'. She notes the variety of ways it has been used in feminist discourses and wonders whether it has not become a barrier rather than an aid to understanding institutions or professions on the one hand, and women's capacity for agency on the other. Sophie Watson takes a similar approach to the concept of 'need', which, though it has been central to feminist demands on the state, has generally been left unexamined. It has been treated as standing outside of discourse, as having a real existence to be identified and measured, rather than as something which plays a major part in any feminist strategy.

This concern about texts and discursive construction is elaborated and expanded in many of the other essays in the collection, pointing to the importance of cultural studies in contemporary feminism. Susan Sheridan provides an overview of current theoretical approaches to cultural studies and then applies them to her reading of one of our great female icons, *The Australian Women's Weekly*. This approach allows her to show how complex a task reading the *Weekly* is for contemporary feminists—who want neither to reject it nor to celebrate it uncritically, but to recognise its importance both personally and culturally.

The question of how women themselves deal with, negotiate and subvert gendered assumptions both about cultural meanings and about creativity is dealt with by Anna Gibbs in her analysis of the many ways in which Gertrude Stein plays with conventions of autobiography in *The Autobiography of Alice B. Toklas*. By not writing her own autobiography, Stein avoids the confessional mode, while managing at the same time to stake her own claim to genius.

Many of the essays in this collection take for granted that this is a postmodern age, and several of them focus on the difficult concept of modernity. This is a key concept in discussions of twentieth-century women but one which also lacks a solid, fixed existence; seeming rather to involve a chimerical collection of changing ideas and practices. What 'modernity' is and was is a recurrent theme in the book. Jill Matthews, Anna Gibbs and Susan Sheridan examine different aspects of its construction and explore in very different ways some of the possibilities and problems it has created for women.

The essays in this collection range across women's studies as a disciplinary, an interdisciplinary and a transdisciplinary enterprise, showing in the process the multiple meanings and locations of women's studies. Different and even conflicting approaches and interpretations run through the volume, centring on the conflict between those concerned with deconstructing terms, including that of 'women', and those concerned with explicating the meanings of the various representations of women's lives and experience. These differences in approach reflect some major underlying debates which threaten to set up a new binary division between feminist theory and women's studies. For some, women's studies has outlived its usefulness: it may have played an important role over the last three decades in putting women back into their disciplines, but it has not succeeded in challenging the main disciplinary paradigms. For some, the challenge continues to be that of deconstructing the patriarchal symbolic, while others are more concerned to extend feminist approaches to technology on the one hand, and to cultural studies on the other.

As editors, we are seeking to encourage debate while maintaining 'women's studies' as the broad field in which these issues are worked through. We need a women's studies that actively questions its own boundaries and approaches as well as challenging the paradigms and knowledges of specific disciplines. At times we have been stunned by the disagreements and tensions involved in different approaches to feminism and to women's studies, at how little they seemed to share. But looking at the final drafts, we believe that the essays show how very productive this cross-disciplinary interaction has been.

We all had the opportunity to talk to each other and to a wider audience when earlier drafts of the papers were presented at an ANU Humanities Research Centre summer school in February 1994. We would like to thank Graeme Clark and the staff at the centre for enabling this to happen. The conflicting ideas about and approaches to both feminist theory and women's studies were initially taken up there and this has allowed for a careful reworking of each paper. Discussion at the summer school made it clear that there are communication difficulties across different disciplines and approaches. Some of these centred on the use of concepts. 'Deconstruction', for example, is used very precisely in philosophy and in literary studies to refer to a Derridean project, while in the social sciences it is used more loosely to refer to the unpacking and questioning of concepts. Poststructuralism has many meanings.

Some of the time, it has seemed to us that women's studies, which regularly complains about the hierarchy of the disciplines which exclude it, is in danger of setting up a hierarchy of its own, with philosophy at the top acting as the gatekeeper for what is regarded as important. Discussion at the summer school focused on this: How far does the practice of 'feminist theory' require a close reading of Nietzsche, Deleuze or Derrida? Is anything more being asked here than an earlier generation expected in relation to Marx or Freud? What is the relation between pure and applied theory? Is it always necessary to go back to the original or is that fundamentalist? If texts play such a powerful role in constructing our world, how do we choose which texts to prioritise? Is it possible to draw on and apply previous feminist work on, say, Foucault or Nietzsche?

Perhaps the one thing we agreed on was the rapidity of change and the need to respond to these changes in the way we think about gender and power (or, as some prefer to call them, sex/sexual difference and violence). In a variety of contexts writers are grappling with the question of whether 'postculturalism' marks a retreat, a denial of the 'structures' which still oppress women. The deconstructionists are grappling with the structures of the symbolic, which are less amenable to change, while those operating in a post-Marxist terrain (Gibson-Graham, Pringle, Watson) see the destabilisation of social structures (whether intellectually or in the 'real' world) as potentially liberating, allowing change to happen in the here and now without waiting for revolution. Lurking here is the question of how far equal opportunity and affirmative action programs have brought 'real' change. While these questions are usually discussed in terms of the general workforce, Julie Ewington carries them into the world of the visual arts. She plays with the multiple meanings of representation, and tracks not only the ways in which it has been useful and helpful to call for equal representation, but also the limits of that call and the new questions it has opened up.

This is very much a collection centring on the humanities and social sciences. As a result, this volume does not provide a comprehensive coverage of contemporary Australian feminist scholarship. Many questions of great importance within feminism and women's studies have been omitted. We do not address environmentalism, eco-feminism, or reproductive technologies, nor do we deal with contemporary feminist legal theory or with the physical or natural sciences. This is not to say that we are uninterested in these areas; rather, we recognise that the field of feminist scholarship and women's studies is far too large and diverse for any one volume to even attempt to include it all.

At the same time, we do think this collection gives a very clear idea of what is increasingly coming to be recognised internationally as 'new Australian feminism', which by Michelle Barrett says is characterised by its 'sympathetic combination of some aspects of psychoanalytic theory (predominantly Lacanian) and a theory of social signification (Barthes, with a "cultural studies" inflection)' (Barrett 1988:xxix). This volume shows also the growing influence of Deleuze and Derrida and the constant development and change which makes this such an exciting and important field.

1

Women's studies, feminist traditions and the problem of history*

Barbara Caine

The current moment in feminist thought and scholarship is very much one of reflection and revision, as ideas, beliefs and approaches which were accepted orthodoxies even a few years ago are subjected to critical analysis and discussion. New approaches to reading, especially the idea of reading against the grain, along with the many forms of deconstruction which are associated with poststructuralism, have provided a variety of critical vantage points from which to reconsider not only accepted deas about the nature of women's oppression, but also the very categories of 'women' and 'oppression' (see Chapter 4).

I want to extend this critical revision to feminism itself and more particularly to the history of feminism, in order to contrast current concerns about stressing the multiplicity of feminisms with an earlier sense of feminism as both a more limited and in some sense an exclusionary term. I want to suggest that there is perhaps some merit in limiting the term and its claims. At the same time, I want to consider the ways in which contemporary interest in multiple readings and in resistance offers new ways of looking at a feminist past. My material is drawn mainly from English feminism, but the general argument applies equally to Australia, Europe and the United States.

In the past decade or so, the meaning of the term 'feminism' and the need to recognise the existence of many different feminisms have become the subject of intensive discussion within the general field of women's studies. This discussion has focused primarily on the question of difference, as the need both to recognise the ways in which ethnicity, socioeconomic position, religion and sexuality differentiate and divide women, and to give different groups of women an adequate voice, has

* I would like to thank Elizabeth Grosz and Rosemary Pringle for their comments on earlier versions of this paper.

become a major theoretical and political concern of feminist scholarship.

For many contemporary scholars, the central issue in this debate is the need to interrogate or reject any essential idea of 'women' as the basis of feminism. Denise Riley has explored the changing and unstable meanings of the term 'women' within feminism over many decades (Riley 1988: 67–95), and other theorists have argued that it is not only possible but positively advantageous to feminism to be freed from any essential notion of women and of a female identity. Judith Butler, for example, argues that the inability of feminists to totalise or summarise 'women' and the constant rifts over the meaning of the term ought to be safeguarded and prized, 'confirmed as the ungrounded ground of feminist theory' (Butler 1992: 16).

While it is acutely aware of the instability of meaning attached to the category 'women', much of the current discussion about feminism seems implicitly to contrast contemporary concerns relating to difference and the existence of many feminisms with earlier periods in which the meaning of the term 'feminism' was stable and uncontested. Historians of feminism, on the other hand, might prefer to suggest that the meaning of 'feminism' is as unstable as that of 'women', having been fiercely contested since its introduction a century ago, and that it too requires investigation.

Indeed, from an historical perspective, the most noticeable feature of the extensive contemporary discussion about the meaning of the term 'women' and about the need to establish a form of feminism which does not require any specific sense of female identity has been the insistence on retaining the term 'feminism' regardless of the ever-increasing range of scholarly approaches and political commitments to which it might refer. Even a very brief survey of the recent history of 'feminism' reveals both how central the term is in current politics and scholarship dealing with gender and women's oppression and how new its widespread acceptance is. By contrast, even the 1970s generation, which was most active in the women's movement and in establishing women's studies, had profound difficulties with the term and often sought to reject it.

The meaning of 'feminism' has, in fact, been fiercely contested ever since the term was introduced in the mid-1890s. The early debate on this issue is all the more interesting because of its focus not only on what feminism meant, but on whether the term was useful: whether it served to assist consideration of women's oppression or to designate contrasting approaches to the emancipation of women.

Just as the meaning of feminism is constantly contested, so too is the nature of feminism's history. Interest in this field is increasing rapidly among historians and literary scholars, but so is debate over its borders, subject matter and central concerns (Offen 1988: 119–157; Cott 1987). These questions are made more difficult and more urgent because any attempt to survey the history of feminism, either within one country or internationally, needs to come to terms with internal disagreement, fragmentation, and rupture. Ironically, histories of feminism thus accord well with the current historiographical emphasis on discontinuity. At the same time, however, historians have to recognise that the frequent rejection of the term 'feminism'—and of any sense of connection with earlier feminists—by women who have embraced the notion of female emancipation indicates that women often find it hard to establish trans-generational links or to set themselves up as legitimating or authoritative figures for each other or for future generations.

The historiography of feminism is hampered by this lack of a functioning feminist tradition. Most forms of political and social thought, and their accompanying political and social reform movements including liberalism and socialism, have developed around certain dominating and legitimating figures and texts, and their ideas and beliefs have been transmitted from one generation to the next (Caine 1994: 25–44). Feminism, by contrast, has never had such a tradition: few of those who have protested about women's oppression in any given generation have known about predecessors—and even those who did rarely acknowledged them.

In some respects, one can trace this lack of tradition to the very oppression and subordination about which feminists were protesting. As women, feminists have lacked the financial and institutional resources to establish schools of thought or formal ways of transmitting their ideas. Because few either received inheritances of any size or were able to earn the sums required to establish colleges or even journals, feminism lacked the institutional framework which allowed groups like the early political economists or the philosophical radicals to become powerful and influential. Even in the mid-nineteenth and early twentieth centuries, when there was an organised women's movement, financing journals—like financing women's colleges—was a major problem.

More significantly, feminist writers, activists and theorists have lacked the power and prestige which would induce members of later generations to seek connection with them to enhance their own status. The differences between feminism and other major late eighteenth- and early nineteenth-century social, political and philosophical movements, like that of political economy, are instructive here. Few nineteenth-century political economists ever wrote without invoking the Great Tradition stretching through Adam Smith and Ricardo to John Stuart Mill. By contrast, although Mary Wollstonecraft was widely recognised even in the nineteenth century as 'the founding figure' of Anglo-American feminism, she was rarely written about. Very few nineteenth-century feminists demonstrated a sense of connection with her (McGuinn 1978: 188–205). Whereas the prominent male philosophers and ideologues of her day were constantly discussed and referred to by those who knew about them and their ideas, Wollstonecraft was not.

As is so often the case in women's history, this silence requires careful interpretation (Allen 1987). While the lack of detailed discussion of Wollstonecraft might suggest that she was unknown, the form of the few references to her which do survive suggest rather that she was carefully and consciously avoided. On those few occasions when she was referred to, she was simultaneously acknowledged and rejected. Thus, for example, the prominent feminist Harriet Martineau, writing in the 1830s and '40s, recognised Wollstonecraft's role as the pioneer feminist—and in the same sentence repudiated her. Martineau was not, she insisted in her autobiography, in any way influenced by Wollstonecraft. On the contrary, she regarded her as unfit to champion her sex. 'Mary Wollstonecraft was, with all her powers, a poor victim of passion, with no control over her own peace, and no calmness or content except when the needs of her individual nature were satisfied' (Martineau 1788: 399–400).

Martineau's disparagement of Wollstonecraft suggests that her main concern was not with Wollstonecraft's writings but rather with her life. In finding Wollstonecraft's conduct not only reprehensible but damaging for feminism, Martineau was reflecting a common contemporary view. Wollstonecraft's *A Vindication of the Rights of Woman* was quite well received by progressive groups when it was first published in 1792. But her reputation was destroyed shortly after her death in 1796, when her distraught husband, William Godwin, published his *Memoirs of the Author of A Vindication of the Rights of Woman* and laid bare her private life. In this work, Godwin stressed her emotional nature and experiences, detailing her attachment to the painter Henry Fuseli and her affair with an American adventurer, Gilbert Imlay, in the course of which she had a child, and after which she twice attempted suicide. He also made clear the unconventional nature of his relationship with Wollstonecraft. They had married only when she was already pregnant and even then the couple had retained separate homes to ensure their independence. Godwin's book triggered widespread condemnation of Wollstonecraft, especially by social and political conservatives who were delighted to be able to point to the unhappy consequences of her unconventional life and her rejection of women's traditional sphere.

While the claim to a connection with Adam Smith or Malthus or Mill automatically conferred legitimacy and importance on male writers, Wollstonecraft lacked the capacity to confer legitimacy on her followers. Whereas questions of private morality had no effect on the public reputation of men, for a woman the merest hint of immorality was enough to erase recognition of her writings. Thus Victorian feminists could continue their adulation of John Stuart Mill despite the fact that he lived with the woman he loved, Harriet Taylor, for some years before he was able to marry her. But they could not contemplate the public acknowledgment of Wollstonecraft.

Although Wollstonecraft was not able to found a tradition and was largely absent from public feminist discussion and debate, privately she seems to have been powerfully present in the feminist imaginary. The first periodical of the English women's movement, *The English Woman's Journal*, for example, never published a single discussion of Wollstonecraft. In 1858, however, its editor, Bessie Parkes, wrote to her close friend and fellow feminist activist Barbara Bodichon to say that she had received a letter from Mary Shelley, who she was surprised to learn was still alive. She described her simply as '*Mary*'s daughter, *his* wife', as if Wollstonecraft's first name alone sufficed to identify her—and as if she was frequently discussed by the two women.[1] Their public silence and private interest add to the impression that knowledge of the details of her personal life was widespread. Indeed, it would not be an exaggeration to say that although Mary Wollstonecraft was not publicly referred to, she haunted nineteenth-century feminism, as a shadowy and disreputable presence powerfully suggesting the close connection between personal and sexual revolt and feminist commitment—a connection which most nineteenth-century feminists sought to deny. While no Victorian feminist would claim direct connection with Wollstonecraft, nineteenth-century feminism is in many ways incomprehensible without her. Indeed, especially in the mid-nineteenth century—when feminism was attempting most strongly to maintain its respectability—there was a marked similarity in the rhythm of discussion of Wollstonecraft, on the one hand, and problems of sexual morality and behaviour, on the other. Somehow Wollstonecraft seemed to come up or be indirectly referred to whenever an issue of sexual mores or conduct arose. Thus while Wollstonecraft did not found a tradition, she functioned as a powerful symbol of the sexually subversive nature of feminism and of the connection between personal rebellion against the oppression of women and the demand for women's rights.

Ironically, the first broad revival of interest in Wollstonecraft occurred in the 1880s and '90s, when changing ideas about sexual morality enabled a number of writers to show her life as a justifiable rejection of convention and a tragic struggle for freedom and authenticity of feeling—and when the term 'feminism' was first introduced. But although the term's introduction suggests the emergence of a coherent identity and outlook, in fact it arose at a time of extensive and divisive debate about the meaning of women's emancipation and the nature and identities of the women for whom emancipation was sought.

Nancy Cott has explored in detail the introduction and adoption of the term 'feminism' in the United States, in the period around 1911–12. She describes how it was embraced particularly by young and progressive intellectuals and college graduates, who welcomed it as a sign of their modernism and their revolt against formalism: it was a way of indicating their intention to transform ideas of femininity by rejecting the notion of womanly submission and nurturance and demanding not only an end to discrimination, but also the sexual and social freedom which would allow them to live their lives to the full (Cott 1987: 37–41).

Cott stresses the ways in which feminism served both to broaden and to question the suffrage campaign, with its stress on personal life and sexual freedom rather than on political rights based on a notion of womanly duty. But the contrast between these two terms sees to me to warrant more attention than she gives them, pointing as they do to a major underlying conflict which became more and more important in women's movements in the early twentieth century.

This is particularly so in England. There, as in the United States, the introduction of the term 'feminism' was a very significant development, suggesting a shift beyond concerns about women's rights towards questions of private life and identity, on the one hand, and cultural ideas and values on the other. But while the introduction of the term apparently brought to the fore a new sense of a feminist identity, there was no unanimity as to what that identity was. On the contrary, the term 'feminist', like its contemporary 'new woman', signalled the breakdown of a consensus about the nature of womanhood which allowed for an unprecedented range and diversity of views, not only about feminism's strategies and goals, but about who women were and what their emancipation meant (Caine 1992: 239–67). The enormous energy that went into defining and debating the meaning of the terms 'new woman', 'feminist', and 'suffragette' during the 1890s and the early twentieth century served not so much to centralise feminist ideas as to exhibit their range, diversity and complexity.

In view of the central place which the militant suffragettes hold in the contemporary feminist imaginary, it is surprising that many of those who first described themselves as feminists sought in so doing to distinguish and differentiate themselves from the suffragettes. The writer Cicely Hamilton, for example, one of the first to label herself a feminist, explained that her 'personal revolt was feminist rather than suffragist; what I rebelled at chiefly was the dependence implied in the idea of "destined" marriage, "destined" motherhood—the identification of success with marriage, of failure with spinsterhood, the artificial concentration of the hopes of girlhood on sexual attraction and maternity'. (Hamilton 1935: 65). Like Dora Marsden, she contrasted herself with the suffragettes, whose primary concern, in her view, was with the external and public world of national politics rather than with the familial and domestic world which circumscribed the lives of women. Indeed, she went so far as to argue that the suffragettes were not part of the wider feminist movement because they 'merely ask for a trifling political adjustment—the vote! rather than fighting for the full humanity and the economic, social and sexual freedom of women' (Marsden 1912: 285).

This question of the suffragettes' position in relation to the general history of feminism is a very important one—and one which serves well to highlight the complexities of both feminist traditions and the politics of naming as it concerns women's emancipation. For many, the idea of feminism has little meaning unless one includes the suffragettes. Their actions, as many historians have argued, served to dramatise both the brutality and the fundamentally sexual nature of male domination— and the complex ways in which women could resist it. Martha Vicinus has shown how militancy offered women a new kind of freedom and expression—and the capacity to engage in suffering and self-sacrifice of a potentially transforming kind (Vicinus 1985).

The tactic of the hunger strike, originated not by the Pankhursts but spontaneously by a number of their followers, provides one of our primary images of the 'meaning' of the suffrage movement—and endows that movement with a complex series of associations with women's vulnerability, purity, spirituality and self-denial which contrast starkly with both institutional and individual masculine violence and power (Tickner 1987: 100–104). There is also a continuing fascination with the suffragettes, particularly the charismatic Emmeline and

Christabel Pankhurst, and with their capacity to represent sexual oppression in such powerful ways as to show that the fight against masculine privilege might be a fight to the death (Holton 1990: 7–32).

For all this, it remains significant that the Pankhursts and the suffragettes never referred to themselves as feminists, choosing rather to appropriate the term first applied to them flippantly in *The Daily Mail*. Perhaps they hoped that their militant campaigning would defeat this attempt to diminish their importance by reworking the term's meaning. What was important for them was the novelty of the word suffragette and the fact that it, like the word 'militant', served to differentiate them from the more moderate suffrage campaign begun in the later nineteenth century by the moderate and 'constitutionalist' group, the National Union of Women's Suffrage Societies. Far from seeking any connection with earlier fighters for women's emancipation, the suffragettes sought to show that they were a powerful new group, unhampered by earlier traditions or by ideas about how women should campaign. They saw the struggles of the nineteenth-century women's movement for better education, legal reform of marriage and political rights not as integrally connected with their own struggle—which they saw as new and radical—but rather as a kind of prehistory.

Just as the suffragettes rejected any connection with nineteenth-century feminism because in their view it had failed to obtain its own objectives, in time they and their campaigns were also rejected. In the inter-war period, the term feminism had wide currency among those actively engaged in the women's movement, one of its advantages being that it allowed them to differentiate themselves from the suffragettes. The model of the suffrage movement, with its insistence on the need to concentrate women's energies on the single objective of the vote, was seen as inappropriate for a movement which was attempting to come to terms with the many different interests and concerns that had become evident once women were enfranchised. 'Feminism' was deemed by many an appropriate term to cover this range of different interests, but a series of adjectives were added to indicate different feminist approaches. The relationship between the immediate concerns of contemporary feminists and those of their predecessors also became a major subject of debate at this time, as feminists argued whether they should continue the earlier demands for equal rights and equal participation in social and political institutions (designated 'old feminism') or whether new concerns which faced women as citizens should take precedence ('new feminism') (Alberti 1992).

In the 1920s, then, the term 'feminism' was widely used within the women's movement but it was used in extraordinarily diverse ways.

Morever, as happened earlier in regard to the suffragettes, the term was used by some whose views seem problematic to later feminists and rejected by others who are today regarded as major feminist theorists. Dora Russell, for example, used the term constantly in her battle for freer sexual relations and for the provision of birth control information and advice. For Russell, 'the important task of modern feminism is to accept and proclaim sex; to bury for ever the lie that has too long corrupted our society—the lie that the body is a hindrance to the mind'. Russell offered lyrical praises of human sexuality, demanding total rejection of marriage in its existing form and its replacement by freer sexual union. In her view, it was marriage which brought inequality into the relations between men and women, by structuring those relations in a particular and hierarchical way. This belief that marriage was at the root of women's oppression was certainly not a new one in English feminism, nor was the advocacy of alternative forms of personal and sexual relations. What Russell added was an emphasis drawn from the writings of sexologists on the importance of (hetero)sexual activity for women. Like many others who shared her concern about birth control at the time, she came close to arguing that only those women engaged in active heterosexual relations had the balance and maturity required to be full citizens. Russell tied her belief in sexual freedom to a powerful advocacy of the ideas of those sexologists and sex reformers who were engaged in a bitter war against single women, celibacy, and women's relationships with each other (Russell 1925: 24–25).

While Russell claimed the term—and used it to cover ideas and beliefs which are reprehensible to many contemporary feminists—it was rejected by Virginia Woolf, the woman whom many feminists now, as in the 1920s and '30s, see as the most important feminist theorist of the early twentieth century. Woolf saw more clearly than anyone else the difficult political issues involved in using the term feminism at that time. She commented on the term and discussed it, raising a number of questions about both its utility and the reasons why it aroused such extraordinary hostility.

Woolf discussed the term 'feminism' and its importance in *A Room of One's Own,* where she sought to account for the intense and irrational anger triggered by any kind of derogatory or critical remark women made about men, and for the use of 'feminist' as a term of complete and even contemptuous dismissal. Deliberately invoking a psychoanalytic framework, Woolf argued that feminist comments and criticisms threatened the very basis of patriarchal power. For the patriarch, 'who has to conquer, who has to rule', could only do so secure in his own belief in himself and his abilities—beliefs which were buttressed by the knowledge that at least half the members of the human race were inferior to him. The role of women within this patriarchal framework was to serve 'as looking-glasses possessing the magic and delicious power of reflecting the figure of man at twice its natural size'. Feminism threatened this by telling the truth about men, and hence brought upon itself the angry cry of wounded vanity (Woolf 1928: 37).

This recognition of the hostility visited upon women like Rebecca West who declared their feminist convictions helps perhaps to explain why Woolf, in *Three Guineas,* rejected the term despite her detailed knowledge of the history of feminism and the women's movement and her extensive organisational and personal feminist connections (Woolf 1938: 184). *Three Guineas* is an extremely complex text, and Woolf's strategy in it warrants careful analysis. Anna Gibbs's reading of *The Autobiography of Alice B. Toklas* by Gertrude Stein (Chapter 10) demonstrates how Stein's rejection of the traditional form and authority of autobiography 'enables a critique of the implicit assumptions of the genre of autobiography and allows for new possibilities in feminine discourse'. In a similar way, one might argue that Woolf's savage comments about the corruption and uselessness of the term 'feminism' and her suggestion that it has served its turn and should now be burnt (Woolf 1938: 117) allow her greater scope to make her critique of the male-dominated society in which she lived—and of the simultaneous oppression and exploitation of women within it. Thus she criticises not only male economic, educational and political privilege, but also the insistence by several prominent men that women have a special duty to carry out the program those men deem desirable, especially in regard to the promotion of pacifism. Woolf insists that the only way women can counter the urge to war which seems to be inherent in so many educational and social institutions is by maintaining their financial independence and hence being able to reject men's demands—thereby endorsing the ultimate feminist program of the time. Her suggestion that the term feminism be burnt—appearing as it does in a passage that connects the struggle of twentieth-century women with that of their nineteenth-century forebears like Josephine Butler—may be intended ironically, an interpretation strengthened by her comment that some words cannot be burnt because they are not yet obsolete: 'Tyrant, Dictator, for example' (Woolf 1938: 118). Woolf's disassociation of herself from feminism may thus be seen as allowing her much greater freedom both to endorse feminist ideals and to criticise masculine privilege and behaviour than she would have had if she had taken an obviously and avowedly feminist stance.

Nonetheless, her discussion of the term indicates a distinct unease with the women's movement. Following on from her arguments in *A Room of One's Own* about women's exclusion from educational and cultural institutions, from material prosperity and indeed from cultural self-representation or expression, Woolf elaborated, in *Three Guineas*, her idea of women as constituting a 'society of outsiders' who cannot see or participate in political and professional institutions as men do (1938: 5–20). Whereas earlier feminists had complained about the ways in which masculinism entailed the sexual subordination of women, Woolf looked at it rather in relation to the professions and social and political institutions. She satirised masculine rituals and behaviours, making a connection between the love of professional costumes, such as legal robes, and the uniforms beloved of soldiers—and fascists. Women, in her view, were not able to participate in such institutions and rituals—nor should they. On the contrary, Woolf insisted that women's marginality was valuable because it gave them 'freedom from unreal loyalties' such as patriotism and nationalism. But her position bore little relationship to the one then prevailing within a women's movement preoccupied with winning access for women to all social, political and economic insitutions (Middleton 1982: 407). Thus Woolf's rejection of the term feminism also accorded with her disagreements with her feminist contemporaries and allowed her to position herself outside the movement while remaining connected with it.

Woolf's ambivalence about the term 'feminism' was shared by many of the most active members of the Women's Liberation Movement in the 1970s. Many of these women made a determined and concerted rejection of the term 'feminist', seeking to differentiate their own revolutionary energies and enthusiasm from the cautious and pragmatic approach of a number of staid and reformist groups which had continued, throughout and after the Second World War, to designate themselves 'feminist'. In seeking to emphasise its concern with political and sexual radicalism, and with a complete social transformation, the Women's Liberation Movement sought to distinguish itself from earlier 'bourgeois' feminists who had sought to improve the status of women within an existing social and political framework. For many in the early 1970s, the term 'feminist' suggested a connection with a despised reformist tradition, limited in its aims and conservative in its demeanour.

This rejection of the term 'feminism' and of any sense of connection with the earlier reformist politics associated with it pointed to some of the contradictory impulses and concerns of the early 1970s. The Women's Liberation Movement, and especially its academic wing, which began demanding 'women's studies', criticised the phallocentric nature of existing academic disciplines and their exclusion of women either as subjects or objects of investigation. History was the subject of particular criticism, which was accompanied by demands for a new field, women's history, to deal with the ways in which women had participated in and contributed to social, economic and political developments. This demand went along with a stringent criticism both of the existing histories of women and a rejection of any approach which stressed the activities and achievements of women in politics, who were regarded as atypical and hence as uninteresting. This rejection included a strong attack on earlier feminists, many of whom were seen as socially privileged, politically conservative and as having little of interest to offer a new generation. Thus the demand for women's history went along with an explicit rejection of any existing feminist tradition.

This hostility to past feminists changed within quite a short time: as the major, even revolutionary, changes sought by the Women's Liberation Movement failed to bring about the immediate transformation of society, some of the impatience with earlier endeavours gave way to a new recognition of the difficulties earlier women had faced in demanding their own emancipation. At the same time, dislike of the label 'feminist' faded and, without any particular fanfare, those concerned about women's liberation came to adopt the older term. Indeed, the term 'women's liberation' has now been almost entirely superseded by a broader use of the term 'feminism'—and many of those who rejected the label most fiercely twenty years ago now accept the designation 'second wave feminists' without demur.

Just as the introduction of the term 'feminist' in the 1890s was accompanied by increasing divisions among those concerned to bring about the emancipation of women, so too its adoption in the 1970s went along with both a new sense of feminist identity and a new range of divisions in the women's movement. In the 1970s, as in the 1920s, feminism came increasingly to be used with qualifiers to indicate the particular kind of feminism referred to. In the 1970s, the two main contending groups were socialist feminists and radical feminists. While 'socialist feminists' sought to indicate their commitment to economic and social transformation and to socialist political objectives, 'radical feminists' tended rather to argue that sexual oppression was the primary and universal form of oppression and that left-wing and socialist parties or groups were themselves implicated in women's oppression. This division between feminists was a major focus of debate and tension throughout most of the 1970s and '80s. It clearly signalled a shift in feminists' focus away from distinguishing themselves from an older and more moderate generation and towards their own immediate political context. This particular division more or less came to an end in the late 1980s, as both socialist and radical feminism gave way to new forms of cultural feminism which developed under the influence of poststructuralist and postmodernist thought (Pringle 1988: 25–31). The very meaning of women's oppression and of feminist politics came to be debated and redefined under the impact of ideas derived from psychoanalysis and the works of Michel Foucault and, as we have seen, as feminists influenced by deconstructionist approaches began to question the very meaning of the term 'woman'. The use of qualifiers is still evident, especially in regard to 'liberal feminism' (see Chapter 2), but increasingly the term is used undefined and unqualified—and with an emphasis on its diversities of meaning and its capacity to encompass multiple approaches, forms of politics and groups of women.

Reflections on the history of feminism emphasise the novelty of the current situation. In contrast to the present project of inclusion, debates about the meaning of feminism over most of the past century have tended to involve efforts at exclusion: at establishing a true feminism in contrast to positions and forms of politics which were deemed (by some who called themselves 'feminists') to be non-feminist. This exclusivism is clearly problematic at a time when feminist scholarship is so concerned to deconstruct rigid notions of truth and to break down the disciplines which foster them. But the emphasis on particular meanings of feminism in the past also served to make feminism a partial and specific project in ways that prevented the kind of violence Ien Ang (Chapter 5) sees as accompanying contemporary attempts to structure the differences among women in ways that allow for some ultimate harmony in the goals of all.

In a similar way, one could argue that conflicts over the meaning and usage of the term 'feminism' demonstrate the marginality of women and their inability to function as legitimating figures for each other. On the other hand, marginality itself confers freedoms and possibilities for reworking the past in accordance with contemporary needs. The history of feminism suggests the need for a new approach to the whole question of traditions which allows recognition of powerful, almost hidden figures like Wollstonecraft as well as well-known and oft-invoked ones like Mill. This approach allows a recognition of the subversive and destabilising implications of feminism which have always made it discomforting.

This sense of the historical complexity of 'feminism' leads one both to celebrate and to question the ease with which the term is used today. Clearly, expanding the framework of feminism to encompass difference and diversity is one of the biggest challenges we face. But one cannot but ask whether, if it sits so easily within contemporary political, scholarly, and disciplinary frameworks, feminism can remain an oppositional discourse—and conclude that the very concept needs to be under challenge, if it is to have any radical potential.

2
Feminism and method
Catherine Waldby

Feminism has entered the academy on the basis that knowledge is not the learned reflection of the world but rather shapes the world in particular ways, for particular interests. Knowledge production occurs within the context of particular kinds of social power relationships, and the question 'whose knowledge, for what purpose' is a crucial one for feminism. Specifically, feminism understands orthodox forms of knowledge production, forms that faithfully observe the distinctions between the academic disciplines and the demands of objectivity, to be deeply implicated in the maintenance of women's social disadvantage. The historical masculine prerogative over academic knowledge production has, it argues, ensured that the forms of knowledge most established in the university extend masculine experience and interests, and work to silence and pathologise feminine points of view.

So feminism has come to contest this prerogative, to find ways to make knowledge which allow and extend feminine experiences and points of view. The elaboration of kinds of academic knowledge which are sympathetic to feminist interests is understood to be an essential strategy in the more general feminist project to secure more social power for women in all spheres of life. Such elaboration gives feminism the means to contest not just the practices of everyday life which disadvantage women, but also the knowledges which inform these practices and which often work to make women's disadvantage seem 'natural' and inevitable, even to women themselves.

This contestation of knowledges has proved to be a more complex matter than it first appears. It raises a series of difficult and shifting questions about relationships between sexed experience and point of view on the one hand, and the forms of academic knowledge on the other. It would be possible, it seems to me, to write a history of feminist methodologies in terms of successive approaches to these questions.

The most straightforward approach to such contestation, one which was common among feminist scholars during the 1970s and is still current in some fields, is a simple reversal. If academic knowledge has until now authorised itself through the exclusion and devaluing of women's experience, then accounts of this experience must be introduced into the disciplines in order to make them pay proper attention to women. This approach suggests that feminist method is primarily archival or fieldwork oriented; the task of feminist scholarship is the uncovering and valorisation of previously devalued historical and oral accounts of women's lives. This is the approach which motivates the historical component of Anne Summers' *Damned Whores and God's Police* and Diane Bell's anthropological study of Aboriginal women's ritual, *Daughters of the Dreaming*, for example. Both works set out to make up a deficiency in the historical and anthropological accounts respectively of Australian society by providing accounts of feminine activity that had been previously ignored.

While it has produced some valuable research and made some important early incursions into what counts as significant social activity, this approach has nevertheless proved inadequate to the task of transforming existing power relationships between feminine experience and masculine knowledge. Accounts of women's experience have been readily accommodated as the claims of a 'special interest group', without disrupting the university disciplines' valorisation of masculine activity as universally significant.

The inadequacy of this strategy derives from two assumptions which have proved increasingly untenable. First it assumes that experience, particularly women's experience of oppression, is radically distinct from academic, disciplinary knowledge and works as its automatic critique. This assumption has been called into serious question by a number of studies which have demonstrated the strong continuities between the terms in which day-to-day experience is understood and the terms of academic knowledges (Martin 1987; Hollway 1984). As the feminist philosopher Iris Young points out, experience cannot be treated as transparent and authentic.

> The discourse we use when we describe our experience is no more direct and unmediated than any other discourse; it is only discourse in a different mode. The narrative form through which even young children learn to relate their experiences, for example, has rules, conventions, and many spaces for the introduction of social assumptions and stereotypes. Often people seem to assume that if we express our authentic experience, we will be free of

ideology, but this is clearly not so: 'ideology operates . . . at the most immediate level of naive experience' (Young 1990: 12).

In other words, the terms of experiential knowledge demand as much critical scrutiny as those of academic knowledge if the relationship between the two is to be thought.

Second, the reversal strategy assumes that the apparatuses of knowledge production are neutral epistemological machines that men simply use to make knowledge whose content is sympathetic to their interests. If this were the case, the methods of knowledge, its rules and procedures, would be as useful for the representation of women's experience as for men's. In practice, much feminist research has encountered a kind of recalcitrance in the use of orthodox methodologies—their observance of narrow but absolute disciplinary divisions, their assumptions about what counts as evidence, their assertion of the necessity of an 'objective' relationship between the scholar and what he studies—which has provoked suspicion about their alleged neutrality. This suspicion in turn has motivated a great deal of contemporary feminist research, based on the proposition that the valorisation of masculine experience occurs not just through content but is located in the process of production of knowledge itself. The very rules and procedures of disciplinary knowledge have been shown to be epistemological devices for the simultaneous inscription and effacement of masculine experience.

These asymmetries in the relationship between feminine experience and masculine knowledge imply that if feminist knowledges are to be brought into existence, women must find ways to make knowledge differently. This in turn requires a detailed knowledge of the complex ways in which masculine experience is valorised and systematised in disciplinary knowledge procedures, so that alternative methods can be thought.

In the following discussion I want to focus on different approaches to the excavation and subversion of one of the most effective methodological devices available to masculine knowledges: the fiction of the disembodied scholar. This refers to the assumption that the scholar is simply a properly trained mind, unlocated in the specific historical experience and social position of a sexed, classed or racially marked body. The device of the bodiless scholar allows knowledge the apparent ability to transcend any particular point of view and the limits of any particular experience. It enables knowledge production to perform a sleight of hand, the 'god-trick', as Donna Haraway puts it, 'of seeing everything from nowhere' (Haraway 1991: 189). It also contributes to the image of scholarly dispassion and disinterest, for a disembodied scholar may only contemplate; he has neither desires nor the ability to interfere.

This device underpins all forms of knowledge which claim a straightforward, factual relationship to the thing known. It underpins, for example, 'factual' accounts of history in which the historian writes as though he stands in an unmediated relationship to past events, an objective 'eyewitness' rather than the provider of a necessarily partial, interpreted account from the point of view of the present. The authority of these kinds of texts derives from this particular kind of authorship. At the same time it facilitates the importation of specifically masculine experience into the 'objective' text. This is so because historically only men have been deemed able to achieve the necessary transcendence of the body, while women have been represented as unfit for scholarship due to the perilous influence of their demanding bodies upon their minds (Lloyd 1984). To return to the example of the 'eyewitness' historian, the ability of this kind of historical writing to privilege military and parliamentary political events as exemplary historical scenes, as the 'facts' of history, is an index of the compatibility between 'objective' scholarship and masculine interests.

The device of the disembodied scholar has presented feminism with particular methodological problems in authorising kinds of knowledge which take feminine experience as their point of departure. How can feminist scholarship find ways to read and write texts that subvert the claims of disembodied scholarship, and so make space for a kind of knowledge which acknowledges itself to be located in sexed experience? Needless to say, this is not a question which can be definitively answered. The permutations of disembodied scholarship are so pervasive and varied in different areas of scholarship that multiple approaches to this question will be required. I will discuss four texts whose related methodologies address this question in particular ways, although they by no means exhaust its implications.

Disembodied authorship and perverse interpretation

One of the effects engendered by the device of the disembodied author is the understanding of academic texts as purely rational, conscious creations with a transparent relationship to the objects they describe. The scholar, as properly trained mind, uses the techniques of his particular discipline—those of observation, measurement and classification in the natural sciences, for example—to ensure that the text he produces about his object of study is a logical representation of that object. The disembodied scholar is the expert consciousness who is able to translate the object into text without the contamination of 'bias', that is point of view. The interpretative practice which accompanies this understanding of text production is one which reads texts as though they were transparent windows through which to see reality, and which pays no attention to the subjectivity of the author or the language he may use.

Hence one of the interpretative methods that feminism has developed involves what might be called 'perverse reading', the reading of apparently transparent and rational texts against the grain of their pretensions. Rather than reading for information or the conscious intentions of the author, feminist readings pursue the ways in which masculine embodied experience is encoded in the metaphoric systems, the imagery, that even the most abstract disciplines rely upon to make themselves intelligible.

This kind of reading is possible because the dependence of allegedly 'rational' abstract texts upon everyday imagery signals the point at which the pure consciousness of the disembodied scholar fails and the author must draw upon his embodied, everyday experiences and modes of thought to address the experience of his audience. At the same time recourse to metaphor and image in a text has implications for the text's meaning which exceed the intentions or control of the scholar. As Treichler (1988) puts it, metaphors are 'contagious': they form chains of association which link different texts to each other in complex ways. This ensures that any text can be interpreted in ways which may bear no relationship to the conscious intentions of its author.

So if the use of metaphor in abstract texts is taken seriously, it can be used as a vulnerable point which lays the text open to disrespectful feminist interpretations, like those of the feminist philosopher Michelle Le Doeuff. Le Doeuff's book *The Philosophical Imaginary* develops methods of interpreting some of the classical texts of philosophy to make them speak about the embodied experience of their practitioners, through an investigation of philosophy's imagery. Le Doeuff notes in her introduction that while philosophy declares itself a strictly rational, conceptual discourse, with a status in direct proportion to its distance from folklore and quotidian modes of thought, its texts are nevertheless laden with banal imagery, 'islands, clocks, horses, donkeys and even a lion . . . in short a whole pictorial world' (Le Doeuff 1989: 1). Because philosophy imagines itself to be pure thought, it deals with the embarrassment of these images by dismissing them as pedagogical, as illustrations used by philosophers to communicate their ideas to non-philosophers. Le Doeuff regards this dismissal as a feint, and proposes instead that the recurrence of such imagery marks the points of difficulty in the drive to systematise a learned text, the impossibility of sustaining a purely rational hermetic discourse without recourse to analogy or to the familiar. Images recur within a logical system because, she writes, 'they sustain something within the system which the system cannot itself justify, but which is nevertheless needed for its proper working' (Le Doeuff 1989: 3).

Le Doeuff uses this approach to investigate, among others, the use of an insular image in Kant's *The Critique of Pure Reason*. Kant refers to philosophy as the 'territory of pure understanding . . . an island, enclosed by nature itself within unalterable limits. It is the land of truth . . . surrounded by a wide and stormy ocean, the native home of illusion' (Le Doeuff 1989: 8). To depart for this island presents dangers for the understanding, for, Kant writes, it courts delusion and humiliation once it leaves the shores of reason. Those who wish to pursue philosophy must renounce the seductive islands of the South Seas, the islands of illusory pleasures and childish trifles.

Le Doeuff notes the implicit threat contained in Kant's insular metaphor and remarks upon the licence that imagery has within the philosophical enterprise.

> This announcement of the sufferings which the understanding will face once it lets itself wander among illusions amounts to no more than an arbitrary decree . . . Images are the means by which every philosophy can engage in straightforward dogmatisation, and decree a 'that's the way it is' without fear of counter-argument, since it is understood that a good reader will by-pass such 'illustrations'—a convention which enables the image to do its work all the more effectively. (Le Doeuff 1989: 11–12)

In other words, Le Doeuff suggests, the image of a safe island in a dangerous sea is used to address Kant's readers in a particular register, to marshal their fantasised identification and anxieties in particular ways. 'How does this island work, on the subjective level?' she asks. The renunciation of sensory pleasure in favour of a well-regulated understanding mimics, she suggests, the itinerary of castration, the psychic promise for men of stable identity and status upon the renunciation of infantile sexual attachment to the mother. More specifically it acts as an emblem of the effort of philosophical production, the (putative) renunciation by philosophers of the experiential, the sensual, in favour of ascetic rationality. It is, Le Doeuff suggests, an 'imaginary of the learned', a figure designed to satisfy a caste of scholars 'marked by the experience of schooling [and] scholastic asceticism'.

Le Doeuff's method demonstrates that even those kinds of knowledge which appear most systematic, most hostile to the everyday and the subjectivity of the scholar, depend on this everyday knowledge and subjectivity for their intelligibility and their operation. It points towards ways in which academic knowledges foster their particular communities and mark their borders through the privileging of kinds of experience only available to particular groups. She summarises this relationship in the following way.

> Imagery and knowledge form, dialectically, a common system. Between these two terms there is a play of feedbacks which maintains the particular regime of the discursive formation. Philosophical texts offer images through which subjectivity can be structured and given a marking which is that of the corporate body. In turn the affectivity which is thus moulded sustains the efforts of philosophical production and [its] system of presuppositions. (Le Doeuff 1989: 19)

Le Doeuff's method of textual analysis allows the identification of how particular discourses make available within them certain subject positions which differentially affect different kinds of readers and writers of those discourses. While she makes only the most passing reference to the sex of the scholar of philosophy, in this essay at least, her proposals about the relationship between insular imagery and castration clearly refer the image to the experience of a learned masculinity. More pointedly, Kant's island, and the disavowal of image and narrative more generally in systematic knowledge, can be read as a textual trace of the cost of instituting knowledge on the basis of a disembodied scholarship. Her essay acts as both an account of this institution, with its accompanying exclusion of perspectives associated with the feminine and the sensual, and as a methodology for the discerning of the textual traces of this exclusion.

Similar methods have been used by feminists to interpret metaphor in scientific discourse. While science makes the strongest claim to systematicity and to a right to represent 'reality', a growing body of feminist scholarship has interpreted scientific texts as indicative of masculine embodied experience through investigations of its 'imaginary'. N. Katherine Hayles, for example, has considered the encoding of masculine experience in the highly technical, mathematical field of fluid mechanics, the physics of liquid flows. She has done so through an historical investigation of the way in which certain concepts of the 'regular' and 'irregular' behaviour of fluids were associated with gendered meanings in the eighteenth century, which in turn conditioned the ways in which turbulent and non-turbulent flows could be modelled mathematically. As Hayles puts it, 'gendered metaphoric networks resonated with fluid mechanics at certain nodal points' (Hayles 1992: 27). What she is referring to here is the recurrence in scientific discourse of binary metaphoric pairs, those of continuity/rupture and conservation/dissipation in the case of fluid mechanics, which both form the terms in which the field is conceptualised and take on gendered connotations. In investigating the connotations of such binary metaphors she is drawing on a widely used feminist method of analysis, which works on the principle described above as the 'contagiousness' of metaphors. This method traces metaphoric networks in a text and considers how they link up with historical ideas about masculinity and femininity.

In this way Hayles discerns the implicit alignment between what counts as 'normal' non-turbulent flow, the kinds of mathematical formulas used to model this normality, and certain ideas about masculinity. She reports the ironic remark of an eighteenth-century mathematician that fluid flows 'are more sophisticated than the most sophisticated lady's character' and observes,

> The irony takes its point from an unstated but implied contrast between the opaque complexity of a woman's turbulent character and the straightforward simplicity of a manly laminar flow. One can see in such comments the kind of systematic identifications that put turbulence, hysteria, complexity, nonlinearity, and duplicity on the female side of the gender dichotomy, while steady flow, rationality, simplicity, linearity, and straightforwardness go on the male side. (Hayles 1992: 27)

The value of these methods of metaphoric interpretation of systematic texts is their ability to trace conceptual relationships between the everyday embodied experience of their producers and the kinds of formal textual abstractions to which such experience gives rise. Knowledge in these methods is not reduced to a projection of socially specific experience, but it is nevertheless demonstrated to owe a certain kind of debt to socially specific experience. Here knowledge is understood to be both constituted by and constitutive of certain subject positions, and the formal aspects of knowledge, the way a text is constructed and interpreted, plays out certain traces of these positions.

Embodied authorship as theatre

This reciprocal relationship between the formal constitution of a text and the kinds of subject positions it enables means that the question of what a feminist, embodied knowledge is must address itself to such formal concerns. What kind of knowledge will enable the position of an explicitly feminine scholar? What kinds of texts are they which no longer rest on a claim of objectivity and disembodiment, and which acknowledge their debt to the experiential?

There is probably no limit to the different ways these questions can be answered. The discussion so far suggests that one strategy might involve the generation of different metaphoric systems which link to explicitly feminine points of view when trying to produce systematic kinds of knowledge about the world. This is the kind of strategy pursued by the feminist scientist Donna Haraway, whose work intervenes in particular areas of scientific discourse—immunology and cybernetics, for example—to suggest ways in which the 'imaginaries' of these disciplines can be reworked. This is further discussed by Zoë Sofia in Chapter 11.

The question of disembodied scholarship can also be addressed directly to the way the scholarly persona inhabits or fails to inhabit the text s/he produces. Some recent feminist work deliberately uses first-person address, an explicitly sexed authorial 'I', as a means of demonstrating the limits of disembodied scholarship. Disembodied scholarship generally locates its pronouncements in a universal, rational point of view, which simply subsumes its reader through its use of the passive voice—'it is evident that', 'we can see that'—which implies that its claims are self-evident and located in the logic of the object under discussion.

What is interesting about the strategy of first-person address is that it could easily appear to be an example of what I have been trying to demonstrate as inadequate, a direct staging of experience against the claims of systematic knowledge. This may well be the case in some instances, but its use in the two texts I want to discuss, Iris Young's essay 'Pregnant embodiment' and Jane Gallop's book *Thinking Through the Body*, seems to have a more strategic value. I want to make a case here that these authors' use of an explicit 'I' counts not as a naive, experiential utterance, an expression of an authentic self, but as a formal and methodological innovation in the way academic texts can be written. Their texts find ways to retain the significance of experience while substantially reworking it, not so much through method but as method.

The use of an explicitly feminine/feminist first person in these texts works as a kind of inversion or parody of orthodox scholarly style, whose bid for objectivity involves the careful effacement of any trace of the author, *apart from his scholarly authority*. In other words, the effacement of the 'I' in such 'objective' texts can be considered as a formal expression of the disclaimed subjectivity of the disembodied scholar. To write academic texts using an explicitly sexed first-person 'voice' is to precipitate other textual effects, to pull one thread out of the knot of disavowed masculine subjectivity which subtends the form of the 'proper' academic text and to find that others have unravelled with it.

I think that Young's essay 'Pregnant embodiment', in which the author uses the phenomenal image of her pregnant body to provide a first-person critique of disembodied scholarship, troubles the formal requirements of the orthodox academic text in a number of ways. First, it collapses the requirement of objectivity, the separation of the subject and object of knowledge, because the author, or at least an aspect of the author's experience, acts as her own subject. Second, it mounts the most direct kind of challenge to the fiction of the disembodied scholar. The most immediate target of Young's critique of disembodiment is the concept of the body which is inscribed in phenomenology, that school of philosophy which tries to think the relationship between knowledge and lived experience. This intellectual project makes phenomenology more sympathetic to the use of the first person as a mode of argument than is found in the sciences or the social sciences. In this sense phenomenology acts as a useful index of the extent to which it is not just the grammatical position of the first person which is at issue, but also the sex of the 'I' who writes and is written. Young demonstrates that phenomenological writing has generally emanated from an implicitly masculine 'I' which still maintains a strong relationship with the device of the disembodied scholar. It is for this reason that she chooses to write as a pregnant 'I' because pregnancy is a bodily state which is inaccessible to masculine experience. Furthermore, pregnancy is understood as the very emblem of embodiment, the state which historically has been used to argue women's inherent inability to transcend bodily concerns and to justify women's exclusion from higher thought.

Young uses her phenomenal account of pregnancy to discuss the limits and exclusions involved in the bodily states of experience assumed by phenomenology. As she notes, phenomenological writing assumes that, apart from states of madness, the self is experienced as unified, as a singularity, and that this unity is the precondition for the intelligibility of experience. Pregnancy confounds this assumption because it is a departure from the apparent singularity of the self, yet does not involve the shattering of the self.

Pregnancy challenges the integration of my body experience by rendering fluid the boundary between what is within, myself, and what is outside, separate. I experience my insides as the space of another, yet my own body . . . The birthing process entails the most extreme suspension of the bodily distinction between inner and outer . . . Through pain and blood and water this inside thing emerges between my legs, for a short while both inside and outside me. (Young 1990: 163)

This confusion between inside and outside is accompanied by the uncertainty of the boundaries of the pregnant body. Phenomenology simply assumes the stability and givenness of boundaries and the body's location of its own specific space, but in pregnancy boundaries shift, so that it becomes impossible to move in the world in the same way as before. Young uses the experience of shifting boundary, and the particular motility and heaviness of pregnancy, to question phenomenology's assertion that an active relation to the world, the performing of tasks and projects, involves an indifference to one's body, an unconsciousness of its limits.

[Pregnancy] makes me conscious of the physicality of my body not as an object, but as the material weight that I am in movement. The notion of the body as a pure medium of my projects is the illusion of a philosophy that has not quite shed the Western philosophical legacy of humanity as spirit. Movement always entails awareness of effort and the feeling of resistance. In pregnancy this fact of existence never leaves me. (Young 1990: 165–166)

By writing not just as an 'I' but as a pregnant 'I', Young demonstrates that the project of phenomenology maintains certain kinds of continuity with those other masculine intellectual projects that organise themselves through the device of the disembodied scholar. By deploying the phenomenal image of pregnancy in her writing, Young reveals the extent to which the silhouette which marks the subject position made available in phenomenological writing is a masculine one, a silhouette which it is impossible for a feminine/feminist philosopher to occupy. Her work suggests that similar investigations could be carried out into other areas of intellectual writing, those of fiction and visual arts criticism for example, that permit the use of the first person while eliding the question of the sex of the 'I'.

Young's point is that all bodies, male and female, pregnant or not, have a weight, a bulk, a visceral presence, and a vulnerable mortality, which render ridiculous the idea of a disembodied consciousness. She drives home this point in the generic shifts in her writing, confounding the characteristic calmness of philosophical argument with scandalous, visceral accounts of the sensations of pregnancy and birth. Her scholarly discussion of the questionable unity of subjectivity is succeeded and disturbed by a violent, phenomenal description of birth.

Increasingly I feel my insides strained and pressed, and increasingly feel the movement of a body inside me. Through pain and blood and water this thing inside me emerges between my legs. (Young 1990: 163)

These generic shifts represent, I think, another important textual 'effect' precipitated by the use of the first person. In a sense Young's text becomes a theatre where two allegedly opposite conditions, that of pregnancy and that of philosophical knowledge, can play out a new relationship, one in which the latter no longer has to distance itself from the former. But for this theatre to work, both these conditions must be made to speak in ways that are intelligible to each other. Young makes pregnancy speak philosophically and philosophy speak in a bodily mode, so that dialogue becomes possible between the two.

Gallop's *Thinking Through the Body* also works as a kind of theatre where formerly contrary genres and voices can be brought into relation. Gallop makes more elaborate use of the first person than does Young, inventing a well-developed persona, a dramatic character who regales her readers with gossipy stories about her affairs with professors, about giving an academic paper in a slinky black dress, about crying over certain books and masturbating over others. She also talks about her intellectual anxieties and misgivings and her experience of the actual stuff of intellectual production, reading and writing and the difficulties they present. These authorial performances are interleaved with close readings of particular texts, primarily those of Roland Barthes, the Marquis de Sade, Sigmund Freud and Luce Irigaray, philosophers who, Gallop says, dare to 'think through the body' in various ways.

Gallop uses this authorial exhibitionism to foreground the contradiction between being a woman and being a scholar. By letting loose a flagrantly feminine/feminist persona in her text she dramatises the scandal of the woman in the academy, the woman, that is, who refuses to conceal or dissemble her sexuality, and who uses this sexuality as a form of knowledge, the starting point for a textual practice. Her use of the first person allows these apparently incommensurable things, sexuality and desire on the one hand and knowledge production on the other, to comment upon and inform each other. Desire becomes the starting point for the elaboration of Gallop's methods of intellectual practice. She writes:

My desire to be an academic, intellectual speaker is a desire to speak from the father's place. Yet the spiritual father's place . . . demands separation of ideas from desire, a disembodied mind. I want to expose the father's desire so that I can take his place but as a sexed subject. (Gallop 1988: 21)

It is for this reason that in her critical rereadings of psychoanalytic and theoretical texts she reads for the failures of consciousness and mastery, for the ways that they constantly subvert their own intentions to be systematic and scholarly, free of the authors' personal investments. In the essay *The Seduction of an Analogy* she traces through an ambiguity in certain of the writings of the psychoanalyst Freud. This ambiguity is found in Freud's employment of both systematic scientific language and a more poetic or metaphoric style. It arises, she suggests, from the ambiguous nature of the psychoanalytic enterprise itself—the ultimate impossibility of knowing if what the patient remembers with the analyst's help is indeed the accurate reconstitution of a real past event, or if it is a story more akin to fiction, so that fragments of memory are used to make up what is effectively a new narrative. This in turn places the scientific authority of the psychoanalyst into question, in so far as he may be engaged in a fictional rather than a therapeutic enterprise.

The point here is that while some of the great fathers of contemporary thought, like Freud, do not successfully master and systematise their field, yet they have produced intellectual work which is of great significance. If this is the case then she can licence her own attempt to write without a bid for such mastery, and hence without dissimulating her position as feminine speaker. It is a means of giving a positive value to what she describes as working from a position of explicit uncertainty, rather than one of (always failed) mastery.

All the texts discussed here represent ways of reintroducing questions of the body, sex and experience to the figure of the disembodied scholar. While each text maintains a strong enabling relationship to the others, their strength derives not from the extent to which they offer methods to be replicated but rather from their deliberately limited, strategic accuracy. They each take precise account of the local conditions of knowledge into which they intervene, the specificities of their disciplines, and find ways to demonstrate the costs and limitations of these conditions for feminist scholarship. This strategic accuracy also represents the limits of their respective enterprises, a recognition that the project in which they are engaged requires multiple, temporary interventions into a volatile field. The political nature of feminist intellectual practice demands that feminist method work as strategy rather than as some stable notion of technique, where procedures guarantee results and can be successfully repeated. It involves the recognition, for example, that the use of a sexed authorial 'I' is not a 'technique' which will guarantee radicalising effects in all cases (see Zoë Sofia's discussion of the non-radical effects of 'gender-bending' on computer networks, in Chapter 11). The efficacy of such strategies depends upon how such enunciative devices can be made to subvert or displace the presuppositions of their specific fields of knowledge, rather than in the simple fact of the devices themselves.

3

Knowing women: The limits of feminist psychology

Elizabeth Wilson

It has become commonplace to think of feminist interventions into the knowledges and disciplinary practices of the university as resting along a continuum. The uneven distribution of feminist practice within the university is not simply random: it has a pattern and continuity. We can say with some degree of confidence that feminist interventions have been more successful, or at least more prevalent, in the humanities than in the sciences. More specifically, there is an already familiar continuum, which starts with the humanities, moves through the social sciences and concludes with the natural sciences, that allows us to map not just the success of feminist interventions but also the chronological emergence of those interventions.

While such a continuum gives a viable account of feminist interventions into the disciplinary knowledges of the university, it also mirrors a more conventionalised and troublesome progression. We are already accustomed to the rhetoric of a ranking system that starts with those knowledges considered to be more interpretive or speculative in their methodologies—the humanities—and proceeds through the social sciences until we come to rest on the allegedly sure and solid ground of the natural sciences. Such a continuum, considered more given than constitutive, has served as a means by which power has been installed across and between the disciplines. We may find ourselves wanting to examine the extent to which we accept the presumptions that authorise this epistemological hierarchy; and more specifically to examine its effects on the way feminist interventions are viewed and constituted.

This epistemological continuum does not simply have effects for feminist interventions *across* disciplines, it also takes up residence *within* disciplines, splintering any one discipline into a spectrum of feminist-friendly and feminist-resistant subdisciplines. Here, I am interested in this continuum, and its effects, as manifest in psychology. The uneven distribution of feminist scholarship within psychology follows the same broad pattern as in other disciplines: those parts of the discipline that are more interpretive, less obviously experimental, and more attuned to the social and cultural constitution of the psyche have provided a more fertile ground for feminist intervention (for example, social psychology, see Wilkinson 1986; developmental psychology, see Gilligan 1982; clinical psychology, see Chesler 1972). It is extremely difficult to find any feminist research at the other end of the spectrum in areas like perception, psychobiology and neuropsychology, where knowledge is taken to be more objective, less interpretive, and less directly relevant to women. Certainly the major feminist reviews of psychology (Deaux 1985; Parlee 1975, 1979; Vaughter 1976) fail to mention these areas, except where they overlap with a readily identifiable feminist politics about female reproductive biology or cognitive sex differences.

My concern is that feminist psychology has too easily accommodated this epistemological continuum and its political effects. Feminist inquiry does not stand before or outside this epistemological ordering; instead feminist politics and knowledges are intimately caught up in its constitutive effects. Specifically, I am interested in why one sort of ground has been more fertile for feminism rather than another. Is there something in certain domains that is inherently more open to feminist contestation? Or is it that the politics of feminist interventions, as currently understood, are best suited to some ground and not others? To ask the question more specifically, why have the more interpretive, less scientific domains been more accessible to feminist intervention? To reply that objective, scientific discourse have been more hostile to feminist intervention, or that feminism has not yet expanded to encompass these discourses, simply begs the question, although it does concur with a certain folklore that takes the sciences to be *intrinsically* more non-, anti- or a-feminist. It seems to me that this particular distribution of feminist interventions is neither natural or preordained; and it is not simply reducible to the structural and epistemological differences between and within disciplines (although this does play a part). Rather it seems to me that this pattern of feminist intervention is an effect of the interplay between the structure of disciplinary knowledges and *the structure of feminist politics*. That is, this continuum of feminist interventions is as much an effect of the type of political interventions that have become commonplace in feminism as it is an effect of the disciplines themselves.

In this essay I would like to examine this interchange between a continuum of knowledges and the politics of feminist intervention within the context of feminist psychology, and use this to illuminate a series of political and epistemological questions that are relevant to the domain of women's studies as a whole. Specifically, I want to examine the imperative in many feminist projects to take women as the object or subject of knowledge without in some way putting the process of knowledge production itself under scrutiny. This injunction has the effect of containing feminist interventions within certain sectors of the epistemological continuum, and foreclosing on feminism's ability to intervene in knowledge production more widely. Feminist interventions in the sciences, in particular, have suffered under the force of this imperative. I will argue in the next two sections that it is the desire to know women, a desire that has fuelled mainstream psychological research since its inception (Lewin 1984), that problematically defines and limits the politics of feminist psychology. It is the uncritical pursuit of 'the woman question' that has established a certain kind of feminist practice in psychology; and this has limited the types of questions that can be asked and the type of politics that can be put into action in psychology. In the final section I will return to a broader perspective and offer some brief concluding remarks on the relevance of a critique of feminist psychology to women's studies more generally.

Knowing women

While there has always been feminist research and criticism in psychology (see Lewin 1984), the emergence of feminist psychology as an acknowledged and identifiable area of research is a fairly recent event. We could locate this emergence somewhere between Weisstein's (1971) polemical, revolutionary attack on psychology and Mednick and Weissman's (1975) more restrained review for the institutionally respectable *Annual Review of Psychology*:

> It then goes without saying that present psychology is less than worthless in contributing to a vision which could truly liberate—men as well as women. The central argument of my paper, then, is this. Psychology has nothing to say about what women are really like, what they need and what they want, essentially because psychology does not know. (Weisstein 1971: 1)

> This selective review on the psychology of women has, as we predicted at the outset, raised many questions. It is perhaps banal, but nevertheless necessary, to stress that there are unresolved conceptual and methodological issues within each area which will have

to be raised again and reevaluated as the field develops. (Mednick and Weissman 1975: 13)

Somewhere between Weisstein's independently published broadsheet and Mednick and Weissman's review for a major psychological journal there was a shift in the way feminist criticism interacted with psychology. No longer a voice from the margins, feminist psychology had become an identifiable research domain with its own set of conceptual and methodological parameters. No longer content simply to criticise the masculinism lying at the core of many scientific psychological projects, feminist psychologists embarked on a series of their own avowedly political projects in social, clinical, developmental and cognitive psychological theory. Their goal: to win back the truth about women from mainstream psychology. In Weisstein's words, to establish *what women are really like*.

The question of what women are really like is, of course, an old one in psychology. Before the influx of women into academic psychology, and the concomitant feminist institutional changes of the mid-1970s (see Parlee 1991), sex differences and female psychology were already major areas of psychological research. Operating as a kind of pre-feminist women's studies, this psychology of women had been dominated by research which purported to provide 'objective' data for a number of socially sanctioned stereotypes about women and their place. Women's inherent masochism; their natural mothering instincts; their inferior motor and cognitive skills (especially when under the influence of hormones); sex differences in brain weight, perceptual–motor abilities, emotionality and IQ were typical sites of concern in the field (Shields 1975). By the mid-1970s much of this had changed—the field had become the domain of *feminist* inquiry:

> The 'psychology of women' here refers to psychological research that is *for* women . . . Sexist research on women is of course still being done, but its creators do not identify themselves as being in the field of the psychology of women. Feminist psychologists' power to define and name their own field has evidently prevailed . . .
> (Parlee 1979: 121)

Nonetheless, feminist psychologists had not defined and named a *new* field; rather they had hijacked one that already existed. This is not a problem per se: my concern is that this appropriation was conducted so uncritically. In hijacking the psychology of women, feminist psychologists not only inherited the content of the field (women), they also inherited the presumptions, limitations and boundaries that made that field coherent. Consequently, what was inside and what was outside the domain of feminist psychology was widely considered to be uncontroversial and self-evident. It was also at this historical juncture that, contra Weisstein's impassioned plea, feminist psychology conceded to psychology's epistemological powers: it granted (feminist) psychology the ability to know women. Through these institutional and epistemological moves, feminism became a qualifier or moderator of the psychological project, rather than its interrogator.

The emergence of feminist psychology from the domain of the psychology of women is an important factor in assessing the political agenda and future possibilities of contemporary feminist research in psychology. If feminist psychology continues to take the category 'women' as its most appropriate object and as its unargued rationale for research, then feminist research in psychology will simply operate within the same logical economy as the mainstream discipline:

> . . . where feminism remains committed to the project of *knowing women*, of making women the objects of knowledge, *without in turn submitting the position of knower or subject of knowledge to a reorganization*, it remains as problematic as the knowledge it attempts to supplement or replace. (Grosz 1993: 207)

For Irigaray (1985b), feminist interventions need to be premised on something other than the question 'What is woman?' The reason for this is not simply that the category 'woman' is problematic. Her more general concern is that to speak *of* or *about* women will return us to a phallocentric logic where the feminine is always necessarily repressed, censored and misrecognised:

> The issue is not one of elaborating a new theory of which woman would be the subject or the object, but of jamming the theoretical machinery itself, of suspending its pretension to the production of a truth and of a meaning that are excessively univocal. Which presupposes that women do not aspire simply to being men's equals in knowledge. That they do not claim to be rivalling men in constructing a logic of the feminine that would still take onto-theo-logic as its model, but rather that they are attempting to wrest this question away from the economy of the logos. (Irigaray 1985b: 78)

Irigaray suggests that rather than pursuing the question 'What is woman?' we should be interrogating those masculinist discourses that define woman as lack, deficiency and imitation in answer to this question. Specifically, we could ask: are the questions of and about woman not caught in an epistemological order that will always deploy the feminine as lack, deficiency and imitation? She argues that the question 'What is . . .?' is a metaphysical question that the feminine exceeds: the question 'What is . . .?' is informed by, and in turn advances, a certain epistemological order where the subject maintains an authoritative relation to his object, where knowledge always pursues a univocal truth, and where the feminine and the object of inquiry are metonymically related (pp. 119–169). Much of Irigaray's own work is an attempt to show how the feminine acts as a disruptive excess to this phallocentric logic in psychoanalytic and philosophical discourse. Her project is to demonstrate how the notion of sexual difference exceeds and disrupts this masculine logic, rather than how the feminine could be articulated through or within this logic. She exploits feminine excess in order to demarcate a possible 'outside' (another scene) of this phallocentric imaginary, to denaturalise and locate its universalist claims. A new theory of woman, feminist or otherwise, is exactly what Irigaray is moving against.

Perhaps the central organising political presumption in a feminist psychology of women is that it can answer the question 'What is woman?' outside the systems of violence and falsity that mark traditional knowledges about female psychology. Feminist psychology takes its modes of knowledge production to be largely uncompromised by the masculinist violences of the mainstream discipline. Up to a certain point this can be granted: the positivist projects of feminist psychology have made important and necessary correctives to the psychology of women. But if we examine this desire to know women a little more closely, we can see that it is always caught in a certain notion of violence. Kirby (1993) gives a careful and astute reading of this desire to know in feminist anthropology. In much the same way as feminist psychologists have done in their own domain, feminist anthropologists have carefully excavated the violences inflicted on the anthropological other in traditional ethnographic discourses. Like feminist psychology, feminist anthropology has been seduced by the security of a well-intentioned feminist politics into believing that it can know the anthropological other outside such discursive violences; that it can step outside the structures of power that inflict these violences. Kirby claims that Donna Haraway's work is exemplary in this regard: that is, Haraway attempts to avoid or resolve the oppositional logic that she takes to be at the core of this process of 'othering'. Haraway has recognised, first of all, that the oppositional logic of anthropological discourse serves to obliterate the specificity of the other (it can only know the other by reducing that other to a version of itself), yet she goes on to claim that a sufficiently self-aware feminist practice can know that other outside such violent obliteration; that a careful feminist ethnographic practice can allow the radical difference of the voice of the other to be heard.

How, Kirby (1993) asks, are we to differentiate this feminist discourse—without violence, without distortion or 'othering'—from the traditional discourses of an objective ethnography that likewise claims to present an authentic, undistorted other? If the desire to know the other (woman) is the desire to master the other (woman), if knowing is always an act of violent digestion and incorporation, then the traditional knowledges of feminist psychology and anthropology will always, necessarily, obliterate the specificity and difference of that other. The sense of crisis for Kirby, is not that feminists should not be doing this (as Haraway suggests), but rather that *they cannot do anything other than this*—every intervention must operate through the violence of oppositional logic. To insist that we can know what women are really like represses, rather than avoids, this act of violence in our practice; moreover, this repression is operating at a time when calls to acknowledge alterity within feminism have never been stronger. For Kirby, the recourse to good and honest intentions will not act as a prophylactic between feminism and violence; rather feminist interventions are forced into a difficult, detailed and confronting assessment of their complicity with that which they contest.

Such an interrogation of feminist methodologies should not be read simply as negative critique: I do not wish to deny that various feminist psychology projects have successfully reduced the prevalence of masculinist assumptions in their methodologies and theories. What I do want to contest, however, is the feminist assumption that this residue of masculinism is safely contained at the periphery of our projects. I want to insist that this residue is irreducible: it cannot be removed completely, nor can it be displaced outside the field of feminist psychology. Moreover, it resides not at the periphery of our projects but at their very core, as their enabling possibilities. Put another way: while the difference between sexist and non-sexist projects may be readily adjudicated, the difference between phallocentric and non-phallocentric projects cannot be so easily ascertained.

The issue, then, for feminist psychology is to examine the effects that the pursuit of the psychology of women has on the types of political interventions that are possible inside psychology. It seems that, to date, feminist psychology has been concerned primarily with 'correcting' the bias of masculinist psychology without adequately acknowledging that feminist psychology is caught in the same systems of logic. Too concerned with a certainty and a truth outside violence and deception, feminist psychology seeks to bring an end to the question of woman: to either affirm it or negate it once and for all. In short, to find an answer that will not proliferate more questions. Feminist psychology takes its subject matter to be correctable and resolvable: it takes itself to be a project with an end. It is these desires for answers and solutions to the question of woman, rather than its interrogation, that keep feminist psychology in a compliant and domesticated role in relation to psychology.

Bodies and brains: Different projects in feminist psychology

If feminist practice in psychology could be something other than knowing women, in what would such different practices consist? In this section I shall briefly demonstrate how the traditional perspectives of feminist psychology constrain the scope and purchase of its critical interventions; and I shall point to different critical possibilities for the future of feminist psychology.

Jane Ussher's (1989) investigation of the psychology of the female body provides an example of the effects of an orthodox and narrow feminist psychology. Potentially an opportunity for an interesting examination of the relation of psyche, body and sexual difference in psychological knowledges, Ussher's book disappoints. Ussher's primary concern is with the female body as it has been misread by the patriarchal forces of biological determinism. Rehearsing feminist psychology's orthodox mode of intervention, which claims to present itself outside modes of violence and distortion, Ussher sets out to release the female body and its psychological effects and determinants from the violence of biological determinism: to show us what the psychology of the female body is *really* like:

> What is essential is that we have an understanding of the truths surrounding cyclicity on female identity, including the effects of menstruation on behaviour and the effects of major life events such as pregnancy and the menopause. These uniquely female experiences should not be ignored or denied, nor should their influence be exaggerated. The silence which surrounds the reality of the female experience needs to be broken. (Ussher 1989: 16)

Ussher's analysis falls directly within the reach of Kirby's (1993) critique of a feminism that takes itself to be outside any discursive constraints and in direct contact with the reality of women's experience. At this point, however, my interest lies in a slightly different direction:

the narrow role of female biology in Ussher's critique. The female body that Ussher (1989) attempts to resuscitate from the discourses of biological determinism is completely circumscribed by its reproductive capacities. The only specificity that the female body has for Ussher is its reproductive capacity: the female body is simplistically equated with a reproductive body. By contemplating the female body only within the cycle of menarche to menopause, Ussher perpetuates the biological determinism she criticises in patriarchal texts. Is it not also the case that the specificity of the female body extends to the skin, the internal organs, the nervous system, bone structure, biochemistry et cetera? Why are the psychological concomitants of the body confined to the processes of reproduction at the expense of digestion, excretion, circulation and so on? To what extent is Ussher relying on a notion of truthful biological accounts of the body, even as she contests patriarchal biology's particular claims? Ussher, like many feminists in psychology, presumes that only those things manifestly codified as female are of concern to feminist inquiry. In such a view, the eating body, the sweating body and the physiologically active body become the domain of a supposedly neutral 'human' biology, and outside the reach of feminist criticism.

It is here that we see the beginnings of different projects in feminist psychology. While neither ignoring nor negating the import of that which is specifically coded as sexed, we must also begin to focus our attention on that which is coded as sexually neutral: we must examine this process of sexual codification itself. Feminist psychology must acknowledge that what we take to be sexually indifferent in psychological knowledges (e.g., psychophysical processes, cognition, the laws of learning) are deeply implicated in masculine interests and desires. Lurking behind every neutral codification, behind every statement of scientific sexual indifference, we should expect an unacknowledged masculinism (Irigaray 1985a, 1985b: 106–118).

By naming man as the common force in the production of neutral scientific truth, Irigaray (1985a) suggests that scientific pursuits are intimately caught up in the male imaginary. The principal characteristics of this male imaginary are: 'production, property, order, form, unity, visibility, erection'. Such an imaginary operates through the domination of stability and solidity, at the expense of difference, reciprocity, exchange, permeability or fluidity: in a word, it is phallocentric. For Irigaray, neutral knowledge always bears the mark of a sexed imaginary and thus, by extension, a sexed morphology:

[Irigaray] conceptualises the imaginary in terms of sex, either male

or female: the imaginary either bears the morphological marks of
the male body, whose cultural products are characterised by unity,
teleology, linearity, self-identity, and so on or it bears the morphological marks of the female body, characterised by plurality, non-
linearity, fluid identity and so on. (Whitford 1991: 54)

For this reason, no psychological knowledge is ever sexually neutral;
it will always carry the markings of the sexed imaginary that has
produced it. It is through this use of morphology, and its deployment
in knowledges, that the body and sexual difference re-emerge as the
essential questions in supposedly neutral psychological discourses. This
allows us to see that all the objective products and knowledges of
psychology are marked as masculine, even though such sexed markings
will always be masked as universal and neutral. Indeed it is the very
mark of neutrality, and the systems of rationality and objectivity that
are put in place to enforce that neutrality, that point to their repressed
masculine origin. Like the psychological defences against repressed
material, the intensity with which sites of neutrality are guarded is a
sign that a certain masculinism is being hidden. For this reason it is
perhaps the most sexually indifferent, the most comfortable and
acknowledged of psychology's objects that should become feminism's
concern; after all, that which requires the most protection is that which
is most vulnerable. The psyche itself, and its modern-day manifestation
the brain, offer just such an intensely guarded neutrality. If the brain
has become the exemplar of a neutral site for determining psychological
truths about sexual difference (e.g. LeVay 1993; Moir & Jessels 1991),
then it is here that we could expect to find the carefully hidden kernels
of masculine desires about psychological functioning.

The brain, as figured in contemporary psychological discourses, is
implicated in a hidden masculinism on a number of different fronts.
Here I can only briefly indicate how we might begin to frame feminist
questions about the neutrality of the brain and cognition. According to
current neuropsychological research, the brain is composed of a number
of important anatomical and functional divisions: between left and right
hemisphere, between verbal and spatial functioning, between lower
brain and upper cortex (Corballis 1983). To take the last of these
divisions, we can say more specifically that the anatomical division
between the lower depths of the brain stem and the upper cortical
surfaces corresponds to a similar division of higher cognition (intellect)
from emotion or bodily sensation (sensibility). The lower brain is
widely considered to be responsible for more 'primitive' psychological
faculties (hate, love, fear, sexual behaviour) and the basic life functions

(breathing, eating, cortical tone). The upper brain, or cortical surface, is understood to be primarily involved in 'higher' psychological functions such as reasoning, spatial skills, language, motor and perceptual co-ordination. LeVay (1993) says of the hypothalamus (a subcortical structure, and the site of his controversial discovery of brain differences between heterosexual and homosexual men):

> People tend to stay away from the hypothalamus. Most brain scientists (including myself until recently) prefer the sunny expanses of the cerebral cortex to the dark claustrophobic regions at the base of the brain. They think of the hypothalamus—although they would never admit this to you—as haunted by animal spirits and the ghosts of primal urges. They suspect that it houses, not the usual shiny hardware of cognition, but some witches' brew of slimy, pulsating neurons adrift in a broth of mind-altering chemicals. (LeVay 1993: 39)

The brain quite literally embodies the hierarchisation of reason and intellect ('the shiny hardware of cognition') over emotion and sensation ('the ghosts of primal urges'). Such a division is not sexually indifferent: it is isomorphic with, and deeply implicated in, the dualistic relation of male over female, mind over body. This brain is not divided anatomically and functionally according to neutral, scientific criteria, but according to a whole series of masculine interests, fears and desires.

On another front, we may find the marks of a masculine imaginary in the discrete and locatable traces and spaces of the mind–brain. The neurocognitive sciences are engaged in an ever-vigilant attempt to shore up the physical and philosophical indeterminacy of the mind–brain by positing real, discrete, locatable traces and spaces within it. These traces and spaces embody a certain kind of mind: that is, the contemporary neurocognitive brain guarantees a mind that is locatable, empirical, rational, knowable, containable and safe. If there is a direct relation between containment, solidity and a certain masculinism (Irigaray 1985b: 106–118), then this brain of locatable traces is the type of brain necessary for the embodiment of a rational, logical and masculine mind. If we were to attribute a sex to this brain, we would have to say that in certain insidious ways it is masculine. Consequently, the issue of localisation (where and how is the mind located in the brain?) has been paramount in the neurocognitive sciences, and questions of sex and the brain have always been ones of localisation and origin: where is sex in the brain? how are functional sex differences anatomically mediated? However, the issue of sexual difference and the brain is a complex philosophical problem that cannot be resolved simply by empirical verification. Where many feminist critiques in this area (e.g. Fausto-Sterling 1991; Rogers 1988) are willing to accept that sex and sexuality are written as present and locatable traces on the brain, that the brain does indeed operate as the origin of psychological and biological difference, I would argue that the very notion of locating sex or the psyche in this manner is the product of a masculine-scientific imaginary. What is not questioned in these feminist accounts is the nature of these neuropsychical traces: what exactly are we looking for in the brain? The interesting question is not 'Is the brain the origin of sexual difference?' but rather 'What have we made of the brain, such that this becomes the question to ask?'

Negotiating limits

> A critique is not a matter of saying that things are not right as they are. It is a matter of pointing out on what kinds of assumptions, what kinds of familiar, unchallenged, unconsidered modes of thought the practices that we accept rest. (Foucault 1988: 154)

While the title of this essay suggests that I would be concerned with a negatively critical account of the limitations and shortcomings of feminist psychology, it suggests something else as well. The limits of feminist psychology do not simply constrain and constrict, they also enable. A critical examination of feminist psychology is not simply a chronicle of wrongdoing, it should also be an investigation of what and where these limits are. What are the boundaries of feminist psychology? To what extent are these boundaries constitutive of feminist psychology? In what way would different limits enable a different kind of feminist psychology? We need to remember that what our projects criticise is, perhaps, less important than what they open up.

I have argued here that the limits of feminist psychology are set by its adherence to the category 'women', and by its reluctance to examine its own complicity in the modes of knowledge production that fuel the mainstream discipline. By authorising a certain kind of feminist intervention that takes women as its proper and only concern, feminist psychology has foreclosed on other projects that could operate under its name. It has been my contention that feminist interventions into those areas of psychology (e.g. neurocognitive psychology) that have previously been figured as outside the scope of feminist inquiry will enable feminist psychology to rethink the nature of its knowledges and the politics of its intervention. More specifically, it will enable us to break out of the constraining and domesticating effects of an epistemological and political continuum that dictates the content and boundaries of feminist interventions in psychology. But what is the relevance of this seemingly local critique of feminist psychology to the broader domain of women's studies? What does a critique of knowledge production in a specific disciplinary domain tell us about the political and epistemological machinations of an interdisciplinary space such as women's studies? Obviously, the feminist critiques of woman (Irigaray 1985b) and the ways in which we can know (Grosz 1993; Kirby 1993) are all vital to the future viability of women's studies. Like feminist psychology, women's studies is constrained by an epistemological continuum that dictates what may and may not count as knowledge within its domain; as with feminist psychology, the necessity for new and different projects in women's studies is becoming more apparent. If women's studies is to consolidate its gains and remain a viable political force in the future, it must remain open to new theoretical endeavours and vigilant lest it repeat and disseminate the same foreclosures, exclusions and presumptions that mark the masculine disciplinary spaces it contests.

It is the mark of success of any feminist endeavour that it can not only launch a critique of certain masculinist presumptions but also acknowledge and examine its own internal modes of production. The viability of women's studies and feminist psychology alike is dependent on our ability to acknowledge that our conditions of possibility do not arise from politically uncontaminated ground. We owe irreducible debts to the systems that we contest. Our dilemma is not simply that we cannot live with the violences of knowledges, but also that we cannot produce without them. If feminism is to intervene effectively into phallocentric knowledges, it cannot do so by claiming a space outside phallocentrism or by demarcating a solid and impenetrable line between itself and that which it contests. Rather, feminism must take aim from within: feminism is not possible and cannot be effective except by inhabiting those structures it contests. Far from being a sign of our weakness, this position is our greatest strength. The challenge that feminist endeavours now face is to forgo the dream of an outside, or a politically innocent position, and to examine our own conditions of possibility as they both enable and constrain our political and epistemological projects.

4

Interlocking oppressions

Anna Yeatman

Oppression has been a central political category for contemporary social movements including the 'second wave' women's movement, the gay and lesbian movements, and the various anti-racist movements. These movements are engaged in both theorising and overcoming the oppression of those whom they represent. This oppression, in turn, is viewed as a social relationship whereby a dominant group or groups subordinate and exploit another group or groups. Oppressive relationships, then, are seen as intrinsic to the cultural and structural forces which shape our action. They can be challenged, but the challenge has to be adequate to its object. That is, it has to become a social force or movement which develops a practical critique of these oppressive relationships. This critique is expressed both as a politics of contestation directed against the existing order and as an effort on the part of emancipatory movements to experimentally produce new and less oppressive ways of relating.

The dynamic of emancipatory social movements is always determined by the historical context in which they operate. In turn, these movements assume an historical force which enters into and changes the specificity of oppressive relationships. Under the influence or pressure of contemporary feminism, for example, many institutions have adopted an equal opportunity approach to women. This certainly reduces old forms of discrimination, but it may introduce new forms. For example, the current equal opportunity rhetoric of an active labour market policy means that government personnel in social security and employment areas encourage women into labour market participation regardless of their carer responsibilities to young children and, perhaps also, elderly parents. As government does nothing to equalise the distribution of these responsibilities among men and women, the effect of an active labour market policy is to push many women with carer responsibilities into particular areas of the labour market which exploit their need for part-time work that can fit around their domestic-carer responsibilities. However, even when the effect of social and legal change is to introduce new forms of oppression, this should not be interpreted as minimising the significance of the formal adoption of anti-discrimination and equal opportunity policies. It still represents an important development in the distinctively modern emancipatory politics of equality.

This is a thumbnail sketch of what I think this category oppression implies, or at least of how it seems to work as a discursive practice within contemporary emancipatory social movements, and specifically within the feminist movement. Where did this category come from? What does it presuppose? Does it have a history we might do well to reflect upon? These are what Foucault (1984) would term genealogical questions. They imply that the category has a history and also that our own reflective, critical inquiry into it is historically positioned in ways which ensure that the questions we may ask of it will not be those that are asked by the inheritors of second wave feminism in five or more years time. The idea of 'interlocking oppressions' itself came into being at a particular moment in the history of feminism. To locate and understand this moment requires a broader genealogy of the category of oppression and of the politico-ethical historical terrain in which a modern emancipatory politics has developed.

Surprisingly in all the literature (theoretical, historical, policy-oriented or autobiographical) thrown up by the emancipatory movements, there is scarcely any critical reflection on the key categories which frame and organise their consciousness: categories such as emancipation, domination, and oppression. Iris Young, in her important *Justice and the Politics of Difference* (1990: 31–32, 37) provides definitions of 'domination' and 'oppression' which make explicit some of the assumptions that have informed 'New Left' rhetorics of self-determination and participation. But she does so in a way which treats these categories—social justice, self-determination, participation, domination and oppression—as formal universals, not as historically specific instances of modern emancipatory movement discourse. She does not explore the historical conditions of possibility of this category consciousness, where have they come from, and how have they changed.

In his analysis of the Enlightenment and its modes of thought, Foucault (1984) argues that when ahistorical universals are appealed to—universals which include the modern emancipatory values of equality, freedom, self-determination and democratic participation—they never exist except as specified in relation to a particular historical context:

> This entails an obvious consequence: that criticism is no longer going to be practiced in the search for formal structures with universal value, but rather as a historical investigation into the events that have led us to constitute ourselves and to recognise ourselves as subjects of what we are doing, thinking, saying. (Foucault 1984: 46)

If, in order to exist as values by which practice is directed, universals have to be specified, and such specification is always historical, it follows that this specification, of self-determination for example, accords the formal value a partial, contingent and arbitrary existence. This is why for Foucault (1984: 45) 'the critical question today has to be turned back into a positive one: in what is given to us as universal, necessary, obligatory, what place is occupied by whatever is singular, contingent, and the product of arbitrary constraints?' On this argument, change is directed at testing the limits of the present by experimenting how we can go beyond them. This is not the revolutionary change of overturning the present order thought to be possible when it is a matter of installing a universal such as freedom or equality *tout court*. This illusion, if we can call it such, makes sense only when it is a matter of establishing this modern order of values and overturning an 'old' aristocratic-monarchical-patrimonial regime.

At this point of time we cannot consider modern values as universals which either get fully established at a particular time of revolutionary change or get progressively established in ways which gradually complete their full actualisation. Rather, we have learnt through bitter experience how each time these values are specified, their terms of inclusion simultaneously construct excluded subject identities. For example, when the French Revolutionaries developed the Declaration of the Rights of Man and Citizen in 1789, their specification of the terms of inclusion within the formal category 'citizen' as referring to 'Man' produced the systemic exclusion of women from this modern equalitarian identity. Joan Landes (1988) argues that this was the first time women had been constructed as a homogeneous category in relation to their exclusion from this emergent modern public domain, and that this exclusion worked to call into being a collective subject, women, who would in turn contest it in the name of equality. Paradoxically, then, the exclusion of women from the rights of man laid the foundations of feminism. Struggles over how the modern universals get specified are central to an emancipatory politics and its histories (for some elaboration of this, see Yeatman 1993). If it is impossible to instantiate formal universals in ways which are all-inclusive—if, that is, their specification must produce new forms of exclusion—these exclusions are then contested in the name of the formal, empty and metaphysical category of equality (my debt to Ranciere here is registered in Yeatman 1993).

Before I turn to a genealogy of the category of oppression, more specifically of interlocking oppressions, within contemporary feminism, the status of oppression as a category of a modern politics of emancipation needs to be further examined.

The modern politico-ethical terrain of 'oppression'

If I am to be oppressed (for example, as a woman, an Aborigine, a lesbian or an unemployed person), two conditions have to be operative. First, I have to be conscious of being oppressed. Second, I have to have a sense not only that things could be different, but that the condition of my oppression contradicts or violates core values which I can assume are widely accepted. Sandra Bartky (1990) makes these points in her important piece 'Toward a phenomenology of feminist consciousness'. 'To be a feminist,' she argues, 'one has first to become one.' In other words, it is the transformation in consciousness, the change from not being to becoming a feminist, that is central to the nature of feminist politics and the processes of change it involves. This process of becoming is never over: one becomes a feminist again and again as one negotiates one's way in relation to the persistence of 'pre-', 'non-' or even 'anti-' feminist practices as these are reconstituted in relation to one's changing self and the conditions of one's situation. This is the central reason Bartky (1990: 20–21) insists on the ethical ambiguity of feminists' situation. Bartky also points out that these processes of becoming a feminist makes sense only in relation to a situation where change is thought to be possible. If there seem to be 'natural' reasons why women cannot be as socially powerful as men, then it makes no sense for women to regard themselves as oppressed. While she takes a Marxist approach in focusing on the material conditions for women's liberation—access to effective means of separating sexual expression from reproductive consequence; and integration into the worlds of paid employment—it is important to recognise that the existence of 'concrete circumstances which would permit a significant alteration in the status of women' (Bartky 1990: 12) is contained in the very modern democratic values of freedom, equality and citizenship.

As we have said already, these values are formal universals. They are enunciated in ways which make it appear that they refer to all who are construed as 'persons' or 'human beings'. This enunciation indicates the metaphysic of these values, the core value of which is equality. However, they exist only as they are specified. The specification always locates the value within an historically specific economy of inclusions and exclusions. These necessarily contradict the inclusive metaphysic of equality, and in so doing provide the basis on which those who are constituted as excluded subjects may proceed to contest their exclusion. Accordingly, the possibility, indeed the necessity, of feminism is contained within the modern political metaphysic.

The development of the formal universals of personhood is a peculiarly modern condition. Even while Greek and Roman antiquity elaborated a conception of the citizen, it did not disturb the fundamental division between slave and free. Along with women and children, slaves were confined to the inner life of the household economy, and status as a free man was reserved to heads of households. Freedom in this picture is intimately bound up with a patrimonial and patriarchal kinship status: the inherited headship of a kinship unit and its property base is the prerequisite for freedom. This, then, is an emergent conception of citizenship which bears all the hallmarks and limitations of an aristocratic social order. Modern conceptions of freedom and equality, on the other hand, are developed in the name of all human beings as creatures able to exercise their reason, and they are directed against an aristocratic and monarchical order of rule. John Locke in his 'Second treatise', (1965: 346, para. 54) argues against a seventeenth-century version of privileged, descent-based freedom and for the 'Equality which all Men are in, in respect of Jurisdiction or Dominion one over another'. Against Filmer's claim that the right of kings to rule resides in their belonging to a line of descent which begins with Adam, an argument which claims divine origins, Locke also claims divine origins but offers a different account of them:

> To understand Political Power right, and derive it from its Original, we must consider what State all Men are naturally in, and that is, *a State of perfect Freedom* to order their Actions and dispose of their Possessions, and Persons, as they think fit, within the bounds of the Law of Nature, without asking leave, or depending upon the Will of any other Man.
>
> A *State* also of *Equality*, wherein all the Power and Jurisdiction is reciprocal, no one having more than another: there being nothing more evident, than that Creatures of the same species and ranks

promiscuously born to all the same advantages of Nature, and the use of the same faculties, should also be equal one amongst another without Subordination or Subjection, unless the Lord and Master of them all, should by any manifest Declaration of his Will set one above another, and confer on him by an evident and clear appointment an undoubted Right to Dominion and Sovereignty. (Locke 1965: 309, para. 4, original emphases)

It is true that Locke's language—'all Men'—betrays a masculinist conception of this freedom and equality. However, against Carole Pateman's (1988) interpretation of the account of the Social Contract offered by such modern political philosophers as Locke, I would argue that masculinism is not the core truth of these modern values, but resides within them as one term of a contradiction. The other term is the inclusiveness of the conception: 'Creatures of the same species . . . born to . . . the use of the same faculties'. This inclusiveness becomes evident when Locke (1965, Chapter 6) makes the right to equality and freedom conditional on the individual's being educated to use *his* (sic) capacity to reason. Locke construes reason as a species capacity and one that is dependent on a social process—education—rather than a natural one.

Here we can see the way in for modern feminists such as Mary Astell in the late seventeenth century and Mary Wollstonecraft in the late eighteenth century. They play the contradiction by arguing that, if women share this species-characteristic of reason, then it follows that they share the same natural state of equality as men. Mary Wollstonecraft made special capital out of Locke's making equality and freedom conditional on education. Why could women not be educated to reason so as to come into the capacity to responsibly exercise equality and freedom? Wollstonecraft also anticipated an important argument of nineteenth-century feminism, namely that if women's primary social contribution lies in mothering, then surely it is important that they be educated to be mothers who can provide the appropriate moral environment and socialisation for sons as future citizens, and daughters as the mothers of citizens. Whether the feminist argument set out from women's sharing the capacity to reason, or from this conception of republican motherhood, the effect was the same: a claim on equal citizenship.

Equally we can see how slaves in the plantation economies of the Americas in the eighteenth and nineteenth centuries would have responded to the contradictions of the Lockeian modern conception of equal citizenship. The right of slaves to learn to read became a central

point of struggle within the ante-bellum order of the Southern plantation economy. Reading assumed this symbolic status because it was
understood as the key to education, and thus the key to the effective
use of freedom and equality. My point here is a general one. The modern enunciation of freedom
and equality as formal human universals was an effective if unintended
invitation by such as Locke to all those excluded by the ways these
universals were particularised to contest this exclusion. Modern democratic discourse calls into being or interpellates the contestatory subjects whose political struggle is directed against the exclusions of this
discourse in the name of equality.

Oppression, I am arguing, exists only when a universalistic and
equalitarian conception of the social order is operative. When this is
the case, the dominant subject positions itself as the instantiation of
the universalistic ideal of a particular type of equalitarian social order.
In Locke's day, this dominant subject was a male household head
belonging to 'the Civiliz'd part of Mankind' (Locke 1965: 331, para.
30), namely the Western part which was beginning to colonise the
globe. All other subjects are interpellated as to some extent lacking the
capacities which characterise the fully developed human being. For
example, uncivilised peoples were constructed as being both unedu-
cated and still in the stage of enjoying property in common; that is,
they had not entered the individualising dynamics associated with the
conversion of the common into private property, a development which
Locke, and the modern political economists such as Adam Smith after
him, saw as the condition both of 'improving' the land through labour
and of the production of wealth. This is how the white settler colonists
in New Zealand, Australia and the United States justified their expro-
priation of the indigenous peoples' land (see Fleras and Elliott 1992).
At this time—from the seventeenth century until the Married Women's
Property Acts in the last half of the nineteenth century in British
jurisdictions—in a different but related sense, married women were also
constituted as unpropertied subjects: since they were positioned under
the authority of their privately propertied husbands, they could not be
citizens in their own right.

To be interpellated as a potentially but not fully human subject is
to have a contradictory status. If those who are interpellated in this
way can show that they can overcome the attribute of lesser development, or that this attribution is mistaken, they can claim admission to
the rights of the human being. On this basis, they can show that the
social barriers—such as the legal denial to married women of the
capacity to own property—to this admission are arbitrary, unfair and

despotic. While the argument against married women's propertyless status was carried by the end of the nineteenth century, it continues to have to be made by indigenous peoples who have come under colonial rule. This is the significance of the Mabo decision conferring the right to 'native title' on the Australian Aboriginal peoples, and of the Waitangi Tribunal in New Zealand, which hears Maori tribal claims to lands expropriated by the Crown. In both cases the modern property order is being reconstituted so as to recognise the validity of collective–tribal rather than individualised ownership. This can be seen as a much more thoroughgoing reconstitution of the terms of modern citizenship than the bestowal of property-owning status on married women, which fell within the privatised and individualised outline of the modern property order.

Women, children, indigenous peoples and the colonised have all been interpellated as potentially but not fully human within the modern universalistic discourse of freedom and equality. With the partial exception of children, all these subjects have contested their exclusion from the status of citizen. While these contestations have related features, they have also their own specificity. Their struggles against exclusion have to assume features which take up and respond to the specificity of their exclusion. Thus, women have to show that their sexed identity as women does not disqualify them from doing what is expected of developed social beings at a particular time, and Aborigines and Maori have to show that the collectivism of their culture does not prevent them from being effective commercial entrepreneurs.

A complication of the contemporary picture is that the successes of the struggles for inclusion on the part of those who have been marginalised by the modern discourse of freedom and equality has brought about a very high degree of formal inclusion. It is no longer legitimate for this discourse to discriminate against any subject on the basis of characteristics unrelated to capacities for citizenship: sex, religion, ethnicity, race, age, sexual preference, and so on. In a sense, ours is the age of the formal completion of the modern ideal of a universalistic humanity. This means that the exclusions work in different and, in a sense, more subtle ways than in the past. One may be the female African-American descendant of a plantation slave and also an acclaimed American writer—Toni Morrison, for example. But Toni Morrison's status is still marked, that is qualified in a way which indicates she is not fully included within the dominant subject term: she is constantly referred to as a black woman writer. While dominant subject modes of social participation have been formally opened to the excluded subjects of modernity, the substantive opportunities of this opening become real for only a minority in each excluded subject group. Most are not able to make full and effective use of equal employment opportunity and anti-discrimination laws. This, then, is the historical terrain of the category oppression. I have suggested that it is in the nature of this terrain to create a multiplicity of oppressed subject positions, and that their struggles against oppression, while different, are linked. Closer historical inspection of the differences and links operative at any particular time would bring out their specificity, and the ways in which the various movements against oppression call each other into being in these differences and links. For example, during the movement for the abolition of slavery led by well-meaning members of the 'civiliz'd' and propertied classes in England and the United States, middle-class women began to apply to their own social condition the metaphors of slavery and emancipation. It was out of Abolitionism that the leaders of first-wave feminism in the United States were recruited, and the Seneca Falls Convention in 1848 was led by two women—Lucretia Mott and Elizabeth Cady Stanton—who had been excluded because they were women from being seated as delegates at the World Anti-Slavery Convention in London in 1840 (see Flexner 1972, Chapters 4 and 5).

Second-wave feminism and the discourse of interlocking oppressions

Until very recently, modern emancipatory politics espoused the idea that the various oppressed subject categories all shared in the status of oppression and that in this they were the same. This was a humanist conception, tied to a utopian belief that it is possible to actualise the modern values of freedom and equality in an inclusive way. If the politics of the variously oppressed subjects was essentially the same politics, oriented by a struggle for this inclusive order, then any one subject could stand in for the rest. Historically this has been the working-class subject. The left socialist and communist traditions of political struggle placed this subject at the helm of the general struggle for human emancipation and the overcoming of the oppressor class.

The workers' movement was understood as standing in for the progressive march of all humanity. Even while workers' movements were organised in terms of specific national contexts, it was assumed that they shared an international identity and universal mission. This allowed for a peculiarly unexamined nexus between workers' and anticolonial or, as they later came to be called, national liberation movements. Notwithstanding their national identity, workers' movements were seen as representing an international humanity, while anticolonial struggles were assumed to be pitted against a rapacious and imperialistic international bourgeoisie.

The idea of a universal human subject was sustained at a number of different levels: by the idea of a universal and international working class, by the idea of an internationally networked and colonising bourgeoisie, and by the idea of a struggle which both combined and condensed national liberation and class emancipatory ideals within particular colonies.

As long as the ethos of emancipatory movements was coloured by an orientation to universal human emancipation, there could be no consciousness of interlocking oppressions. For when working-class, feminist and anticolonial movements are oriented in this way, they subsume the specificity of their struggles within the general project of advancement of humanity. These movements are accepted as genuine emancipatory movements only to the degree that they accept this leadership. For a consciousness of multiple and interlocking oppressions to be possible, the idea of universal human emancipation has to lose legitimacy. This occurred with the effective challenges in the postcolonial era to the assimilationist character of the universal or humanist subject. Although one cannot say exactly how the ground was prepared for this, a series of historical events helped to delegitimise the assimilationist ideal of a unitary human subject: the Jewish holocaust brought about by one of the most civilised Western nations; the murder and forced prison exile of millions of people in the name of communism in Stalin's Soviet Union; the increasing force and legitimacy of the postwar anticolonial movements, for example in Algeria and Vietnam. In the 1950s and '60s, these movements signalled their difference from the two great binary forces of world-historical humanist politics—capitalist liberal democracy, and communism—in the non-aligned movement of independent nations.

These developments are not sufficient to explain the emergence of a politics of difference. While they helped to discredit the modern, universalistic idea of the human subject by showing how its exponents could wreak terrible violence in the name of this idea—e.g. the United States defended its military intervention against the Vietnamese anti-colonial struggle as being on behalf of democracy in Vietnam—this in itself does not accord positive value to difference. On the contrary: it can simply license a reinstatement of the universal human subject, this time comprising a universe of free and equal independent nations. A politics of difference does not refer to multiplicity as signifying this kind of pluralism. Rather it implies incommensurable differences which cannot be subsumed under the one universal category. It is impossible to understand how this kind of difference can develop without there being a fundamental challenge to what is presupposed by the idea of a unitary national or, indeed, human subject.

Feminism poses this fundamental challenge because it represents an emancipatory subject who cannot stand in for the whole in the way that the working-class and national-liberation movements can. Feminism suggests that there is an oppressor–oppressed relationship within a class, within a nation, and, therefore, within humanity. It follows from this that there is no unitary emancipatory interest for the universal subject.

This could be appreciated once the idea of the working class as the emancipatory agent of humanity had lost credibility. It lost credibility on two major counts. The first of these I have already indicated: the way in which this universalism underwrote the totalising conception of communism and its violent exclusionary practices. The second of these is the problem of representation, a problem the 1960s 'New Left' movement insisted upon in its argument for the value of each individual's participating in the decisions governing his or her life (see 'The Port Huron Statement' in Jacobs and Landau 1966: 160). Essentially, the New Left was rejecting the inevitability of a need for the working class to be represented, classically by a centralised, top-down party apparatus. According to its analysis, the interests of the Party inner-circle leadership were not the same as those of ordinary working-class people and hence that the Party did not represent the working class.

Once the idea of an agent representing the emancipatory interest of humankind could no longer command legitimacy, feminism as a social movement could come into its own in the sense of representing of those who are cast always as the part, not the whole. As we have seen, this cuts both ways. That is, feminism not only demonstrates that the national community is internally fractured, but this internal fracturing applies also to feminism's own identity, as representing the interests of women.

However, the problem of representation cannot be conjured away as second-wave feminism has discovered: when we speak on behalf of women, who are 'we', and which women are these? The problem is not solved by restricting 'women' to mean only those who share one's own position as, for example, a white, middle-class, able-bodied, educated woman. The issue is still there: who is speaking on behalf of whom? The conditions of participation can be as wide as possible; the issue is still there.

As long as a humanist emancipatory politics persisted, a subject could be positioned as both black, for example, and woman, but this meant she had to subscribe to the most heavily marked of these identities and its politics. For a black woman this meant subscribing to black subject status and its contestation. For a working-class woman this meant subscribing to working class subject status and its contestation. In each case the feminine subject within the oppressed race or class was asked to subordinate her own distinctive claims to what would further the well-being and good of the whole race or class. This guaranteed to white, middle-class women the leadership of feminism, for they were the only women whose subject status threw into relief the condition of women as a marked term and oppressed group. This is no longer the case. As of the 1980s, it is possible for multiply oppressed subjects to claim the multiplicity of their oppressed-subject statuses. Thus, for example, an African-American feminist such as bell hooks brings out what it means to be black and woman, a positioning different from that of black man or white woman:

> As a group, black women are in an unusual position in this society, for not only are we collectively at the bottom of the occupational ladder, but our overall social status is lower than that of any other group . . . we are the group that has not been socialized to assume the role of exploiter/oppressor in that we are allowed no institution-alized 'other' that we can exploit or oppress. White women and black men have it both ways. They can act as oppressor or be oppressed. Black men may be victimized by racism, but sexism allows them to act as exploiters and oppressors of women. White women may be victimized by sexism, but racism enables them to act as exploiters and oppressors of black people . . . As long as these two groups or any group defines liberation as gaining social equality with ruling class men, they have a vested interest in the continued exploitation and oppression of others. (hooks 1984: 14–15)

Other categories of multiply oppressed women have taken up this discourse of interlocking and multiple oppressions. For example, diasporic postcolonials such as subcontinental Indian women working in American higher education (e.g. Mani 1989), non-English-speaking-background women in Australia (e.g. Gunew 1993), Australian Aboriginal women (e.g. Huggins 1993), and lesbian black and Jewish women in the United States (see Bulkin and Smith in Bulkin et al. 1984) have all taken up this discourse.

By the end of the 1980s a literature that explores how coloniser and middle-class status had inflected dominant-group feminism had

developed (see Miller 1990; Armstrong 1990). This literature contributes to a history of how women of dominant-subject class-race-ethnic
status have invented feminism in their own image, and have 'othered'
women who do not hold to this status. This literature is a response to
the emergence of a politics of difference within feminism, and reflects
a crisis of legitimation for dominant-group women's leadership of
feminism that will not go away. Feminism is now exposed in its own
internal differences and ruptures just as the elaboration of a feminist
consciousness within race and ethnic communities has exposed their
lines of fracture. In both cases, the ideal of a unified movement is
revealed as a fiction. The ongoing existence of the movement is now
subject to a lively, visible and legitimate politics of contestation as to
how this movement is to be represented and by whom. The only
adequate response has been to make the differences manifest by having
differently positioned feminists participate in deciding how the movement gets represented. While this may help to make the problem of
representation explicit, it does not dispense with it.

The idea of interlocking oppressions can be made over to a version
of the universal, humanist subject. This happens when it is argued that
an accumulation of oppressed statuses—as woman, black, lesbian,
working class, etc.—makes one a better representative of all oppressed
subjects than those who are 'less' oppressed could be. Alison Jones and
Camille Guy show how this tendency reframed the radical feminism
of the 1980s in New Zealand:

> Radical feminism was able to achieve a kind of settlement despite
> these divisions, through providing a framework which both rein-
> forced the basic certainty of women's shared oppression, as well as
> encompassing its diversity.
>
> The conciliatory but ultimately unsatisfying solution was the idea
> that 'all women are oppressed but some are more oppressed than
> others'. This as expressed in a highly simplistic and moralistic form:
> a hierarchy of oppressions was espoused, with the more oppressed
> at the bottom, and the less oppressed at the top. The more oppressed
> were to be listened to: not because we needed to understand what
> they had to say, but because their membership of certain suffering
> social categories gave them the moral edge. (Jones and Guy
> 1993: 306–307)

Here the most oppressed become a martyred elect of suffering subjects
who accuse the non-elect of contributing to their subject status. Many
positioned as 'oppressor' subjects in this politics use the victim's
accusation much as they would a confessional, which once visited

releases them back into an unreflective enjoyment of their dominant-group status.

Jones and Guy point out that the additive model of oppression cannot grasp the contextually varying and contradictory nature of the relationships of oppression. It is not simply that many women are contradictorily positioned across the relationships of oppression: A is a woman, but she is also white, middle class and lesbian, for example. Just what these positions mean are contextually dependent:

> This is fairly evident in the issue of 'heterosexual privilege'. Lesbian women with no children and highly paid jobs experience different forms of power from heterosexual women with children and low paid jobs (similarly, poor and wealthy lesbian women) . . . Or take the situation of the young female pakeha lecturer who is verbally abused and physically intimidated by a male Maori student, who publicly uses sexual terms to express his anger at what he perceives as her racism. The power relations circulating in these relationships are not adequately understood in abstract and rigid hierarchies of gender, race or class. (Jones and Guy 1993: 309)

This emphasises that nothing privileges our identity or its utterances before they come to be heard within particular historical and locational contexts of communication and struggle. This is why I and others take issue with identity politics where identity is assigned a given and prior status according to the politics of difference. We cannot know who we are until we act, and our action always takes place in a particular context of relationship to and dialogue with particular others. What the action means will depend on the narratives I and these others retrospectively give it. Since we will be assigning meaning interactively, that is in an interlocutory relationship to each other's narratives, it is all too likely that this meaning will be both contested and changing.

The idea of interlocking oppressions, then, presupposes the general modern political context where oppression is a core category of emancipatory-movement consciousness. Historically, it presupposes the end of an assimilationist era, an era in which the universal idea of the human subject was represented by subjects positioned in gender, class, race and ethnic terms as dominant, and where, by the same token, subjects who were positioned in these terms as oppressed found themselves unable to operate within the terrain of the universal human subject. To be sure, where they could, oppressed subjects attempted to join the club of the universal human subject by adopting various projects and strategies of assimilation. These efforts at assimilation were important in tabling the value of difference, because it turned out that assimilation for oppressed subjects on the terms of dominant-group subjects is a costly business. The rules of the game worked to constantly impress on oppressed subjects attempting to assimilate—e.g. the first generations of women professionals—their inadequacy in relation to expected practice and style. For oppressed subjects, assimilation meant trying to be like dominant-group subjects, with the end result that they could neither respect nor value the things that made them different. This can be psychologically destructive. Much of the leadership of second-wave feminism are daughters of women, many of them 'ethnic', who attempted assimilation through education and/or occupational success. These daughters inherited the contradictions as well as the achievements of the projects of their mothers' efforts at assimilation. This may have enabled them to attempt something other than assimilation: a politics of difference. Close examination of the black rights movement in the United States since the 1920s would permit some exploration and testing of this hypothesis, as would a sociological enquiry into the backgrounds of second-wave feminists.

In any case, the idea of interlocking oppressions came into being at the same time as that of a politics of difference. It may turn out that we cannot do without the metaphysical presupposition of a universal human subject. For example, the categories 'cultural', 'historical', 'social' seem to depend on such a presupposition. What is at issue is whether we can develop a critically reflexive awareness of how this presupposition works. If we make it uncritically, then we subscribe uncritically to the exclusions to which the inevitable specification of this universal gives rise. If we are aware that these exclusions must follow, and that their contestation is important, we can work to enable this contestation.

5

I'm a feminist but . . .
'Other' women and postnational feminism

Ien Ang

For some time now, the problematic of race and ethnicity has thrown feminism into crisis. I am implicated in this crisis. As a woman of Chinese descent, I suddenly find myself in a position in which I can turn my 'difference' into intellectual and political capital, where 'white' feminists invite me to raise my 'voice', *qua* a non-white woman, and make myself heard. Anna Yeatman (Chapter 4) suggests that voices such as mine are needed to contest and correct the old exclusions of the established feminist order, and that they will win non-white women authorship and authority within a renewed, less exclusionary feminism. In this sense, feminism acts like a nation; just like Australia, it no longer subscribes to a policy of assimilation but wants to be multicultural.

I want to complicate this scenario by looking at the *problems* of such a desire. Rather than positively representing a 'Chinese' or 'Asian' contribution to Australian feminism—which would only risk reinforcing the objectification and fetishisation of 'Asianness'—I want to argue that the very attempt to construct a voice for self-presentation in a context already firmly established and inhabited by a powerful formation (what is now commonly called, rather unreflexively, 'white/Western feminism') is necessarily fraught with difficulty. To me, non-white, non-Western women in 'white/Western' societies can only begin to speak with a hesitating 'I'm a feminist, but . . .', in which the meaning and substance of feminism itself become problematised. Where does this leave feminism? Feminism must stop conceiving itself as a nation, a 'natural' political destination for all women, no matter how multicultural. Rather than adopting a politics of inclusion (which is always ultimately based on a notion of commonality and community), it will have to develop a self-conscious politics of partiality, and imagine itself as a *limited* political home, which does not absorb difference within a

57

pre-given and predefined space but leaves room for ambivalence and ambiguity. In the uneven, conjunctural terrain so created, white/Western feminists too will have to detotalise their feminist identities and be compelled to say: 'I'm a feminist, but . . .'

The politics of difference and its limits

In the early days of the second wave, feminist theory and practice were predicated on the assumptions of women's common identity *as* women, and of a united global sisterhood. It was the universalisation of white, middle-class women's lives as representative of *the* female experience which made it possible for modern Western feminism to gather momentum and become such an important social movement. In this sense feminism, like any other political philosophy, is an 'interested universalism' (Yeatman 1993), based on the postulate that women have common experiences and share common interests *qua* women.

Today, it is precisely this homogenising idea of sisterhood which has come under increasing attack within feminism itself. After all, not all women share the same experience of 'being a woman', nor is shared gender enough to guarantee a commonality in social positioning. As Elizabeth Spelman (1988: 14) rightly states, 'even if we say all women are oppressed by sexism we cannot automatically conclude that the sexism all women experience is the same'. This is an important realisation which undermines any reductionist, essentialising definition of 'women's oppression' as a universal female experience. It also means the end of the authority of the category of 'women' as the 'natural' binding factor for feminist politics. Instead, as Judith Butler (1990: 3) notes, '*women* has become a troublesome term, a site of contest, a cause for anxiety'.

It is now widely acknowledged that differences between women undermine the homogeneity and continuity of 'women' as a social category: differences produced by the intersections of class, race, ethnicity, nationality, and so on. So 'difference' has become an obligatory tenet in feminist discourse in the 1990s, and feminism's ability to 'deal with it' is often mentioned as a condition for its survival as a movement for social change. The so-called politics of difference recognises the need to go beyond the notion of an encompassing sisterhood, and acknowledges that feminism needs to take account of the fact that not all women are white, Western and middle class and take into consideration the experiences of 'other' women as well. In Australian feminism, this trend is evidenced in important recent publications such as *Intersexions: Gender/Class/Culture/Ethnicity* (Bottomley et al. 1991), *Living in the Margins: Racism, Sexism and Feminism* (Pettman 1992) and *Feminism and the Politics of Difference* (Gunew and Yeatman 1993). What does it mean, however, to 'deal with difference'? Pettman (1992: 158) suggests among other things that it means 'recognising unequal power and conflicting interests while not giving up on community or solidarity or sisterhood'. But this sounds all too deceptively easy, a formula of containment that wants to have it both ways, as if differences among women could unproblematically be turned into a 'unity in diversity' once they are 'recognised' properly. Yeatman (1993: 241) suggests that the politics of difference should encourage 'the complexity of dialogue' between differently situated feminists (e.g. Aboriginal and Anglo-Australian women) who are not positioned as mutually exclusive selves versus others, but 'who understand themselves to be complexly like and different from each other'. However, isn't 'women' being surreptitiously smuggled back in here as the essential way in which the interlocutors are assumed to resemble each other?

The way difference should be 'dealt with', then, is typically imagined by the feminist establishment through such benevolent terms as 'recognition', 'understanding' and 'dialogue'. The problem with such terms is first of all that they reveal an overconfident faith in the power and possibility of open and honest communication to 'overcome' or 'settle' differences, of a power-free speech situation without interference by entrenched presumptions, sensitivities and preconceived ideas. It is a faith in our (limitless?) capacity not only to speak, but, more importantly, to listen and hear. Spelman, speaking to fellow white feminists, relentlessly questions the (white) feminist ability to listen in this regard: 'Is the reason we haven't heard from them before that they haven't spoken, or that we haven't listened? (. . .) Are we really willing to hear anything and everything that they might have to say, or only what we don't find too disturbing? Are we prepared to hear what they say, even if it requires learning concepts or whole languages that we don't yet understand?' (Spelman 1988: 163). Spelman's very phrasing brings to bear a deep and disturbing gulf between 'us' and 'them' (i.e. 'other' women). This suggests that 'difference' cannot be 'dealt with' easily, and can certainly not just be 'overcome'.

Therefore, I want to stress here the *difficulties* of 'dealing with difference'. These difficulties cannot be resolved through communication, no matter how complex the dialogue. Indeed, the very desire to resolve them in the first place could result in a premature glossing-over of the social irreducibility and inescapability of certain markers of difference and the way they affect women's lives. To focus on *resolving* differences between women as the ultimate aim of 'dealing with difference' would mean their containment in an inclusive, encompassing structure which itself remains uninterrogated; it would mean that 'these differences must comply with feminism's (. . .) essentialising frame' (Kirby 1993: 29). In such a case, difference is 'dealt with' by absorbing it into an already existing feminist community without challenging the naturalised legitimacy and status of that community *as* a community. By dealing with difference in this way, feminism resembles the multicultural nation—the nation that, faced with cultural differences within its borders, simultaneously recognises and controls those differences amongst its population by containing them in a grid of pluralist diversity (Bhabha 1991). However, reducing difference to diversity in this manner is tantamount to a more sophisticated and complex form of assimilation. As Chandra Talpade Mohanty puts it:

> The central issue (. . .) is not one of merely *acknowledging* difference; rather, the more difficult question concerns the kind of difference that is acknowledged and engaged. Difference seen as benign variation (diversity), for instance, rather than as conflict, struggle, or the threat of disruption, bypasses power as well as history to suggest a harmonious, empty pluralism. On the other hand, difference defined as asymmetrical and incommensurate cultural spheres situated within hierarchies of domination and resistance cannot be accommodated within a discourse of 'harmony in diversity'. (Mohanty 1989: 181)

To take difference seriously, then, we need to examine the sources and effects of the threat of disruption Mohanty talks about. Concretely, it would mean a focus on how the gulf between mainstream feminism and 'other' women is constructed and reproduced, and paying attention to, rather turning our gaze away from, those painful moments at which communication seems unavoidably to *fail*.[1] Rather than assuming that ultimately a common ground can be found for women to form a community—on the *a priori* assumption that successful communication is guaranteed—we might do better to start from point zero and realise that there are moments at which no common ground exists whatsoever, and when any communicative event would be nothing more than a speaking past one another. I want to suggest, then, that these moments of ultimate failure of communication should not be encountered with regret, but rather should be accepted as the starting point for a more modest feminism, one which is predicated on the fundamental *limits* to the very idea of sisterhood (and thus the category 'women') and on the necessary *partiality* of the project of feminism as such.

In other words, I suggest that we would gain more from acknowledging and confronting the stubborn solidity of 'communication barriers' than from rushing to break them down in the name of an idealised unity. Such an idealised unity is a central motif behind a politics of difference which confines itself to repairing the friction between white women and 'other' women. The trouble is that such reparation strategies often end up appropriating the other rather than fully confronting the incommensurability of the difference involved. This is the case, for example, in well-intentioned but eventually only therapeutic attempts on the part of white women to overcome 'our own racism' through consciousness-raising, a tendency particularly strong in some strands of American liberal feminism. White feminists worried about their own race privilege typically set out to overcome their feelings of guilt by identifying with the oppressed other. Thus, Ann Russo (1991: 308) claims that her ability to 'connect with women of color' is greater when she faces the ways in which she herself has been oppressed in her own life as a white, middle-class woman. She would be less able to empathise, she says, if she would see herself 'as only privileged' and 'as only an oppressor', because then she would see herself as 'too different' from 'women of color'. In other words, the white woman can become a 'politically correct' anti-racist by disavowing the specificity of the experience of being a racialised 'other', reducing it to an instance of an oppression essentially the same as her own, gender-based oppression. This form of appropriation only reinforces the security of the white point of view as the point of reference from which the other is made same, a symbolic annihilation of otherness which is all the more pernicious precisely because it occurs in the context of a claimed solidarity with the other. The very presumption that race-based oppression can be understood by paralleling it with gender-based oppression results in a move to reinstate white hegemony. Such a move represses consideration of the cultural repercussions of the structural ineluctability of white hegemony in Western societies. (I have used the terms 'white' and 'Western' in an overgeneralising way here, but will specify them later.)

Of course, the most powerful agents of white/Western hegemony are white middle-class males,[2] but white middle-class females too are the bearers of whiteness which, because of its taken for grantedness, is 'a privilege enjoyed but not acknowledged, a reality lived in but unknown' (Cathy Thomas, quoted in Frankenberg 1993). To her credit, Russo (1991: 308) is aware of the possible ramifications of this shared whiteness: 'While white feminists have directed our anger at white men for their sexual (and other) atrocities, there remains a common historical and cultural heritage which carries with it a certain familiarity and even subconscious loyalty to our skin and class privilege.' These comments elucidate the fact that white privilege does not have to do necessarily with overt or explicit forms of racism, but with a much more normalised and insidious set of assumptions which disremember the structural advantage of being white, and which generalise specifically white cultural practices and ways of seeing and being in the world as normal (Frankenberg, 1993).

The extent to which this white self-exnomination permeates mainstream feminism should not be underestimated. It is a core, if unconscious, aspect of (white/Western) feminism, which appears unaware that even some of its apparently most straightforward ideas and beliefs reveal its embeddedness in particular orientations and tendencies derived from 'white/Western' culture. For example, the well-known maxim 'When a woman says no, she means no!' to articulate the feminist stance on rape and sexual harassment invokes an image of the ideal feminist woman as assertive, determined, plain-speaking and confrontational. The slogan does not just speak to men (who are commanded to take no for an answer), but also implicitly summons women to take up these feministically approved qualities and mean no when they say it. However, these qualities are far from culturally neutral: they belong to a repertoire of rules for social interaction which prizes individualism, conversational explicitness, directness and efficiency—all Western cultural values which may not be available or appeal to 'other' women. Asian women, for example, may well deal with male dominance in culturally very different, more circuitous (and not necessarily less effective) ways. In other words, far from being culturally universal, 'When a woman says no, she means no!' implies a feminist subject position and style of personal politics that are meaningful chiefly for those women who have the 'right' cultural resources. I am not saying that the maxim itself is ethnocentric; what is ethnocentric is the assumption that it represents all women's experiences and interests in sexual relations (arguably it doesn't even represent those of all 'white/Western' women). Even more perniciously, this universalist feminist assumption implicitly finds wanting all women who do *not* have these cultural resources. As a result, these different women are, as Mohanty says about Third World women, 'stripped of their existence as concrete historical subjects living, working, acting and fighting in particular societal circumstances, and are objectified as a generalised, always-already oppressed "other woman" (e.g. the veiled woman, the chaste virgin)' (Mohanty 1984: 353), against whom Wester women become elevated as the self-professed avant-garde of liberated womanhood (see also e.g. Chow 1991; Jolly 1991; Kirby 1993; Ong 1988).

In acknowledgment of the need to deconstruct such universalising assumptions of white/Western feminism, feminist theorists have begun to concern themselves with the issue of representation, of 'who is permitted to speak on behalf of whom'. If speaking in the name of the other is no longer politically acceptable, how then should the other be represented? Or should white feminists refrain from representing 'other' women at all? Would the problem be gradually solved if more 'other' women would start raising their voices and presenting 'their' points of view? Here again, the implicit assumption is that a diversification of discourse would eventually lead to a broader, more inclusive representation of 'all' women. However, what implications the resulting contestatory discourses can and should have for feminist politics remain glaringly unresolved. In other words, where does the emanating 'complexity of dialogue' lead us?

Let me address this question through an example, again derived (mainly) from American feminist criticism. As is well known, there has been much controversy in the academy about the cultural and sexual politics of the pop singer Madonna. Her many white feminist defenders see her as a postmodern protofeminist heroine, a woman who manages to create a cultural space where she can invent and play with daring representations of feminine sexuality while remaining in control and in charge (see Schwichtenberg 1993). While white critics have generally appreciated Madonna in terms of her clever subversion of male dominance,[3] however, the black feminist critic bell hooks argues that Madonna's gender politics can only be interpreted as liberating from a 'white' perspective:

> In part, many black women who are disgusted by Madonna's flaunting of sexual experience are enraged because the very image of sexual agency that she is able to project and affirm with material gain has been the stick this society has used to justify its continued beating and assault on the black female body. (hooks 1992: 159–160)

According to hooks, what Madonna's white feminist fans applaud her for—namely her power to act in sexually rebellious ways without being punished—cannot be experienced as liberating by the vast majority of black women in the US, as dominant myths of black females as sexually 'fallen' force them to be 'more concerned with projecting images of respectability than with the idea of female sexual agency and transgression' (hooks 1992: 160). In other words, hooks contends, Madonna's status as a feminist heroine makes sense only from a white woman's perspective, and any deletion of this specification only slights the black woman's perspective.

The point I want to make is not that the white feminist interpretation is wrong or even racist, or that hooks's view represents a better feminism, but that we see juxtaposed here two different points of view, constructed from two distinct speaking positions, each articulating concerns and preoccupations which make sense and are pertinent within its own reality. The meaning of Madonna, in other words, depends on the cultural, racially marked context in which her image circulates, at least in the US. Nor can either view be considered the definitive white or black take on Madonna; after all, any interpretation can only be provisional and is indefinitely contestable, forcing us to acknowledge its inexorable situatedness (Haraway 1988). Nevertheless, a reconciliation between these points of view is difficult to imagine. And this is not a matter of 'communication barriers' that need to be overcome, of differences that need to be 'recognised'. What we see exemplified here is a fundamental *incommensurability* between two competing feminist knowledges, dramatically exposing an irreparable chasm between a white and a black feminist truth. No harmonious compromise or negotiated consensus is possible here.

This example illuminates the limits of a politics of difference focused on representation. The voice of the 'other', once raised and taken seriously in its distinctiveness and specificity, cannot be assimilated into a new, more totalised feminist truth. The otherness of 'other' women, once they come into self-representation, works to disrupt the unity of 'women' as the foundation for feminism. This is the logic of Butler's (1990: 15) claim that '[i]t would be wrong to assume in advance that there is a category of "women" that simply needs to be filled in with various components of race, class, age, ethnicity, and sexuality in order to become complete'. That is, there are situations in which 'women' as signifier for commonality would serve more to impede the self-presentation of particular groups of female persons—in this case African-American women struggling against racist myths of black female sexuality—than to enhance them. White women and black women have little in common in this respect. Teresa de Lauritis (1988: 135) has put it this way: 'the experience of racism changes the experience of gender, so that a white woman would be no closer than a Black man to comprehending a Black woman's experience'. So we can talk with each other, we can enter into dialogue—there is nothing wrong with learning about the other's point of view—provided only that we do not impose a premature sense of unity as the desired outcome of such an exchange.

Considering white/Western hegemony

But there is more. It is clear that, while white critical discourse could afford to be silent about the racial dimension of the cultural meaning(s) of Madonna and could assume a stance of seeming racial neutrality,[4] hooks (1992) is only too aware of the marginal situatedness of her own point of view. She does not share the sense of entitlement which empowers white women to imagine a world in which they are 'on top', as it were, successfully turning the tables on men (white and black). Yet this is the quintessence of the all-powerful fantasy Madonna offers white women. Black women like hooks operate in the certainty that they will *never* acquire the power to rule the world; they know that this world—white-dominated, Western, capitalist modernity—is quite simply *not theirs*, and can never be. This fundamental sense of permanent dislocation, this feeling of always being a foreigner in a world that doesn't belong to you,[5] is what all those who are 'othered'— racialised or ethnicised—in relation to white/Western hegemony share.

It is important to emphasise, at this point, that white/Western hegemony is not a random psychological aberration but the systemic consequence of a global historical development over the last 500 years—the expansion of European capitalist modernity throughout the world, resulting in the subsumption of all 'other' peoples to its economic, political and ideological logic and mode of operation. Whiteness and Westernness are closely interconnected; they are two sides of the same coin. Westernness is the sign of white hegemony at the international level, where non-white, non-Western nations are by definition subordinated to white, Western ones. It is the globalisation of capitalist modernity which ensures the structural insurmountability of the white/non-white and Western/non-Western divide, as it is cast in the very infrastructure—institutional, political, economic—of the modern world (Wallerstein 1974). In other words, whether we like it or not, the contemporary world system is a *product* of white/Western hegemony, and we are all, in our differential subjectivities and positionings, implicated in it.

We are not speaking here, then, of an *ontological* binary opposition between white/Western women and 'other' women. Nor is it the case that white feminists are always-already 'guilty' (another psychologising gesture which can only paralyse). But the fracturing of the category of 'women' is historically and structurally entrenched, and cannot be magically obliterated by (white) feminism through sheer political will or strategy. As a consequence, in the words of de Lauretis (1988: 136), 'the feminist subject, which was initially defined purely by its status as colonised subject or victim of oppression, becomes redefined as much less pure [and] as indeed ideologically complicitous with "the oppressor" whose position it may occupy in certain sociosexual relations (though not others), on one or another axis'. Complicity, in other words, is a structural inevitability which we can only come to terms with by recognising it as determining the *limits* of political possibilities, not as something that we can work to undo (by consciousness-raising, for example). In other words, it is important to realise that the white/'other' divide is a historically and systemically imposed structure which cannot yet, if ever, be superseded.

Until now I have deliberately used the term 'other' to encompass all the disparate categories conjured up to classify these 'others': for example, 'black women', 'women of colour', 'Third World women', 'migrant women' or, a specifically Australian term circulating in official multicultural discourse, 'NESB (non-English-speaking-background) women'. Of course these different categories, themselves labels with unstable and shifting content and pasting over a multitude of differences, cannot be lumped together in any concrete, historically and culturally specific sense. In structural terms, however, they occupy the same space insofar as they are all, from a white perspective, relegated to the realm of racialised or ethnicised 'otherness', a normalising mechanism which is precisely constitutive of white/Western hegemony. As we have seen, feminism in Australia and elsewhere is not exempt from such hegemonising processes: in most feminist theory, too, whiteness is the unmarked norm against which all 'others' have to be specified in order to be represented. Spelman (1988: 169) points this out astutely: 'Black women's being Black somehow calls into question their counting as straightforward examples of "women," but white women's being white does not.'

What difference can a politics of difference make in the face of this fundamental, binary asymmetry? Sneja Gunew (1993: 1) claims that '[t]he dismantling of hegemonic categories is facilitated by the proliferation of difference rather than the setting up of binary oppositions that can merely be reversed, leaving structures of power intact'. This postmodern celebration of a 'proliferation of difference' as a utopian weapon in the destruction of hegemonic structures of power is also proposed by Jane Flax, as in this oft-quoted statement:

Feminist theories, like other forms of postmodernism, should encourage us to tolerate and interpret ambivalence, ambiguity, and multiplicity as well as expose the roots of our needs for imposing order and structure no matter how arbitrary and oppressive these needs may be. If we do our work well, reality will appear even more unstable, complex and disorderly than it does now. (Flax 1990: 56–7)

For reasons which will become clear, I am generally sympathetic to Flax's emphasis on ambivalence, ambiguity and multiplicity as theoretical principles in our approach to 'reality'. But she surreptitiously displays another form of psychological reductionism when she ascribes the imposition of order and structure to the obscurity of 'our needs', and suggests that we should learn to 'tolerate' ambivalence, ambiguity and multiplicity. To be sure, the consequence of Flax's postmodern equation of 'doing our work well' with making reality 'appear even more unstable, complex and disorderly' is an underestimating of the historical tenacity and material longevity of oppressive orders and structures, such as those entailing sedimented consequences of white/Western hegemony. This postmodern optimism, I suspect, can only be expressed from a position which does not have to cope with being on the receiving end of those orders and structures. Flax's 'we', therefore, can be read as a white 'we': it is white needs for order and structure which she implicitly refers to and whose roots she wants to expose (and, by implication, do away with), and it is only from a white perspective that 'tolerating' ambivalence and disorder would be a 'progressive', deuniversalising step. The problem is, of course, that the order and structure of white/Western hegemony cannot be eliminated by giving up the 'need' for it, simply because its persistence is not a matter of 'needs'.

From the perspective of 'other' women (and men), then, there is no illusion that white, Western hegemony will wither away in any substantial sense, at least not in the foreseeable future. The nature of global capitalist modernity is such that these 'other' peoples are left with two options: either enter the game or be excluded. At the national level, either integrate/assimilate or remain an outsider; at the international level, either 'Westernise' or be ostracised from the 'world community', the 'family of nations'. This ensures that the position of the non-white in a white-dominated world and the non-Western in a Western-dominated world is always necessarily and inescapably an 'impure' position, always dependent on and defined *in relation to* the white/Western dominant.[6] Any resistance to this overwhelming hegemony can therefore only ever take place from a position always-already 'contaminated' by white/Western practices, and can therefore only hope to carve out spaces of *relative* autonomy and freedom *within* the interstices of white/Western hegemony.

It is in this historical sense that the hierarchical binary divide between white/non-white and Western/non-Western should be taken account of as a master-grid framing the potentialities of, and setting limits to, all subjectivities and all struggles. Feminists and others need to be aware of this systemic inescapability when 'dealing with difference'. This is where I find Flax's insistence on ambivalence, ambiguity and multiplicity useful, not to celebrate 'difference' as a sign of positive postmodern chaos, but to describe the *necessary condition of existence* of those who are positioned, in varying ways, as peripheral others to the white, Western core. There is no pure, uncontaminated identity outside of the system generated by this hegemonic force. Despite hooks's largely autonomist stance on the African-American political struggle and counter-hegemonic practice (see for example, her essays in hooks 1990), it is clear that the very construction of Black identity in the US is intimately bound up with the history of slavery and segregation, just as contemporary Aboriginal 'identity' in Australia cannot erase the effects of 200 years of contact and conflict with European colonisers (see Attwood 1989), and the 'identity' of Third World nations, mostly postcolonial, cannot be defined outside the parameters of the international order put in place by the unravelling of European colonial and imperial history. The irony is that while all these 'identities' are effected by the objectification of 'others' by white/Western subjects, they have become the necessary and inescapable points of identification from which these 'others' can take charge of their own destinies in a world not of their own making. Ambivalence, ambiguity and multiplicity thus signal the unfinished and ongoing, contradictory, and eternally unresolved nature of this double-edged process of simultaneous objectification/subjectification. Seen this way, the politics of difference, while bitterly necessary now that 'other' voices are becoming increasingly insistent, has not resulted in a new feminist consensus and never will. There will always be a tension between difference as benign diversity and difference as conflict, disruption, dissension.

Australian whiteness, the postcolonial and the multicultural

I have used the terms 'white' and 'Western' rather indiscriminately so far. This is problematic, especially given the rapidity with which these terms have become 'boo-words', signifying irredeemable political incorrectness. To counter such sloganeering and to clarify my argument, I should stress that I have used these concepts first of all as generalising categories which describe *a position in a structural, hierarchical inter-relationship* rather than a precise set of cultural identities. Thus, being white in Australia is not the same as being white in Britain, France or the United States, as whiteness does not acquire meanings outside of a distinctive and overdetermined network of concrete social relations. Even who counts as white is not stable and unchanging—we should not forget, for example, that in the postwar period Southern European immigrants to Australia (Italians, Greeks) were perceived as non-white, thus 'black'! Whiteness, then, is not a biological category but a political one. Therefore, we need to go beyond the generalisations of generic whiteness and undifferentiated Westernness if we are to understand the specific cultural dynamics in which these interrelationships are played out in any particular context. In other words, analysing and interrogating the culturally specific ways in which whiteness, including white femininity, has been historically constructed and inflected in Australia is a necessary condition if Australian feminism is to effectively deuniversalise the experience of white women in feminist theory and practice.[7]

Australia is implicated in the global configuration of white/Western hegemony in ways which are particular to its history—of European settlement and Aboriginal genocide, of the White Australia policy, official multiculturalism, and the current 'push toward Asia'. Despite this, Australia remains predominantly populated by Anglo-Celtic people, who inhabit exnominated whiteness in this country. Its main social institutions and basic cultural orientations are identifiably Western, and as a nation it is categorised in the international order as a part of 'the West'. Yet it is important to note that Australian whiteness is itself relatively marginal in relation to world-hegemonic whiteness. The fact that Australia itself is on the periphery of the Euro-American core of 'the West' (and as such is often forgotten or ignored by that core), produces a sense of non-metropolitan, postcolonial whiteness whose structures of feeling remain to be explored. Meaghan Morris (1992) has begun to capture the distinctive ambiguities of Australian whiteness with the term 'white settler subjectivity', a subject position which, Morris notes, oscillates uneasily between identities as coloniser and colonised. In this respect, Australian whiteness is itself steeped in a deep sense of the ambivalence, ambiguity and multiplicity so valued by Flax. Here again, however, it doesn't get us very far to celebrate these conditions as inherently positive principles. Rather, they signal a historically specific cultural predicament which has led Morris

(1992: 471) to describe the Australian social formation as both 'dubiously postcolonial' and 'prematurely postmodern'. I want to suggest that the precariousness and fragility of this antipodean whiteness, so different from (post)imperial British whiteness or messianic, superpower American whiteness, inscribes and affects the way in which white Australia relates to its non-white 'others'. I will finish this essay then, by sketching briefly how Australian feminism is implicated in this.

Being Asian in Australia necessarily implies a problematic subject positioning. It is well known that the White Australia policy effectively excluded Asian peoples from settling in the country, because Australia wanted to be white, an outpost of Europe. Since the abandonment of this policy, however, 'we' are allowed in. And the politics of multiculturalism even encourages us to contribute to the cultural diversity of Australia. Still, the presence of Asians is not naturalised. A while ago I bumped into a middle-aged white woman in the supermarket. Such small accidents happen all the time; they are part of the everyday experience of sharing a space, including national space. But she was annoyed and started calling me names. 'Why don't you go back to your own country!' she shouted. I am familiar with this exhortation: it is a declaration of exclusion racialised and ethnicised people have to put up with all the time. But what does such a comment mean in Australia? I want to suggest that, placed in the larger context of Australian cultural history, the racism expressed here is not just ordinary prejudice. There is a measure of spite in the insistence with which this white woman proclaims Australia as her 'home' while emphatically denying me the right to do the same thing. It shocked me, because I thought this kind of thing was possible in Europe, not in a settler society such as Australia. In declaring herself to be a native threatened by alien immigrants, she displays an historical amnesia of (British) colonialism which actively erases the history of Aboriginal dispossession of the land. In other words, in her claim that Asians don't belong in this country, she simultaneously reproduces, in a single appropriative gesture, the exclusion of Aboriginal people. A disturbing bunker mentality is expressed in this peculiar double-edgedness of white Australian ethnocentrism, a mentality of tenaciously holding on to what one has which, I suggest, is sourced precisely in the precariousness and fragility, the moot legitimacy and lack of historical density of white settler subjectivity.[8]

Australian feminism has to take into account this two-sided antagonism, in which white Australia constitutes and asserts itself by demarcating itself from the immigrant on the one hand and the indigene on the other by racialising and/or ethnicising both, naturalising its own claim to nativeness in the process. It is clear that an Australian feminist politics of difference needs to dismantle and deconstruct the hierarchical relations involved in this complex and contradictory, three-pronged structure of mutual exclusivism, in which 'white' is the constitutive centre. This quotation from anthropologist Margaret Jolly typifies the problematic as it is currently seen through 'white' feminist eyes:

> There is the general problem of white feminists dealing with Australian women of colour, the rainbow spectrum of ethnic identities resulting from a long process of migration. *But the problem is more acute* with indigenous women because they identify us not so much as Anglo-inhabitants of Australia, but as the white invaders of their land. There is a strong and persistent sense of racial difference and conflict born out of the history of colonialism in our region. (Jolly 1991: 56; emphasis added)

My quarrel with this comment is that it reinstates the white feminist subject as the main actor, for whom the Aboriginal other and the migrant other are two competing interlocutors, kept utterly separate from each other. One result of this is that the differing relations between indigenous peoples and various groups of settlers remains unaddressed,[9] and that the Anglo centre—*its* problems and concerns pertaining to identity and difference—remains the main focus of attention. In intellectual terms, this amounts to a non-dialogue between the postcolonial and the multicultural problematic, the serial juxtapositioning of the two conditional entirely upon the distributive power of the hegemonic Anglo centre. From a white (Anglo) perspective, it may be understandable that priority be given to Anglo-Aboriginal relations (as Jolly suggests), as it is this relation which marks the original sin foundational to Australian white settler subjectivity, which can now no longer be repressed. However, this intense investment in the postcolonial problematic—which is the locus of the distinctively Australian quandary of 'white guilt'—may be one important reason why there is so little feminist engagement with the challenge of constructing a 'multicultural Australia'. 'Migrant women', lumped together in homogenising and objectifying categories such as NESB, are still mostly talked about, not spoken with and heard (Martin 1991); they remain within the particularist ghetto of ethnicity and are not allowed an active, constitutive role in the ongoing construction of 'Australia' (see for example Curthoys 1993). Multiculturalism remains, as Gunew (1993b: 54) complains, 'the daggy cousin of radical chic postcolonialism'.

It is this context which makes it problematic to construct an 'Asian' voice in Australian feminism. Despite the regular presence of Asians in contemporary Australia and despite the recurrent official rhetoric that Australia is 'part of Asia', Asianness remains solidly defined as external to the symbolic space of Australianness, in contrast with Aboriginality which—certainly since Mabo—has now been accepted by white Australia, albeit reluctantly, as occupying an undeniable place, however fraught by the injustices of history, in the heart of Australian national identity. To define myself as Asian, however, necessarily means writing myself out of the boundaries of that identity and into the margins of a pregiven, firmly established Australian imagined community. The only escape from this ghetto, from this perspective, would be the creation of a symbolic space no longer bounded by the idea(l) of national identity; a space, that is, where 'Australia' no longer has to precede and contain, in the last instance, the unequal differences occuring within it. Of course, such a space is utopian, given the fact that 'Australia' is not a floating signifier but the name for an historically sedimented nation-state. Yet the imagination of such a space is necessary to appreciate the permanent sense of displacement experienced by racialised and ethnicised people, including, I want to stress, Aboriginal people.[10]

What does this tell us, finally, about the feminist politics of difference? As I have already said, too often the need to deal with difference is seen in the light of the greater need to save, expand, improve or enrich feminism as a political home which would ideally represent all women. In this way, the ultimate rationale of the politics of difference is cast in terms of an overall politics of *inclusion*: the desire for an overarching feminism to construct a pluralist sisterhood which can accommodate all differences and inequalities between women. It should come as no surprise that such a desire is being expressed largely by white, Western, middle-class women, whom Yeatman (1993) calls the 'custodians of the established order' of contemporary feminism. Theirs is a defensive position, characterised by a reluctance to question the status of feminism *itself* as a political home for all women, just as Australia will not—and cannot, in its existence as a legislative state— question its status as a nation despite its embrace of multiculturalism. Yeatman herself, for example, considers the politics of difference as an 'internal politics of emancipation *within* feminism' (1993: 230, emphasis added). In this conception, difference can only be taken into consideration insofar as it does not challenge the rightfulness of feminism as such. Feminism functions as a nation which 'other' women are invited to join without disrupting the ultimate integrity of the nation. But this politics of inclusion is born of a liberal pluralism which can only be entertained by those who have the *power* to include, as pointed out poignantly by Spelman (1988: 163): 'Welcoming someone into one's own home doesn't represent an attempt to undermine privilege; it expresses it.'

Taking difference seriously necessitates the adoption of a politics of *partiality* rather than a politics of inclusion. A politics of partiality implies that feminism must emphasise and consciously construct the *limits* of its own field of political intervention. While a politics of inclusion is driven by an ambition for universal representation (of all women's interests), a politics of partiality does away with that ambition and accepts the principle that feminism can never ever be an encompassing political home for all women, not just because different groups of women have different and sometimes conflicting interests, but, more radically, because for many groups of 'other' women other interests, other identifications are sometimes more important and politically pressing than, or even incompatible with, those related to their being women.

Yeatman (1993: 228) acknowledges the necessary partiality of the feminist project when she points to the incommensurability of its insistence on the primacy of gender oppression with the political foci of movements against other forms of social subordination. It is this structural incommensurability that feminists need to come to terms with and accept as drawing the unavoidable limits of feminism as a political project. In short, because all female persons 'do not inhabit the same sociohistorical spaces' (Chow 1991: 93), (white/Western) feminism's assumption of a '"master discourse" position' (ibid: 98) can only be interpreted as an act of symbolic violence which disguises the fundamental structural divisions created by historical processes such as colonialism, imperialism and nationalism. As Butler (1990: 4) puts it, 'the premature insistence on a stable subject of feminism, understood as a seamless category of women, inevitably generates multiple refusals to accept the category'. It compels us to say, 'I'm a feminist, but . . .'

6

Dancing modernity

Jill Julius Matthews

In the past twenty years and more, much admirable history has been written of the lives and experiences of women. The absence of women from the historical drama has been redressed. The curtain of silence and invisibility has been raised, revealing a stage strewn with suffering bodies set against backdrops of repression, punishment and control; of collusion, bad faith and false consciousness; of reaction, struggle and heroic resistance. Such revelation has been essential to the pursuit of equality, dignity and even some sense of autonomy for women. But the very success of this feminist historiographical project has thrown up new problems, new complexities that cannot be addressed in the same ways as before. In particular, the question 'Who are these women?' has become insistent as feminists have felt compelled to abandon the essentialist paradigm of earlier analyses.

An important aspect of this shift has involved a reconsideration of the nature of power. The image of woman as eternal victim or resisting heroine opposing the might of a universal and monolithic patriarchy is no longer an adequate way to understand either the meaning of the historical experiences of femininity or how gender constitutes the social world. The 'women, resistance, and revolution' model (Rowbotham 1972) that was so important to early feminist historiography has been worked to its limit. Its benefits have been incorporated into newer methods that its difficulties have made necessary, and it has been effectively replaced by models that are better able to deal with the multiple dimensions and meanings of women's lives, the differences among women, and the constitution of feminine subjectivities. The earlier model emphasised the simple one-way effect of the gender power of men against women. This has been put aside in favour of an examination of power as a much more pervasive and productive and localised force. The early work rediscovered the lost women of history,

74

and set in train a project to redefine the meaning of history so that women should never again be overwhelmed by the dominance of masculine meanings. The second phase carries on that task of redefinition by making problematic and destabilising all the orthodox historiographical categories, including the very categories of gender used by the early feminists. One particularly useful way of unsettling these orthodoxies has been to look away from the history of struggle and to seek out women's pleasure.

In this essay, I wish to tease apart some of the meanings of femininity in a specific time and place, to understand how young Anglo-Australian women came to understand themselves as modern. Beyond an analysis of women as universal victims, colluders and resisters, I want to bring to the surface some of the particular, feminine pleasures of the 1920s. The meanings given to those pleasures, and the discourses in which those meanings were embedded, are able in turn to sketch in some of the boundaries of possible Australian womanhood in the 1920s. Rather than working within the dialectic of oppression and resistance that was common to the earlier phase of feminist historical work, I want to analyse the way that changes in women's leisure and pleasure activities were central to processes of modernisation and constitutive of modern feminine subjectivity. Specifically, I am looking at one aspect of the process whereby young Anglo-Australian women in pursuit of fun and amusement came to embody a certain meaning of modernity. To address this process of change, I will first of all discuss three key terms: modernity, the body, and everyday life. Second, I will look at one moment of the process that brings together these three terms: the dance craze of the 1920s.

Modernity, the body and everyday life

Marshall Berman in his book *All That Is Modern Melts Into Air* (1983) identifies three terms embraced by the notion of the modern: the socioeconomic process of modernisation, the aesthetic of modernism, and the historical experience of modernity. The first two processes have been extensively but separately addressed, resulting in rather problematic historiographic models. Analyses of modernisation tend towards a deterministic progressivism, while discussions of modernism are usually directed to elite high culture. The third term, the historical experience of modernity, which links or is implicated in the other two processes, shows promise of being able to avoid those problems and to suggest an understanding of social change on a vast scale that does not obliterate either human agency or the determination of social structures.

The experience of modernity is also a term that allows the recognition of diversity through the notion of embodied experience. That is, modernity is lived and experienced through bodies that are coded by class, race, ethnicity, gender, sexuality and religion; moreover, those bodies are themselves part of the experience, they too change and become modern. In particular, I would suggest, modernity is carried by and inscribed on the bodies of people, initially women, pursuing happiness and seeking self-respect and fulfilment.

The body has been a popular topic of academic analysis over the past several decades, but it has only recently been subjected to historical analysis. This lack of interest has been due, in large part, to perceptions that the female body, apart from its work of reproduction, is unchanging and ahistorical, that it is a mere epiphenomenon of more important historical processes, or that it is simply a surface and essentially trivial. Ordinary women and the physical amusements of their daily lives have usually been read historically as symbols of the meaningless, the merely entertaining or, at most, as part of the circus which deflects attention from the lack of bread. Women's bodies, beauty, pleasure and sexuality have been read as insubstantial ornaments or even as corrupt impediments to more serious pursuits. Against this, my broad aim is to show how such apparent trivia are centrally implicated in the transformation of Australia into a modern society, and how fundamental issues of subjectivity—of desire and self-affirmation—find their meaning in these processes of change in everyday life.

The history of everyday life has had a chequered career, emerging most recently out of the 'new social history' and subject to many of the charges under which that study has long suffered: that it is antiquarian, subjectivist, shapeless and hence meaningless. Some of these criticisms are indeed valid for some works dealing with the history of everyday life. But feminist history has breathed new vigour into the discussion, primarily by elaborating a more comprehensive understanding of 'the political'. This has been helped by a judicious grafting of certain aspects of Foucault's analysis of power which have more authoritatively articulated or clarified directions that feminism had already undertaken. In particular, there has been a valuable interactive development of the notion that the personal is political and of the importance of the local as a site of analysis and action.

Foucault's four methodological precautions concerning the analysis of power and domination might well stand as useful guides for the work of feminist historians of everyday life (Foucault 1980: 96–100).

First, he suggests, analysis should not be concerned with power in its central and general operations, but in its local and concrete manifestations. Second, analysis should not be concerned with intentions, but with how power actually works in practice. Third, power should not be understood as a static substance owned and used to impose its owner's will, but as a protean substance always in motion, passed on by being used. Fourth, analysis of power should not be a deductive or descending process, starting at the centre and seeking to discover how that power permeates and affects all the elements of society down to its base; rather, one should start with the autonomous dimensions of local mechanisms of power and examine the steps by which they are made use of or harnessed by more and more global mechanisms of power.

Foucault's attention to the 'microphysics of power' has been adapted and in part challenged by Michel de Certeau's (1984) discussion of everyday life. De Certeau is concerned to show how resistance to Foucault's all-enveloping networks of discipline is possible, and he seeks his answer in an analysis of the apparently trivial practices of everyday life. This, for him, is a space in which 'the network of an antidiscipline' becomes possible as people make do and create ways of operating which deflect and evade the power of the disciplinary technologies in which they are caught. 'The weak must continually turn to their own ends forces alien to them' (De Certeau 1984: xix).

What I am addressing here is a sense of the embodied experience and practices of everyday modernity. I am seeking to tease out some of the ways in which the desire to be modern was lived by young Anglo-Australian women; how those practices of their everyday lives that were infused with such desire were 'a creative use of the conditions of constraint' (Fiske 1992: 156) and resulted in a sense of pleasure and self-affirmation; and how such desire was simultaneously annexed by other mechanisms in the creation of the network of disciplinary powers of modern Australia. In one small and specific story, I am toying with questions about how the subjective and the social meanings of being a woman in modern Australia were created; and how modern Australia itself was created. The specific period I am addressing is that between the wars, and the specific desires and practices I concentrate on are those of dancing.

The dance craze

In the stories of themselves when young (Hooton 1990), many white Australian women born around the turn of the century tell of their desire to be modern. For these writers and hundreds more, the 1920s have been carefully boxed into a simply coded memory and story: the mad, roaring, decade of dancing, the era of jazz and modernity. Such coding limits the range of experience presented in their texts, and stereotypes the meanings they attach to it. Nonetheless, their stories still bear the lineaments of power and desire.

From their reminiscences, it would seem that during the '20s only those young Anglo-Australian women who were sick or religious—especially Methodists—were not drawn into the pleasures of modernity. The women remember their delight in the arrival of aunts who are modern; they tell of their older sisters who are modern; they become modern themselves, making their own short slinky dresses and bobbing their hair, often against their father's wishes; some smoke cigarettes and take to drink; and they all dance. A young apprentice seamstress tells of the basement storeroom becoming a dancing academy during the lunch hour, with the women and girls practicing popular ballroom dances (Miller 1983: 13). A middle-class university student claims 'a party without dancing would have been no party at all', and elaborates the range of dancing occasions from private house dances to the Palais de Danse to supper dances to balls (Fitzpatrick 1983: 173–174). A country girl evokes the trembling excitement of the arrival of urban, modern, dancing femininity into the farmhouse kitchen on Friday nights (Corbett 1983: 138–139).

There is, of course, no moment of beginning to the modernity that these young women remember yearning for. For each of them, modernity arrives, in the '20s, already constituted, already embodied in she who is modern, who dresses in fashion, who dances. But it is still as yet a fragile thing, a contested form, occupying an uncertain place amid other possible representations. What is modern in suburban Collingwood may well be out of date to the dancing crowd at the Crystal Palace. What seemed modern at the time might well fall back into the old-fashioned in a later retrospective overview. Or that overview might grasp the moment of the modern at an even earlier time. Certainly, while each of these women identifies a particular embodiment of modernity, their stories also tell of the antecedent means of its constitution, the tools for body writing (de Certeau 1988) which carve out the space for it to occupy and carve the body to fit that space. They tell of movies, vaudeville, gramophone records, jazz bands, clothing, beauty culture, radio, cars, and dancing. All of these tools of modernity have their own independent histories but it seems to be the fusing of them all into the 'dance craze' that the women identify as the meaning of the '20s and the heart of their desire to be modern.

The dance craze had begun before the First World War, around 1911. The cities of Australia were only a season behind England and America (Bisset 1979; Johnson 1987; Andrews 1979; *The Victorian Dance News*). The excitement, along with descriptions of the dances, arrived with each mail boat; with professional dancers and musicians touring the world performing and teaching both privately and on the vaudeville circuits; with the steady stream into Australia of dance-crazed visitors and immigrants; with the visits of the American Fleet in 1908 and again in 1925. Those visitors who continued travelling took back with them Australian creations, like the Kangaroo Dip, to add to the great whirligig. Ragtime was played at private parties in homes around Sydney before 1910 and was the rage of public dances by 1913. Tango Teas were danced at the Tivoli on the eve of the great war and 'teas dansantes' were held every afternoon in the big city hotels, restaurants and department stores. Good dancers taught their friends and built up small businesses, along with a vast army of dressmakers, hairdressers, manicurists, cosmeticians, shoemakers, electricians, chalk manufacturers and sellers, clothing hirers, florists, record and sheet music importers, and piano tuners and players. Some with stronger entrepreneurial ambitions set up enormous public dance halls catering for more than 2000 dancers at the one time: the Crystal Palace Dance Hall, Salon de Luxe, Centennial Palais de Danse and White City Ballroom in Sydney; the great St Kilda Palais de Danse, Leggett's Ballroom, the Windsor and the Albert Hall in Melbourne. In the tens and teens a menagerie of dances tumbled over each other into exhilarating exhibition: the Bunny Hug, the Grizzly Bear or Texas Tommy, the Turkey Trot, the Black Bottom, the Camel Walk, the Lame Duck. Each lasted a year or two, was the subject of impassioned performance and aghast moralising, then was replaced by a newer step. The dance styles that fitted the new music were progressively regularised and sanitised, though for some they were never cleaned up enough.

Dancing declined during the war, with many dancers and musicians enlisting or engaging in war work, but it did not disappear. In 1917 a new jazz emerged from New Orleans and arrived in Australia by the end of that year: a hot jazz, eccentric, violent. Its popularity soared with the return of troops with disposable income from deferred pay, and from the reopening of shipping lanes that let entertainers return to their Pacific-rim and world circuits. Belle Sylvia and Her Jazz Band, listed as Australia's first jazz band, toured Ben Fuller's Vaudeville Circuit in 1918. The Globe Theatre in Sydney held a 'Jazz Week' in 1919, featuring bands, dancing and two films, one locally made, *Does Jazz Lead to Destruction?*, and the other an American film starring

Irene and Vernon Castle, *The Whirl of Life*. This pattern of mixing the two entertainments of live dancing and silent pictures became increasingly popular and profitable throughout the '20s until the advent of the talkies from 1929 changed the shape of the picture industry and the Depression knocked the bottom out of the vaudeville business. For the '20s, however, the dance craze was constantly stimulated by the combination of the two media. On the screen, both Australian and American films showed contemporary dance scenes in society settings, and certainly showed off the latest in evening dress. On the picture theatre stage, vaudeville performances including modern ballroom and fancy dancing were interspersed between the films. Many of the larger picture palaces employed full-time cinema ballets and orchestras, and smaller theatres hired jazz bands and revue acts. A world of excitement, music, movement and glamour was opening up to a mass audience that had never before had access on such a scale.

A music historian claims of early Australian jazz that, 'to the general public, jazz was dance music (or a dance) characterised by violent movement, abandoned delight, profanation of established decencies, the essence of vulgar, modern America' (Johnson 1987: 11). A more technical description of the way jazz inscribed the bodies of its followers with the marks of modernity is given by professional dance teacher A. H. Franks (1963). For him, post-1910 social dancing underwent two crucial changes: first, the abandonment of classical foot positioning, most particularly the replacement of the turned-out position by a posture having the feet in a straight line, allowing for a walking, gliding movement. This encouraged closer, more intimate, more sensual dancing, and made 'good' dancing more accessible without extensive and expensive training. Franks identifies the second change as rhythm: '[before 1910] no matter what the dance, the main attraction lay in the actual steps, and in some cases the exhilarating movement. After 1910 the main impetus came unquestionably from the rhythm rather than the movement, although frequently the two were now combined as never before' (p. 176). Through the very way they moved, women's bodies now became visibly modern.

Dancing boomed from the early 1920s, with dance halls mushrooming throughout the suburbs, newly built or converted from institutes and local halls, while dancing tea rooms and pie shops transmuted into cabarets and night clubs. Australian orchestras playing syncopating rhythm or refined jazz tried to keep their jobs against a wave of American and British hot-jazz bands. By invoking the White Australia Policy and capitalising on popular and official racism and prudery, the Musicians' Union succeeded in having Negro jazz bands prohibited from entry into Australia after 1928 (Bisset 1979: 41–46). But from 1923 to 1928, white and black American bands defined the meaning of jazz for Australian audiences and called at least some young people into the pleasures of an international modernity.

In the boom year of 1926, the Charleston hit town and was promoted by theatrical entrepreneurs, department store managements, newspapers, and the great galaxy of dancing establishments. In all the capital cities, dances were held every afternoon and evening of the week except Sunday. On Sundays, friends gathered around gramophones and kept on dancing. Peppy, jazzy music and the foxtrot, one-step, quickstep, and tango were the core of the ever-changing variety of modern ballroom dancing, with many so-called vulgar, abandoned and sexual contortions escaping from the standard steps. Hot rhythm and joyful sensuality were what the fans wanted; barbaric rhythm and illicit sexuality were what the critics abhorred; a regular beat and dignified and graceful movement were what the professional dance teachers tried to impose.

After a year or so more, the dancing craze began to fade. In Foucault's terms, local pleasures were becoming harnessed into more and more global mechanisms of power. Immigration laws, by-laws, civic regulations, entertainment taxes, labour awards and alcohol regulations were the mechanisms of control introduced or newly policed by state and local leaders with slow but cumulative effect. The Depression ate into the disposable cash available for dancers as well as sending many 'mushroom ballrooms' and associated businesses to the wall. The anti-dance moralists and the dance entrepreneurs reached a compromise in the form of self-regulation. Professional dance associations were organised, able to discipline members and deny legitimacy to unregistered teachers. They gained control of dance competitions and exhibitions; they established the rules of acceptable behaviour, and defined and policed the meaning of dancing. Between state regulation and association pressure, the dance hall owners and managers ran respectable shows. The modern was no longer a glorious, giddy future to be embraced enthusiastically, but a present that simply was.

In this schematic story of the rise and fall of the dancing craze in Australia, there are three major interlocking grids of power and desire at play on the bodies of young women. Such grids display the operations of increasingly more abstract mechanisms of disciplinary power and at the same time reveal the local practices by which the imposition of such discipline is subtly subverted to extract a constrained pleasure and self-affirmation. The first such grid deals with political economy;

the second with moral discourses of femininity; the third with female subjectivity.

Political economy

The dancing craze was not just an entertainment to be consumed by increasing numbers of young women and men across the spectrum of Australian social life. It was also an entertainment to be produced. As dancing became increasingly public and commercialised, it provided employment for large numbers of young, and a few older, women. It is hard to track down the precise numbers, since much of the work occurred in the informal or local economy and slipped through the net of formal enumeration (Matthews 1983). As well, the categories used in official accounts were too broad to catch such uncertain trades. More telling than census listings is another listing, by Marjorie Hollinshead, of *Some Professional Dancers of, or from, Queensland and some Teachers of the Past and Present* (1963). Identified in this alphabetical listing is the oldest surviving school of dancing in Queensland, founded in about 1894. Thereafter, one can read across the entries the proliferation of dancing schools, catering primarily for children. Each school had a public performance program, if only an annual display, and many built up small companies which performed at charity benefits, pantomimes, plays and revues. Until a 1928 Act prohibited children under 14 from appearing professionally except during school holidays, troupes of juvenile performers toured the state on the various vaudeville circuits. Many of the graduates of these schools continued in the industry: in ballet troupes in legitimate live theatre; on the vaudeville circuits and with tent shows and boxing shows; in metropolitan, suburban and country picture theatres; in seaside shows and public recitals; some even made it into the pictures. They also became teachers: working as assistants in established dancing academies, setting up their own schools, taking classes in public and private schools, girls' clubs and factories, training debutantes. Their dancing skills ranged through tapping, limbering, musical comedy, character, song and dance, physical culture, eurhythmics, fancy dancing, Cecchetti method (or Russian Ballet technique, a forerunner of what is known today as ballet), as well as ballroom dancing (modern and old-time).

For many women, the work of dancing was fitful and rough; for some, it provided a sufficient living. In the late '20s, one cinema dancer recalled that, 'The girls in shops only got 30 shillings or so, but at the Capitol we got four pounds 10 shillings (or 90 shillings) a week' (Fisher

1990: 38). The peak age for performers was between 14 and 25 and, according to the censuses, well over 70 per cent were single. Clearly, dance-related occupations were viewed as a bit of excitement, and possibly good money, to be gained in the time between leaving school and marrying. It was also a business with sufficient specialist niches to sustain a career or be returned to in later life.

For ballroom dancers, there was another mode of income earning. Many of the large dance palaces held competitions, copying American entrepreneurs who had inaugurated them in 1914. In Australia they continued well into the 1930s. Prizes included cash, cars and suites of furniture, as well as auditions for theatre and picture companies. Champions often moved into professional teaching or management after winning a title. Teachers of champions could expect an influx of eager and ambitious pupils. With such rewards beckoning, vote rigging apparently caused occasional disturbances. To regulate this, as well as all other aspects of the dance industry, professional associations of teachers began forming in the early 1930s. Their brief involved the standardisation of steps, which led quickly to the establishment of examinations in the three main branches, Ballroom, Operatic and Theatrical. They spoke often of the 'dignity of their profession', and sought means to curb the 'rough conduct' of patrons in ballrooms, and to abolish 'charlatanism' and 'unsportsmanlike methods' among teachers (*The Victorian Dance News*).

From this account of dancing as work, what is most significant for my purpose is that large numbers of young women were earning a living in the inter-war years by displaying their variously uncovered bodies in public, and that this activity was relatively respectable for an increasing proportion of Australian society. Certainly, it was respectable enough for the children of the middle and upper working classes to be sent in their droves to dancing classes and to permit them on the public stage in school performance. These classes were not of the old establishment style, teaching upper-class children genteel accomplishments, cultivated behaviour, and the morals and manners of fashionable society. Nor were they working-class training grounds for future theatrical performers and a refuge of the demi-monde. Rather, they were part of a modern educational program involving health, movement, fitness, and musical appreciation. Within this program, the acceptability of dancing classes came from two particular sources. First, the very popularity of dancing as a mass entertainment meant that large numbers of people had contact with it and were not corrupted. This gave the profession a visibility it had not had before—in particular, a visibility to cross-gender and cross-class audiences. It enabled dancing to cast off its earlier associations with masculine voyeurism on the one hand and upper-class social discipline on the other. Second, the profession's own regularisation of itself and its active pursuit of respectability were relatively successful, despite or perhaps because they tamed the craziness of the dancing '20s.

Moral discourses of femininity

That respectability was hard won. Dancing was not just an occupation and a pastime, it was also the focus of ideological and moral debate. Throughout the 1910s, 1920s and into the 1930s, dance floors were a battlefield upon which the diverse forces of rectitude and tradition opposed the motley cohorts of modernity and pleasure. Skirmishes were fought particularly fiercely over possession of women's bodies. In mid-1925, Australian newspapers reported that the Irish clergy had banned dancing. Earlier in that year, the South Australian Methodist Conference had sought to ban mixed dancing in church halls, a move soon followed by the General Conference of the Methodist Church of Australia. Among Catholics, there were similar condemnations of dancing, although they took care to keep alive the sectarian connotations of the terms 'wowser' and 'puritan' and to distance themselves from them. All sects were appalled by the abandon induced by jazz, the sensual and barbaric music, the voluptuous movements of the dances, the semi-nudity of female dancers and the paganising style of the whole entertainment. Civic authorities and the medical profession also weighed in. A nostalgia column in 1936 asked: 'Do you remember? . . . When suburban councils banned the Charleston and several people were reported to have died from doing this dance. Doctors said that this dance was undermining the health of those dancing it' (*The Victorian Dance News*, 9 April 1936: 11).

All sides to the public debates about jazz professed a contempt for pleasure for its own sake and accepted a hierarchy of moral and aesthetic values based in a simple opposition between good and bad, right and wrong. Because jazz was pleasurable, to be acceptable it had to attach to itself redeeming and uplifting features; otherwise, censorship would be necessary. As well, there was a second hierarchy of personal worth to which all sides adhered, involving a contrast between self-responsibility and gullibility. There were categories of people defined as less responsible and needing protection—youth, especially young women, were deemed easily manipulated. There were other categories of people who were defined as essentially amoral and whose corrupting influence needed to be constrained—most particularly working class and black entertainers and their promoters. The two hierarchies of values and persons fused along a vertical axis of power, and pleasure was inevitably caught in a discourse of censorship. The only significant questions were: where to draw the line, how elastic were the boundaries of the good, and who must be protected from the bad.

But, curiously, in the practices of everyday living, anybody could attain a certain respectability simply by proclaiming belief in the need for such a line. This allowed dancers to continue in their pleasures by diverting into unexpected channels the disciplinary powers exercised upon them. Of course, such practices left fully intact those powers and indeed strengthened them through explicit compliance/complicity. A very rigid knowledge of pleasure was installed globally, a knowledge based on a seemingly monolithic and totalitarian moral-aesthetic principle. Only one true standard of art, as of life, was ever possible. Heterogeneity must either be absorbed into that standard or expelled and condemned. Difference could not be allowed simply to be. Whether one proclaimed oneself to be for the status quo or for the avant garde, for the old or for the new, one's stance towards all the rest was equally rejecting. Even within one's own aesthetic realm, the same critical rejecting mode prevailed: there was trained and practiced art, over which one struggled, and there was rubbish, mere escapism, an amateur pastime, idle pleasure.

Thus, guardians of the classical tradition in music condemned jazz; proponents of jazz argued for its worth in moral and aesthetic terms consonant with the classical tradition, condemning tin-pan alley's popular tunes, and drawing invidious comparisons between white and black jazz. Guardians of polite traditions of social dancing condemned the jazz dance craze; the arguments of the proponents of modern ballroom dancing advanced the cause of jazz in terms consonant with the values of that tradition, claiming that 'dancing, properly executed, is neither vulgar nor immodest, but, on the contrary, the personification of refinement, grace and modesty' (Castle 1914: Foreword). Necessarily, they condemned 'cheap cabaret entertainers' who lured impulsive youth into emulating vulgar dancing, and they urged cooperation 'with our guardians of civic decency [to] aid them constructively in the elimination of the coarse, the uncouth, the vulgar, and the vicious' (Marbury in Castle, 1914: 28).

As well as drawing modern dancing into the circle of the good by creating a boundary against the bad, the jazz apologists also distinguished between real dancers—experts, professionals, registered teachers and their pupils, people who passed accredited dancing exams—and mere followers and patrons, men and girls out for a good time. The policing of these two boundaries, of art and of the artist–audience relation, became the source of legitimation for and the task of the various associations of professional dancing teachers formed during the inter-war years, although these organisations could not claim adequate control over the dance floors of Australia until well into the 1930s.

Female subjectivity

I have used in this discussion the subordinate appellation 'men and girls' since, among the dancing professionals, men were dancers, women were partners. The dance floor was an important site for the constitution of a specifically modern heterosexuality and heterosocial-ity. Writing of middle-class amusements in America during the same period, Kathy Peiss has argued that 'Women's experimentation with individuality was shaped by their situation as contingent consumers, as half of a heterosexual couple' (Peiss 1990: 113). Women were girls, and the lesser half, but good pals nonetheless. So, together, the men and girls out for a good time kept on trying to have one. They had no organised public voice, they participated in the debate with their bodies and feet. The young women, especially, engaged with the serious moral questions of modernity in daily life in their families, and occasionally with women police, church officials and even sententious passers-by. At issue was the need to be able to distinguish the good woman from the bad, and for each woman to know how to present herself on the right side. After the First World War, the distinguishing marks shifted so much and so often that it became increasingly hard to do so. Ivy Arney and her Aunty Max knew that 'Being fashionable was quite distinct from being "fast", which applied to those who smoked or wore make-up beyond a light dusting of face powder' (Arney 1987: 75). The weekly newspaper *The Graphic of Australia* tried to draw the line with a lighter hand in its 'Girls' Gossip' column from the 1920s:

> Cigarette smoking in a woman may be pardoned if the smoker knows how and where to do it. High heels are not out of place in a ball or drawing room, but are the worst possible taste for street wear and, furthermore, bad for the health. Even rouge and powder may be pardoned if they are so delicately manipulated as (to quote an old jingle) to 'look like what they ain't'. (*The Graphic of Australia* 11 March 1920: 9)

But sometimes, firmness remained necessary.

No women belonging to the first grade of society, either in Melbourne or elsewhere, consume cocktails in public cafes instead of afternoon tea. It simply is not done. In fact it is a fashion usual to the half world. Nor do the best people—that is to say, of the feminine gender—puff cigarettes in public places. (*The Graphic of Australia* 6 April 1920: 9).

Perhaps if any one thing can be said to mark the experience of modernity for young Anglo-Australian women in the inter-war years, it is the gradual physical erosion of the space, and the fear, of that 'half world'. Good girls and bad girls henceforth occupied the same territory; one could not simply read their status from their bodies. For the women themselves, the multiple negotiations around mass entertainment, the commercialisation of leisure, and the meanings of their bodies—around the pleasures and disciplines of dance, fashion, and beauty culture—shifted both economic and moral boundaries, changing the shape of the social space in which women could pursue self-respect and fulfilment, in which they could dance and desire and be drawn into the modern.

7

Reading the *Women's Weekly:* Feminism, femininity and popular culture

Susan Sheridan

The power of media representations of femininity, with which any woman must reckon in the production of her sexed subjectivity, her sense of self as female, has been a constant preoccupation of contemporary feminism. Indeed, one of its founding texts, Betty Friedan's *The Feminine Mystique* (1963), made media representations of femininity its central object of criticism. Thirty years later, Naomi Wolf's *The Beauty Myth* echoed the arguments as well as the title of Friedan's book: false ideals promulgated by the mass media conceal the real truth of women's lot, not least from women themselves. Although she took account of changes in women's situations in the US since the early '60s, and gave weight to the economic and social functions of these media myths as well as to women's psychological vulnerability to them, Wolf's central point is the same as Friedan's: that media representations of femininity are by and large inimical to the feminist goals of improving women's well-being and freedom. The specific American contexts in which these texts were produced has not limited their wide circulation throughout the Anglophone world, and their line on the mass media is still a first base in many people's understanding of feminist critiques of the status quo.

Naming the enemy, however, is a limited strategy. Any one-dimensional account of the situation of women is open to objections that it is oversimplified (this one, for instance, that it is monocausal, it ignores women's secondary position in the paid workforce), and that it assumes a homogeneous class of 'women' (ignoring differences of class, race, age and sexuality). Naming the media as the enemy is problematic for feminism because it assumes most women to be the dupes of ideological brainwashing processes and takes no account of the kinds of pleasure they might take in consuming these representations.

Many feminists have moved away from this approach, while still recognising the immense power of the media. They are asking more broadly conceived questions about the status of these representations in our culture, questions that go beyond the modernist dichotomy between serious and popular culture and its gendered associations ('masculine' creativity and reason contrasted with 'feminine' mindless consumption). They investigate how media representations actually 'work'—in the functional sense (whose interests they serve), in the more technical sense of how they are constructed and circulated, and finally in the sense of how people interact with them to produce their self-understandings as social subjects.

Feminism and cultural studies

One way of expressing this change of perspective is to say that the study of media representations has become central to cultural studies, which takes the meanings of modern social experience as its field and explores the ways in which gender, class and other social differences are produced in various sites within this field. This discipline has emerged concurrently with that of women's studies, so that the kinds of questions which feminists want to ask about women, femininity and the media are central to cultural studies' concerns with the structures of meaning in everyday life.

Cultural studies is a broad field of inquiry which can encompass media studies and studies of popular culture, past and present, so as to include everyday practices and cultural habits as well as texts and institutions. A feminist research agenda in cultural studies might be described as 'articulating the relationship between different sites [of the production of gender] and making connections between the body, everyday practices, institutional inscriptions and cultural habits' (Craik 1990: 174; 1992: 89–98). In this context, the cultural 'representations' mentioned at the beginning of this essay have to be understood as including not only the images or textualisations of modern social experience, but also the processes of their production, circulation and consumption. A 'cultural studies' approach to these questions also involves attending (at varying levels of abstraction) to the experience of these processes: to the way people produce the meanings of their social existence in interaction with cultural representations.

This aspect of cultural studies may involve ethnographic studies of the way people actually use cultural materials in making sense of their lives, including giving particular forms to their dreams and fantasies. However the production of meaning can also be approached through a study of cultural texts themselves, and the way they construct for readers a variety of positions from which to identify or understand. Cultural studies borrows from both sociological studies of behaviour and literary studies of signification. Because popular cultural forms were for so long seen as trashy and unworthy of analysis, there has been a tradition in media research on soap opera, for instance, to focus on the audience rather than the text—to prefer 'good' (because 'real') audience over 'bad' (because unrealistic) text. In textual studies, a related and opposite tendency has emerged, of designating certain textual forms as themselves good because they are said to display features, such as openness of form, which are considered progressive: some recent work on 'women's genres' like soap opera belongs to this tendency, where the open feminine text occupies the place of the good textual object (Brunsden 1990: 67–8).

Reading the *Women's Weekly*

To illustrate some of these features of popular cultural studies and how they are implicated in feminist analyses, let me describe a research project that I am engaged in, a study of the *Australian Women's Weekly* during the twenty-five years after the Second World War.[1]

The principal material or source for our study is this long-running women's magazine, a gender text if ever there was one, which has often been very conscious of its function to train women in femininity and of its self-constructed status as an Australian cultural institution.

Our approach to this material is twofold. On the one hand, we take a 'textual' approach, investigating how the magazine works as a text, both verbal and visual, including the relation between its direct advertising functions, its 'training and advice' functions and its provision of materials for fantasy and aspiration. On the other hand, we take a thematic 'historical' approach, tracing the *Weekly's* particular constructions of events, technologies and cultural habits and their changes over time. But we also want to bring these metaphorical hands together, to articulate relationships between the discursive world of the magazine and the social world it addresses, through the figure of 'the Australian woman' who is hypothesised on its every page. This approach differs from most historians' raids on magazines for evidence of social changes because we insist on the importance of the context of the whole magazine and the way it addresses its audience.

We are interested in the way changes in domestic life in Australia, as well as popular preoccupations like the Royal Family, are presented to a targeted population by a particular medium. We are interested in the way the *Weekly*'s readers are constructed as having certain values, desires, needs and self-perceptions, and the way they are invited to occupy certain feminine subject positions. These positions incorporate gender-coded responses to a huge range of matters, from patriotism to how you do your laundry, from good mothering practices to appropriately feminine jokes and anecdotes. We aim to analyse the way in which a diversity of social codes and cultural discourses construct an ideal of Australian womanhood and domestic life, and to trace the tensions and contradictions in that ideal—for instance, the way it incorporates elements of both glamour and domesticity, and the way fine differentiations of social status (to which women are supposed to be attuned) are constantly used to create the ideal type—the white, Anglo-Saxon, Protestant, middle-class married woman—by the exclusion of all the opposite 'others' implied by these terms.

In doing this study we operate with a notion of 'text' which partakes of both audience and representation, in that it examines the way texts construct preferred reading positions (positions from which the material makes the most sense) or ideal reader-identities, like 'the Australian housewife'. The theoretical framework we use draws from recent literary theory this concept of the textual construction of readers or reading positions, and from social theory the concept of the production of self or subjectivity through negotiating with such discursive constructions. In this way we can put into operation the notion of the *Weekly* as one among many possible sites for the production of gender, and can show what possibilities and constraints it constructs for its readers to produce meanings of their lives and dreams, of their sexed subjectivity as women.

Theoretical frameworks and problems

This emphasis on people *producing* meanings through their negotiations with cultural representations marks the theoretical debt which our feminist project owes to the structuralist framework within which cultural studies began in the 1970s. Drawing on the work of earlier British socialist writers Richard Hoggart and Raymond Williams, which defended working-class popular culture against the dominant assumption that the only 'culture' of value was that of the elite, the Birmingham Centre for Contemporary Cultural Studies developed a positive engagement with mass-mediated popular culture, including its

American versions. Here the work of Stuart Hall and others complicated the earlier model of class conflict with the politics of race and gender. In theoretical terms, they rejected not only the liberal humanist idea of culture as the expression of 'the human spirit' but also the economistic Marxist model of culture as the reflection of ruling class interests and 'mass culture' as the sedative pap designed to be consumed by the workers. Instead there was an emphasis on notions of ordinary people's agency in contesting and producing cultural meanings. As Meaghan Morris puts it:

> This means studying not how people *are* in a passively inherited culture ('tradition') but what they *do* with the cultural commodities that they encounter and use in everyday life ('practice') and thus what they *make* as 'culture'. Inflected by post-structuralist theories of reading as well as by empirical audience research . . . this shift enabled a crucial redefinition of popular culture not as a stratum (the 'low') one of aesthetic practice but as a social 'zone of contestation', in Hall's famous phrase—the ground in and over which different interests struggle for hegemony. (Morris, 1992: 10)

Two major themes emerge here—indeed, two senses of 'agency'. First there is the sense of people making rather than passively receiving meaning through their exchanges with cultural commodities, a *production* that is part of the same process as, rather than set in opposition to, *consumption*. Here consumption is defined as the appropriation of cultural meanings rather than the acquisition of goods. Second, there is the political agency implied by the notions of struggle and contestation, *resistance* and *subversion*.

This second cluster of meanings of agency has proved tricky for cultural studies, coming as it does from a political vocabulary of collective action against an identifiable opponent and based on the demystification of dominant ideologies. But notions of struggle and contestation are somewhat out of place in this context, for cultural commmodities mostly reinforce people's construction of themselves as individuals rather than collectivities, and they work at the levels of the unconscious and fantasy at least as much as of rationality, to stitch us into whatever patterns or promises of harmony are culturally available.

In combination, these revised notions of consumption and resistance in cultural theory have encouraged a certain romanticised reading of everyday consumption practices as 'resistant': Morris gives as an example the way the book *Myths of Oz,* by John Fiske, Bob Hodge and Graeme Turner, reads aspects of Australian popular culture—male pub culture, family barbecues, tourist trips to Uluru—as if they were marginal practices, resisting some kind of ruling-class ideology in the way youth subcultures are shown to do in British cultural studies. She argues that the book's male authors can only purport to uncover as the 'subjugated popular' what is in fact the dominant suburban patriarchal culture by ignoring feminist critiques and their own investment in this culture (Morris 1990: 470–480; 1992: 13).

The notion of resistance is most appropriately applied to identifiable social subcultures. The British feminist Angela McRobbie has argued that subcultures are less relevant to working-class girls than 'the intimate world of magazines' which they can use 'as a means of creating their own space in the school, the youth club or even in the home' (McRobbie 1991:xvii). In other words, girls and women are more likely to construct out of the cultural commodities available to them an imaginary social space rather than a material 'subculture'. McRobbie's later studies of young women in Britain place more emphasis on the way magazines and other cultural commodities offer them an individualised femininity that works on those levels of fantasy which much cultural criticism has been quick to dismiss or denigrate. Janice Winship's work on women's magazines draws comparable conclusions about taking seriously their functions of entertainment and escape, while using the solutions they proffer as a way of reading back from media texts to locate the social contradictions of women's lives, such as the tension between 'work' and 'home'—contradictions which neither individual women nor women's magazines can resolve (Winship 1983: 44–65; McCracken 1993).

It would be perverse to regard a hugely popular magazine like the *Australian Women's Weekly* as marginal and resistant in the subcultural–political sense. Femininity and domesticity may well be marginalised by masculinist high culture, but the *Weekly* rarely contests this. Instead, it follows the time-honoured practice of claiming and valuing the separate space reserved for women by patriarchy. It elaborates a suburban domestic culture in which women are dominant and feminine values and behaviours are reinforced—implicitly, in order to resist the domestic irresponsibilities and everyday sexism practised by 'their' men. The virulent masculinism and misogyny of everyday Australian culture are given minimal recognition in cartoon jokes against women's extravagance, nagging and so on; they are also implicitly recognised in the many readers' letters which tell stories at the expense of 'the mere male' and his myriad incompetencies.

Women, modernity, mass culture

However light on criticism, the *Weekly* is very strong on pleasure and advice. While there is little chance of our romanticising its contestatory possibilities, in steeping ourselves in the study of popular culture for women feminist critics run the risk of romanticising it as a repository of 'women's culture'. Alternatively, there is the constant temptation to denigrate the whole enterprise from that very critical high-culture position against which the feminist defence of women's traditional cultures is directed.

It is undeniable that a major influence on the way we read and analyse the texts of popular culture is the legacy of the denigration of the popular in dominant discourses about modernity. In these discourses, culture is constructed dichotomously—the elite opposed to the mass—and valued accordingly. Gender designations are never very far away from these dichotomies, and it can be argued that not only 'women's genres' but all events and objects designated 'popular' or 'mass culture' are denigrated and 'allegorised as feminine'. Rita Felski and others have written about 'woman' as the figure of mass culture in the discourses of modernism, a figure associated with a taste for things sentimental and moralistic (Felski 1990: 54–70; Huyssen 1986: 188–207).

Continuities of this discourse within postmodernist cultural criticism have been traced by Meaghan Morris in such figures of speech as the 'seduction' of commodities and 'distraction' versus contemplation. Morris argues that the opposition between women's modernity and their traditionalism, as it appears within this postmodernist theory, is anachronistic, since women—especially women as consumers—are part of modernity. Pointing out that the home has long been one of the major experimental sites of modernisation, she suggests that it is the theorist, rather than the woman herself, who is in danger of shutting the door on (post)modernity and retreating to old debates (Morris 1988a: 193–225; Morris 1988b: 3–29).

Lesley Johnson argues that this modernist cultural critique underpins Betty Friedan's *The Feminine Mystique,* and she traces its persistence in feminist cultural studies in the tendency to stay with this dichotomous construction of gender, either by reversal (positively valuing the feminine) or by incorporation (showing that 'women' actually do possess the valued 'masculine' qualities) (Johnson 1993). The danger in attempting to answer the modernist critique of women's magazines by defending their promulgation of a distinctively feminine world in the face of rampant masculinity is that one assumes the existence of a genuine, authentic femininity, whether it is thought to be expressed in a text like the *Women's Weekly*, or distorted and mystified by it.

Femininity and feminist criticism

The feminist questions we bring to our study of the *Australian Women's Weekly* are both historical and contemporary. We want to know how women in the 1950s and '60s were presented to themselves in this period of the baby boom and the suburban dream: What range of issues and interests was constructed around the domestic ideal? What recognition was there of dissatisfactions with it? What, indeed, were presented as its satisfactions? Its aspirations? To whom was it made available? As feminist questions, they need to tread the fine line between a critique of oppressive representations of femininity and an appreciation of women's concerns with domestic maintenance and personal satisfactions, their pleasures and desires. As critics we need to be able to switch focus back and forth between the critical eye that can see the way women's magazines construct female subjectivity as a problem—and ourselves as providing the answer (Ballaster et al 1991: 172–173)—and the pleasures that readers (and we ourselves) take in the way these 'answers' are presented (Coward 1985).

As a way of teasing out the implications of the issues that confront feminist cultural critics speaking about women's popular cultural forms, we can consider questions of the critic's enunciative position: From where do we speak, to whom and for whom? If 'representation' is our game in both its senses—as depiction, in the social sense, and as standing in or acting as proxy for a constituency, in the political sense—then we have to ask who and how we 'represent'. In posing this question for critics generally, Gayatri Spivak argues that the role of the critic as proxy, speaking on behalf of class interests, as an agent of power, has outlived its usefulness and should be abandoned (Probyn 1993: 7). This Marxist concept, which also appears in the notion of the cultural critic as 'organic intellectual', expressing the interests of an emergent social class, is often the one implicitly claimed by feminists. Elspeth Probyn points out the difficulties of claiming to speak in the name of women, as their proxy—and the paradoxical necessity of this claim as a ground for feminism. She proposes that, to cultivate a sense of the specificity of this mode of speaking, we ask ourselves the necessarily double and urgent questions of feminism: not merely 'Who am I?' but 'Who is the other woman?' That is, what 'other' does my self-definition require for its coherence? What 'other' is necessarily excluded from this definition of woman?

In relation to the *Women's Weekly* project, we could ask this same double question: not only 'Who is the other woman, the "ordinary Australian housewife" addressed by the magazine?' but also 'How do I name her? As a "cultural dope" who cannot see how she is being exploited by the media? As a postmodern consumer to whom these images are more real than the real? As a potential subversive asserting the value of traditional femininity in the face of everyday sexism?' All of these need to be recognised as possible constructions of the subject/consumer in feminist cultural studies. Then there is the question of who I am, reading the *Weekly* from a different time, place and politics. How do these positionings become part of the story I have to tell about it?

Ambivalence and kitsch

I have found it most productive to approach this question through interrogating my own responses to the material. At a discussion I attended about working with women's magazines, we talked about the way we read them, the way we position ourselves and are positioned by their discourses.[2] Ambivalence—between enjoyment and revulsion, pleasure and critique—was a common response, an ambivalence which seems to come from occupying multiple reading positions. Most obviously, there is oneself as feminist critic, and oneself as participant in patriarchal femininity, both inside (complicit) and outside (oppositional). In the case of historical materials like the *Weekly* in the postwar years, there is also a nostalgic memory of past selves—myself at sixteen, my imagined identification with my mother at that time, and so on—which can also be ambivalent, as much a 'sickness of home' as a longing to return to it.

This ambivalence can become outright rejection for the feminist critic who finds a kind of 'doily gentility' dominating these representations of women. Reading old *Women's Weekly*s I often feel more revulsion at this kind of femininity than I do admiration of say, my mother's generation's skill in doily-making; an admiration that I should cultivate as a (certain kind of) feminist committed to revaluing women's traditions. So I worry: Am I feminist enough to undertake this task? I am reminded here of Beverley Kingston's ironic question, also asked in the context of a discussion about using women's magazines: Should a feminist knit? Should she knit in public? (Kingston 1977: 27–33).

In dealing with these materials, the spectre of Edna Everage is never far away, that simultaneous celebration and vilification of the suburban housewife which is also deeply misogynist. Jean Duruz, in her paper 'Laminex dreams', discusses the problems of listening to women's dreams in the context of a peculiarly Australian version of the modernist critique of mass culture/femininity, that attack on suburbia to which Barry Humphries' satire belongs; and she points out the dominance of a notion of 'taste' in this discourse (Duruz 1994: 99–110). This leads me to suggest that my ambivalence might be called 'kitschy', an attitude of amused disgust at things considered over-the-top 'bad taste' or, if not exactly in bad taste, then belonging to the 'doily gentility' of oppressive femininity.

Rita Felski shows that there is an historical association between kitsch and women's literary genres (sentimental treatments of romantic love, birth and the family), and more generally with a '"feminine" love of ornamentation, exemplified in the various forms of bric-a-brac and "knick-knacks" bought to beautify the . . . domestic household' (Felski 1990: 56). She discusses the attribution of kitsch to certain kinds of objects by that particularly patriarchal cultural pessimism about modernity—the familiar association/denigration of mass culture and women. In this context, kitsch as the enjoyment of bad taste is an awkward position for me as a feminist critic to occupy, precisely because my social identity as a woman has been constituted by things like the *Weekly*. It is not a simple pleasure, as presumably cultural slumming is for white middle-class male intellectuals, but a complex relation to something that is both close to me and also distant, not just historically but politically.

Does this ambivalence mean, then, that we are condemned endlessly to repeat the dichotomies of modernism? Can we use them differently? One possibility is suggested by Kathy Ferguson's expansion of the aesthetic definition of 'kitsch' into a political stance. She identifies political kitsch as 'a basic faith' that all is, or can be, well in the world—a form of subjectivity that 'allows one to belong too well to one's place', an offer of plenitude or redemption, depending on one's temperament or politics. She suggests that 'a certain amount of kitsch' may be necessary for the maintenance of any kind of political faith, although its seriousness and its promises can be undercut by irony (Ferguson, 1993: 67). She quotes Milan Kundera, from whose postmodernist novel, *The Unbearable Lightness of Being*, this notion of kitsch is taken:

Kitsch . . . must derive from the basic images people have engraved on their memories . . . [for example, of children playing].
Kitsch causes two tears to flow in quick succession. The first tear says: How nice to see children running on the grass! The second tear says: How nice to be moved, together with all mankind, by children running on the grass!
It is the second tear that makes kitsch kitsch.
The brotherhood of man on earth will be possible only on a base of kitsch. (Ferguson 1993: 181–2)

Read 'the sisterhood of woman' for 'the brotherhood of man' in this passage, and the temptations of feminist kitsch are immediately discernible. Consider the role of the media in incessantly engraving such images in the memory, and one basis for an unholy alliance between feminism and popular culture becomes evident.

From this point, two directions are possible in exploring our particular emotional involvements with the phenomena we examine. Such involvements can be described as a kind of complicity with those phenomena, perhaps because they are still so generally derided. One direction would be to explore the perverse pleasures of playing off the enjoyment of kitsch against irony. There is a curious kind of affection involved in recognising what these reassuring images of femininity are all about—and a certain complicity is thereby assumed between reader and object. There is something close to what is often called 'camp' about this affectionate yet distanced recognition of gender being made up before one's very eyes. For a feminist reading of popular texts like the *Weekly*, what is camp is the knowledge that gender-bending is possible, that gender is all performance, not the fixed femininity and masculinity that these texts present us with (Sedgwick 1990: 156; Butler 1990). In homosexual camp, it is glamorous images of femininity that attract, but what about the domestic images, that other stock-in-trade of women's magazines? What is the attraction in dressing down, not dressing up, femininity?

Nostalgia and cultural history

In addition to this 'camp' kind of complicity, there is also nostalgia. I have observed in discussing the *Weekly* project with other women of my generation ('baby boomers') that this affectionate complicity with the materials of our inquiry is intensified when they are connected with our own pasts in some immediate way. This is all the more powerful when 'we' are feminists reclaiming, however critically, the texts of a past 'women's culture'. Here we are in the terrain of nostalgia, regret for a lost past, that occurs as the result of a present perspective on that past.

Nostalgia involves desire, loss, longing, and a certain pleasure as well as pain in those emotions. A Greek compound which translates roughly as pain for the loss of home, nostalgia can be double-edged, both a sickness for home and a sickness *of* home (Gunew 1988: 35–46). I think that the nostalgia operating around a cultural text, like the *Weekly* of the 1950s and '60s, has several dimensions: for those of us of a certain age, there is the autobiographical desire to contruct a 'fable of origin' of our youth in the '50s and '60s; but there is also a less historically specific nostalgia for a fantasised past, for images of home and of the maternal.

The desire to revisit our own pasts, and to use the *Weekly* as the occasion to construct a 'political fable of origin', is deeply implicated in our writing of a social and cultural history of the period. The *Weekly* is a powerful icon for those of us who learned a distinctively Australian femininity with and through it in the 1950s and '60s. We were the first generation to be constructed by the media as consumers first and foremost: this was a crucial factor in the gap between our generation and our parents' (formed by Depression and war), and the *Weekly* was a major pre-TV apparatus for doing this. It also played a major role in constructing us as *teenage* consumers, with its special 'Teenagers' Weekly' supplement. We were also 'Americanised' with unprecedented intensity, and the *Weekly* did its bit in this process through movie gossip, some fiction, fashion, and pop psychology.

We tell our stories of this time within a context of other, conflicting stories already told. There is the dominant myth of the '50s as the decade of conservatism, in which women's place was supposed to be in the home. We learn to see this in relation to Lees and Senyard's (1987) account of the 1950s as the apotheosis of the (male) Australian dream of house, car and family wage. Another text is *Baby Boomers* (both book and film), which constructs this period very much within a sentimental nostalgic mode, seeing 1950s childhood as a safe suburban space, a utopia of benevolent regimentation in which girls were no more restricted than boys, and 'reffo kids' good-naturedly learned, and taught their postwar migrant parents, to be Australians (Townsend 1988). We learn something else from Lesley Johnson's work on con-structions of the female subject as individual, but also as 'woman' above all: we learn that there were contradictions operating to enable the emergence of the potentially dissatisfied female individual. This is the woman who figures so prominently in the myth of the '60s, a story of everything starting to move again, when Australian women got the contraceptive pill and returned to the workforce in droves. She is also the emergent feminist subject who, in the late 1960s, took this identification with the category of 'woman' literally and made it the basis of a political position (Johnson 1993: 154). This fable of origins, then, is 'political' in that it is written from a vantage point that is not only older but feminist; not 'more of the same' but different politically from the dominant ideology of the past's texts.

The desire for a fable of origins also has an unconscious level, one which gives another dimension to nostalgia and its presence in such a study as ours. Sneja Gunew, in her essay 'Home and away: Nostalgia in Australian (migrant) writing', writes that nostalgia begins in the desire for beginnings, for lost origins, and ultimately in the desire for the lost maternal presence. She identifies nostalgia's prevailing motif of a utopian return to 'within the walled city of the maternal'—to a fantasised refuge (Gunew 1988: 41). It might, of course, be objected that this sort of study (of the *Weekly*, or of 1950s TV) easily becomes just another way of talking about our mothers, and, as one critic has put it, 'a mode of regression to an imaginary, if utopian, infancy' (Morris 1988b: 27–28). This is all the more likely to happen in a genre directed to women. Concepts of the maternal in feminist theory link it to the 'mute body', the silent woman, the mother whom feminism sometimes fantasises itself enabling finally to speak (Modleski 1991: 48).

The image of woman in the *Weekly*, especially in the 1950s, was centrally maternal (and a nostalgic attraction to that image surely operates for male as well as female readers). This may be linked with the *Weekly*'s self-presentation as a national symbol, supposedly inclusive in a maternal way. There is a nostalgic, 'regressive' pleasure in being so included in a national space gendered feminine-maternal. The *Weekly*'s construct of 'Australia' may be attractive because it is so unlike the images of the masculinist Australian Legend revived in the 1950s.

Romanticising suburban Australia has its own attractions in this context. A study of the *Weekly*, like visual exhibitions of the domestic styles of the 1950s and 1960s, is likely to be widely read as a text of 'Australiana'. Popular-cultural texts are considered acceptable if they speak to us of the past, if studying them can be seen as a populist kind of history, and can be read as an appreciative farewell to a bygone era.

Yet this would not be a satisfactory position for feminist critics to adopt. In her work on nostalgia, Gunew is concerned to show how nostalgia, from a 'migrant' or 'other' position—nostalgia for a different home—can be used to reread Australian literature by rendering uncanny its familiar versions of home/mother/land so that we must examine them and not take them as given. This challenge can be applied as well to a feminist reading of the *Weekly*, as a challenge to defamiliarise this specifically Australian popular text in the same way, to render the world it constructs uncanny, strange, so as to denaturalise its common sense, its 'average Australian women'. The double question of feminism returns here—not only Who am I? but Who is the other woman?—to remind us that there are other frames of reference, other subjectivities, made invisible by the discourses of this particular medium.

8

Number magic: The trouble with women, art and representation

Julie Ewington

Art and life have altered remarkably for Australian women artists in the last twenty years. Arguably, women are now more active as professional artists here than in comparable Western countries like the United States, Germany or the United Kingdom, with painters, sculptors, photographers, printmakers and installation artists working in greater numbers than ever before. Susan Cohn, Olive Cotton, Rosalie Gascoigne, Joan Grounds, Fiona Hall, Narelle Jubelin, Emily Kngwarreye, Lyndal Jones, Bea Maddock, Mandy Martin, Sally Morgan and Susan Norrie are only a few of the well-known contemporary Australian artists who are women. This turn to professional art by women marks a decisive break with the past. It is a special consequence of the broad demographic and social changes of the postwar period, supported by articulate and active feminist teachers, groups and campaigns.[1] While many women engaging in important cultural work still deliberately eschew the professionalisation of feminine creativity, the challenges posed by the artistic practice of women working in the public domain constitutes the most distinctive transformation in Australian arts practice of the last generation. Quite simply, they have made a different world from their mothers.

In the 1990s, Australian women artists enjoy the unusual, even unique, circumstance of official endorsement. Feminism, in the historical context of rapidly expanding public and private patronage in the last twenty years, suggested an expanded interpretation of citizens' democratic rights, and thus brokered equal opportunity and affirmative action policies in the arts. The climate of developing equal opportunity legislation in the 1980s in Australia offered one solution to the continued marginalisation of women artists and was seized as a useful tool. Since 1984, the argument that women artists suffer the same kinds of discrimination as women in other areas of employment, and that their

Affirmative Action for Women in the Visual Arts at the 1984 Biennale of Sydney, Art Gallery of NSW, protesting at the absence of women artists in the exhibition. (Photographer unknown)

access to professional life is discouraged, has generally been conceded. If the social revolution of feminism remains incomplete, frustrating the fonder hopes of the heady late 1960s, at least the bureaucrats ('femocrats') instituted the same concrete gains for women artists as were achieved in other areas of Australian social life.

Acquiescence to feminist demands for 'equal representation' was bound up in the generally egalitarian tenor of Australian public culture, but the consequences of this development were particularly marked in this country because of the great importance of government to the Australian arts. In 1994, it is accepted wisdom that women should be equally represented in major exhibitions such as the Biennale of Sydney (for Australian artists, at least), Australian Perspecta, the Adelaide Biennial of Australian Art, the Asia-Pacific Triennial and the Art Gallery of Western Australia's Craft Triennial; in international delegations; and in programs administered by the Australia Council and other bodies, which fund fellowships, project grants, overseas travel and studio residencies, and exhibitions.

Equal opportunity and affirmative action policies are not an expression of social power, however, but depend on exclusion from it. They would not exist if women were as valued, encouraged or rewarded as their male colleagues. They are not. Nor would I be obliged to refer in this text to 'women artists' if their practice were completely socially

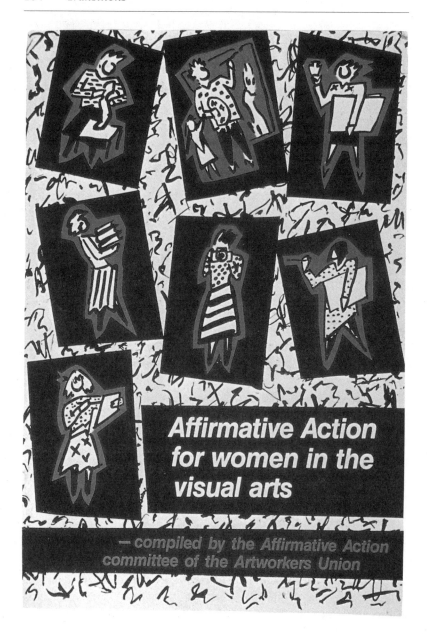

Affirmative Action for women in the visual arts

— compiled by the Affirmative Action committee of the Artworkers Union

accepted. Despite official recognition of the claims of women to training, employment and recognition, women working as artists do not enjoy the same access to professional life as men, nor are they encouraged to think of themselves as authentic artists. Women artists are still the exception rather than the norm. A deep suspicion of women as active cultural agents remains embedded in Australian society, and the questions about women's participation in Australian art and culture which have emerged may characterise the remainder of the 1990s.

In this essay I want to examine the current predicament of Australian women artists. Women insist on access to professional opportunity, but many are convinced that only legislative prods will gain full recognition of their achievements. The common denominator of women's demands is the argument from equal opportunity, particularly in employment, rather than a commitment to an explicitly feminist art practice. On the other hand, the venerable notion of artistic achievement as the sole criterion for assessing an artist's practice continues to war with discourses around 'representation': put simply, democratic theory insists on the inherent equality of every citizen, but traditional notions of artistic practice emphasise remarkable achievements by extraordinary personalities, often described as 'geniuses', a clearly male group (Battersby 1989 *passim*). Thus while women argue in the professional arena for recognition of their work, they must struggle, subjectively, to secure their sense of themselves as artists.

Ten years after the Australia Council's affirmative action policies were instituted, the merits of the quest for equal representation of women in the arts are ripe for reassessment. I will argue that despite the gains offered by equal opportunity and affirmative action programs, such legislation cannot resolve the fundamental problems for women of practice as an artist. Equal opportunity is a useful tactic, blocking off certain avenues of discrimination and steering institutions towards desirable outcomes for women. But equal opportunity most characteristically addresses equal employment opportunity, and involves a set of specialised tactics which, useful as they are, cannot by their very nature embrace all the problems women encounter in other arenas of social and cultural life. Finally, I will argue that the strategies which will enable women artists to enter into full possession of their powers lie with more complex intersections of the subjective and public life. The reconfiguration of social practice and cultural forms which will change women's experience of artistic work will be undertaken on different terrain: at the level of artistic discourses, and through the experimental exemplars of women's art practice.

The trouble with 'representation'

Australian artists are well aware of the difficulties of appeals to equal opportunity arguments, as a fascinating discussion with the Guerrilla Girls during their gorilla-suited appearance on a panel at the 1992 Adelaide Festival Artist's Week revealed. This New York activist group of women artists and arts workers has successfully advertised the professional difficulties of women through a hilarious series of widely published posters, an achievement which has considerably embarrassed the liberal pretensions of American art institutions. But in Adelaide, Australian feminists noted the limitations of notions of democratic access to professional life, arguing that success in conventional terms is still regarded ambivalently by a movement seeking radical social change. Indeed, at the other end of feminism's political spectrum from the Guerrilla Girls, the English performance artist Bobby Baker spoke about the merits of collaborative activities by women in extra-professional networks in the UK.

Feminist strategies within culture have been debated for twenty-five years. One influential opinion in the 1980s held that earlier emphases on practical questions about equal opportunity had given way to more fundamental problems of image production and the social construction of the audience. As British art historians Roszika Parker and Griselda Pollock argued: 'Practical strategies have become strategic practices' (Parker and Pollock 1987: 52). The important notion of feminists strategically addressing artistic discourses and institutions was thoroughly canvassed in Australia as in other Anglophone art centres: indeed, the key transatlantic text was reprinted in *Lip*, the influential Australian feminist arts journal of the late 1970s and early '80s (Marsh 1993: 63–64; Barry and Flitterman 1980: 164–165).

In the phrase 'women and representation', and the several different meanings of the term peculiar to the visual arts, lies part of the confusion of equal opportunity and of the hopes held out for it. Let me unpack these fascinating complexities. First, 'representation' in its most technical sense refers to picturing, especially European cultural traditions claiming to faithfully record appearances as if external appearance were the sum total of the person. The ferocity of recent debates concerning the depiction of women in art and contemporary mass media depends, in part, on the underlying conviction that Western modes of picturing are fundamentally, literally, 'realistic', and somehow capture the 'real person'. Feminists objecting to these 'representations' of women sought other forms of imagery, literally re-presentations. They argued that traditional modes of picturing are not natural or inevitable, merely 'naturalistic', and that it was essential to recognise 'art as socially determined representation/ signification', as Parker and Pollock argued the case. In short, cultural constructs and artistic forms are not eternally fixed but may be changed (Parker and Pollock 1987: 45). This conviction has inspired women to a remarkable flowering of experimentation in the last twenty-five years with modes of picturing women (including refusing to image them at all). Not surprisingly, the most concentrated experimental site has been photography, the key picture-making practice of the twentieth century, and in this important project Australian women artists have been very active. Key contributors include Sue Ford, Helen Grace, Anne Ferran and Julie Rrap, but as Catriona Moore demonstrates, feminists understood the significance of photography very clearly and exploring ways of harnessing its powers was an early, multi-faceted and continuing project (Moore 1994).

The second sense of 'representation', in which individuals were seen as 'representatives' of all women, was characteristic of the politics of the early Australian Women's Liberation Movement and of the ethic of 'sisterhood'. But as feminist artists organised slightly later than the original women's groups (the first Women's Art Group was founded in Sydney in 1973, five years later than the original Women's Liberation group), they were less subject to the earlier rhetoric of solidarity. In fact, nowhere is the distinction between women as individuals and as members of a group more sharply registered than in the practice of art, a cultural practice relying precisely on individual idiosyncrasy rather than on shared capabilities. This contradiction persists as a major difficulty for equal opportunity arguments in the arts: it is perfectly absurd to demand that practitioners of an art which in its most traditional form depends on individuals mining their individual histories, desires and abilities, should be seen as somehow characteristic of their sex. In recent years the notion that all women share identical interests has been almost entirely rejected by feminism as it has come more and more to recognise the diversity of Australian women and Australian feminisms (see Chapters 4 and 5). However, despite the traditional privilege which art accords to the individual project and achievement, a sense of shared interests has subtended affirmative action arguments. The implicit belief has been that women artists, curators and managers would nurture the interests of other women.

It has become clear, however, that the struggle to ensure greater participation by women artists in public life is fundamentally not about representation but about access to opportunity. Women artists do not 'represent' anyone in the sense that a parliamentarian represents a constituency or a unionist her colleagues. This is not a frivolous comparison. Affirmative action policies rest on the assumption that access to education, employment, housing, medical treatment and other amenities is the right of all citizens. Injustice can be demonstrated when access to particular jobs, schools, housing programs or hospitals is shown to have been denied to individuals who have the right to them. In the context of the visual arts, it is possible to show that a woman should be granted entry to art school but not that she is a better artist on graduation than her male colleagues or that her work is of greater value. This is a matter of judgment, subject to an unpredictable complex of attitudes and preferences. All that can be proven is that consistently fewer women artists are exhibited or funded, given the size of the available pool of talent. In short, whatever the sense of representation engaged, women may argue with certainty that their interests are not being served at present, but cannot state with equal confidence how they might be better served within the current discursive and institutional regimes of art.

Moreover, even successful affirmative action policies may be distasteful in their personal implications: women artists are no more willing than their counterparts in other professions to welcome patronage on the basis of gender, insisting on success on the basis of merit. Indeed, such is the traditional intimate connection between the artist's ego and her work that selection on the basis of gender is especially unacceptable in this profession. Women artists of earlier generations have been particularly scornful of affirmative action policies, and of quotas in particular. In one sense, the opponents of affirmative action, and feminists upholding it, have pursued different ends while recognising the force of similar arguments: gender is no guarantee of achievement.

The glass ceiling and the troubling status of women artists

In the 1990s the social environment of the visual arts is far wealthier and more confident, and certainly more politically complacent, than it was in the 1970s when the original agitation for increased opportunities for women artists occurred. The extensive social critiques of the post-Vietnam period favoured the interrogation of even such relatively remote corners of Australian life as the visual arts. The almost complete absence of women from public life shocked artists influenced by the Women's Movement into action: affiliation, discussion, research, publication, and agitation for improved opportunities. In the mid-1990s the situation is very different. Twenty-five years ago the possibility that an individual woman might be successful as an artist was debated; today it will generally be accepted. As a result of this (modified) success, women are now much less likely to agitate for change, feeling with some justification that the 1970s and '80s was the period when feminist action was necessary, and that existing safeguards protect women from gross injustice. Only at the most elevated levels of achievement is the presence of women unusual: retrospective exhibitions at major museums, like Bea Maddock's at the Australian National Gallery in 1992, are very rare; major monographs are almost exclusively reserved for (living) male artists; and only in 1993 was Jenny Watson chosen as the first woman to be the sole representative of Australia at an international exhibition, the 1993 Venice Biennale, the world's most prestigious contemporary art event.

I would argue that Australian cultural discourses are still deeply masculinist and that gender remains a crucial factor in assigning value to the work of artists. Despite the enhanced artistic status of women, a tenacious association exists in Australian culture between excellence in the visual arts and notions of creative genius, or what the British artist Mary Kelly has described as '. . . the aura of genius and madness and originality and maleness that surrounds the artist auteur' (Parker and Pollock 1987: 53). At this intersection, irresistible forces meet an immovable object: the growing sophistication and reputations of women come up against the entrenched social belief that creativity in the visual arts is the prerogative of men, not merely contingently, as in football, but essentially and irreducibly. Despite the successes of many individual women as artists, there is evidence of persistent resistance to them by many arts institutions, both public and private. Equal opportunity policies have not reversed the pattern whereby the proportion of women selected for major exhibitions falls far below the proportion of women practitioners in the field. The Federal Sex Discrimination Act cannot touch arts organisations directly, as they are independent and self-regulating; moreover some states have never implemented equal opportunity principles in the arts. The Australia Council is not satisfied with the response to equal opportunity policies, but can take no action. This resistance is not merely a matter of institutional imposition. It also operates at the level of the individual subject, both female and male. Equal opportunity arguments are particularly powerless in the arts, where attitudes about artistic achievement and value change only very slowly, and where the general proposition informing equal opportunity programs—that the predisposition to succeed in any field occurs in both sexes—is clearly not yet accepted.

This is not the case with all art forms. A comprehensive sociology of women in the arts in Australia has yet to be written, and it is as yet imperfectly understood why some art forms are more feminised than others. For example, women writers are much more prominent in our culture than women artists. This was not always the case, but resulted from changes in literary discourses and forms accomplished over a century ago. On the other hand, women conductors of symphony orchestras are still extraordinarily rare. In the visual arts, social factors which once prevented women from professional life as artists are gradually changing. But the situation in public life, and internalised representations of women as lesser artists than men, continue to militate against complete acceptance of women as genuinely creative visual artists.

In the 1990s, the status of women artists as a group is improving, but very slowly. Few women are employed in full-time, tenured and senior positions in art colleges, places which are extremely important in Australia since they guarantee income and often sustain artists attempting experimental work. Teaching positions are also highly influential: they set for future generations the appropriate styles of artists. Women artists expect to earn less than their male colleagues; they receive mid-career exhibitions and retrospectives much less frequently than male artists, so that in 1993 the Visual Arts/Crafts Board of the Australia Council noted that retrospective exhibitions for women should be a priority; and women are under-represented in major museum collections.[2] Despite their recent achievements, women artists and arts administrators are subject to the same attitudes as women working in other industries: expectations of them are lower, and the responsibilities they are given are less taxing than those assigned to men.

However, a response to equal opportunity programs has been demanded in the arts. At heart, the public culture of Australia is thoroughly egalitarian and a deeply felt belief exists that cultural life can be arranged equitably by the rational application of progressive policies. As a consequence, contemporary Australian culture is profoundly influenced by public debate about the participation of women (and other social groups), and a species of social engineering is encouraged in the belief that an acceptable and equitable allocation of public resources and individual satisfactions can be achieved. Women now make up approximately one-third of all exhibitors/participants in cultural programs, though they far outnumber men as consumers of the arts. It would seem that one-third is a quasi-magical number, for it is the proportion of women tacitly agreed to be acceptable in many fields of public life. An excellent recent example is the decision of the

Australian Labor Party in 1994 that by 2003, 35 per cent of candidates preselected for winnable seats should be women. The frequency with which this one-third fraction occurs in the visual arts is extraordinary, whether in advertisements, group shows in commercial galleries, or even in exhibitions by the larger museums, which ostensibly support the principles of equal opportunity for the purposes of grant applications to the Australia Council. This is not simply a quota imposed from above. Not only are organisations satisfied with the situation, but many women also appear to agree with this perception of the 'acceptable' numbers of women in artistic life. Otherwise, how can we account for the persistence of this almost unexamined fraction in major museums?

Even more remarkably, this magical fraction has barely altered in the last decade since the introduction of equal opportunity policies, despite the continuing overwhelming dominance of women graduating as professional artists. Despite the increasing pool of available female practitioners, and despite the ten-year history of official adherence by the Australia Council, the federal funding agency, statistics drawn from major national exhibitions indicate that selection processes for artists to be presented to the public, outside the explicit run of official affirmative action policies, continue to favour men. It is extremely unusual for the number of women to equal men even in the major exhibitions which have received Australia Council funding. For example, since 1984, women have constituted half of the exhibitors in the Australian Perspecta on only one occasion—when a special 'women's section' was presented. Even more remarkably, women made up only 13 of 31 exhibitors in the Australian section of the inaugural Perth International Crafts Triennial at the Art Gallery of Western Australia, although demographic studies have consistently shown that women account for around 67 per cent of craftspeople (Throsby 1986). The curatorial decisions for each exhibition depend on a number of factors—artistic, logistical, financial—and demographic parity is no automatic guarantee of success. Nevertheless, the distance between official government policy and the exhibitions supported by its major agency is striking.

This discussion of the intersection of visual arts practice and affirmative action is simultaneously an instance of the desirability, and the profound limitations, of liberal policies of access and equity. Official policies cannot prevent the persistence of social patterns discouraging women from confidence in their creative powers, encouraging them to relinquish work for the sake of their partners' careers, or dissuading from practice women who also wish to parent children. In the visual arts, as in other arenas, it seems that a 'glass ceiling' prevents women from becoming more active. This phenomenon is currently much discussed, identifying informal and unofficial (indeed counter-official) habits of mind and practices which suggest that if women are visible at all they are too visible, and that even a small proportion of women will be seen to dominate an enterprise. It is known from numerous studies in educational institutions and social groups that considerable anxiety is attached to increased recognition of women. Characteristically, women are seen as excessively numerous even if they are in the minority, and as taking up too much time, space and attention even if they are, objectively, less demanding than their male counterparts. These patterns have been tracked from the nursery to high school, from large corporations to political parties.

Contemporary Australian attitudes to artists participate in these social practices. In the visual arts they take the particular form of favouring group/theme exhibitions by women over one-person exhibitions; give credence to masculine rather than feminine subject matter; and reserve the highest esteem for male artists. In such a cultural milieu, affirmative action programs are unable to insist on the representation of women artists in numbers that are consistent with their actual presence and contribution in the arts community. Legislation will always be frustrated by contradictory social attitudes, and the demand that an artist's work be of a certain 'quality' is essentially tied to perceptions about gender.

Disparities between the achievements of women and their participation in public life trouble the assertively egalitarian traditions of Australian culture, now committed to access and equity policies for minority groups, whether classified by age, class, ethnicity, geography or gender. The intransigence of the arts industry in the face of this strong female presence is all the more intriguing given tactical successes by Australian feminists in the arts who have harnessed industrial demands rather than engaging in philosophical debates. Instead of directly addressing feminist criticisms of visual arts discourses and tackling entrenched notions of the male monopoly on excellence, Australian feminists have maintained a non-prescriptive agnosticism. Australian arts feminism is not a theoretically and politically naïve discourse, on the contrary, 'political practice' in the arts is a set of very generously drawn, catholic notions, benefiting from the political vigour of the Australian Women's Movement, the eclectic intellectual climate of Australia and lively parallel debates in the US and the UK. The complex relationships between imagination, creativity, the specialised arena of the art world and society in general are customarily treated with sensitivity, and a habitual protocol of tolerance has embraced the broadest conceptions of feminist practice in the arts. This flanking tactic has served women artists well, up to a point. But eventually the deficiencies of the implied liberal individualist rationale for women's involvement in the arts is revealed: it cannot address fundamental issues concerning the place of women in culture.

If recognising talent remains the sign of a cultivated society and fostering it a matter of public responsibility, the position of women artists will continue to be of great interest. This is the quandary: it seems that there is no option other than to accept equal opportunity policies, which counter barriers to professional success and attempt to increase the numbers of women participating in public life as artists. But they are unable to address the institutions, histories and customs constructing culture. (The machine is being asked to perform differently but the apparatus remains intact.) We must refine the usual arguments concerning women artists, though, and ask more pointed questions of arts institutions. For instance, art colleges training large numbers of women but failing to employ them after graduation may be interrogated about their employment policies; women taxpayers may inquire why public funds do not purchase works by bona fide artists who are women or provide child-care facilities for arts events; and cultural critics will interest themselves in aspects of contemporary culture favouring masculine individuals, interests and discourses, as well as the invention of feminine discourses.

Who am I?

Successful professional practice should have enabled women to experience wide confirmation of their self-esteem as artists. It is striking, for example, that the valuable Moët and Chandon Award for younger artists, judged anonymously though eschewing explicit policies of gender equality, has consistently been awarded to women artists since its institution in 1987. Unhappily, women artists still value themselves less highly than do men. A survey of occupational patterns suggests that women consider themselves less 'authentic' as professional artists than their male colleagues: approximately twice as many women as men work in the traditionally feminised crafts, particularly in textiles, the lowest-ranked medium in the contemporary hierarchy; women artists still apply less frequently to the Australia Council than men for the most prestigious and valuable awards, the Creative Artist Fellowships, apparently assuming that modesty is the appropriate feminine posture. However, the proportions of women in other categories have risen considerably over the last decade, partly in response to the council's own affirmative action strategies. Significantly, when women do apply for assistance they continue to ask for less money than men.[3] If seeking to excel, to be a 'tall poppy', is difficult for an Australian woman, pursuing extraordinary achievement as an artist is doubly difficult, since the field is dominated by notions of excellence deriving from stereotypical constructions of the artistic ego as gigantic, impassioned, impervious to criticism, semi-divine and thoroughly male.

Alternative constructions of feminine artistic practice are developing, however. I cannot rehearse here the entire catalogue of experiments achieved by feminist artists. But it is important to note that within the last thirty years the landscape of artistic practice by women has altered irrevocably, and that these developments have profoundly affected contemporary art. An expanded account of the feminine imagination, and of the objects of feminine desires, has sustained an explosion of possibilities. Insistence on the distinction between female and male subjects underpins a number of key strategies in contemporary art by women, strategies encompassing new subject matter, an expanded range of working practices, and experiments with the form and location of feminine subjectivity. It is the latter, paired innovations which interest me here. For instance, women have developed works concerning their passion for their children; their bodily functions, including the previously taboo matters of menstruation, orgasm, childbirth, aging; sexual relations with both women and men; the constitution of women as primary objects of sexual desire, especially through the mass media; and the practice of domestic labour and crafts. These are now important themes in art by women, and each implies subject positions, both as makers and as audiences, previously absent from Western cultural life. To cite just one example: Mary Kelly's *Post-partum Document,* 1975–1979 (UK), seen in Australia in its entirety in 1982; *The Lovely Motherhood Show,* 1979, by the Women's Art Movement, Adelaide, coordinated by Jude Adams; and Helen Grace's film *Serious Undertakings,* 1983, all engaged with the 'problem' of motherhood from feminist perspectives, giving utterance and images to previously 'invisible' social experiences.

In each case, these new or (expanded) themes have aroused considerable opposition as inappropriate for art, a criticism stemming from the belief, deeply embedded in Western culture, that the universal subject is masculine. In this view, art is neither gendered nor embodied, and men and women participate equally and with identical interests in its practice, a view strenuously challenged by feminist artists, historians and critics. They argue that as the artist is gendered and embodied, then not only will different subject matter arise, but the subjective experience of art will also differ. Feminists have been aware of the difficulties of adopting, as authentic practitioners, the conventional artistic subjectivity of the West, which insists on mastery of both subject matter and methods. Thus they have used a number of sophisticated strategies and devices investigating alternative subjectivities, ranging from collaborative work to forms of decentred utterances which reject the artist's persona as the primary focus of the work. In these works the very marginality of women (social and cultural) has been mobilised to interrogate existing assumptions about artistic practice.

I am also interested in an attitude more directly parasitic on, and parodic of, traditional stereotypes of the artist. The work of the Australian painter Jenny Watson since the early 1980s has consistently engaged with traditional configurations of the persona of the painter, the archetypal artist of the Western tradition. Jenny Watson's works appear as self-obsessed as any man's. But unlike male painters, for whom egoism is a birthright, Watson is a delinquent in the house of genius, playing a dangerously double-edged game between the personal and the political. Consequently her work has attracted both critical acclaim and deeply sceptical responses. Curator Judy Annear writes of Watson's 'cultivated naïvety' and also of the 'obsessive narcissism' of her paintings, both key factors in reactions to Watson's work (Annear 1993: 12–13). It is clear that Watson's flagrantly reiterated egoism, remarkable in a woman, and her roughly made, sequined and collaged fabric paintings, which deliberately reject notions of 'finish', are infuriating to certain audiences.

Assuming a naïve stance is a venerable feminine ploy. The simultaneously infantile and mature aspects of Watson's paintings, the child–woman persona she cultivates in her work and appearances, and her frequent identifications with Lewis Carroll's Alice in Wonderland, alert us to the knowing ambiguity embedded in her work. In adopting Alice as her alter-ego, Jenny Watson resembles the writer Dorothy Hewett's archetype of the expressive Australian woman, a doubly dangerous grotesque in this notoriously masculine and taciturn society. As Judy Annear has remarked, Jenny Watson 'has chosen to transgress and transcend the conventions of painting and to dignify the feminine imagination' (Annear 1993: 12). Watson's insouciantly feminine, ironic self-portraits deliberately draw attention to the improbability of a woman parading her desires and experiences: her dreams, her passion for her horses and her cats, her loves and their loss, her travels and her enmeshment in the international art market.

Watson also explores the theme of her situation as an artist in many

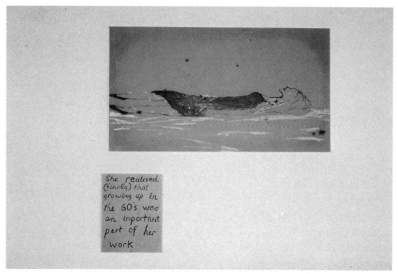

She realised
(finally) that
growing up in
the 60's was
an important
part of her
work

Jenny Watson *Left for dead + She realised (finally) that growing up in the 60s was an important part of her work*, 1992, Oil on taffeta with netting and sequins plus synthetic polymer paint on stretcher, 79 × 146 cm, 50.5 × 40.5 cm.

works. She goes out of her way in her work to reject conventional social estimations of women's appropriate modesty. Significantly, these works have coincided with postmodern critiques of the artistic subject. Australian artists first became interested in theorists like Roland Barthes and Michel Foucault, who suggested a diminished importance for individual authorship, in the early 1980s. At that time Watson began brazenly to parade her persona as an artist. Not only are many paintings self-portraits, but Watson's prominent signature and an outsize copyright symbol underline the artist's presence in/on the work. Thus Jenny Watson's work is doubly significant: she asserts that the artist is a woman, visible, identifiable, almost a contradiction in terms, a figure Rozsika Parker and Griselda Pollock characterise as '. . . a perverse hybrid struggling to conform to incompatible stereotypes' (Parker and Pollock 1987: 87), but her work also implies the specificity of all subjectivities. For the artist who may be a woman may also be a man. At any rate, the artist is no longer semi-divine and abstract but socially specific and thoroughly embodied. This redefinition, implicitly and often explicitly present in the work of many women, constitutes a hefty challenge to traditional notions of the identity of the artist. For deeply embedded in the conventional artist's career, set in its highly elaborated social contexts and resistant to alteration by the mere reiteration of

Jenny Watson *Eternal Youth + This painting is in the process of being purchased by a museum*, 1992. Oil on velvet with ribbon, false horse tail, synthetic polymer paint on stretcher, 152 × 76 cm, 50.5 × 40.5 cm.

feminist political demands, is the constitution of the Western artistic persona as male.

Why should this be so? For the excellent reason that until recently the stereotypical artist has been a man, though historically women always practised as artists. Thus there is no aspect of the profession of art which is not subtended by expectations about the proper place of men in it. The very practice of art, and its reception, have been thoroughly imbued with attitudes originating in and continuing the social experience of men. These include the expression of masculine forms of sexual desire as the social norm; expectations about successful reception; and the belief that the usual colleagues of artistic practice will be other men. Robert Hughes, the influential Australian-born art critic of *Time* magazine, implicitly subscribed to these attitudes when he described Jenny Watson's painting at the Venice Biennale as 'whiny postfeminism' and remarked that the powerful sexual works of the veteran American sculptor Louise Bourgeois were 'sometimes over-praised for feminist reasons' (Hughes 1993). In each case association with the specific interests of women was sufficient to invoke Hughes's critical disapproval. He did not directly address the works themselves.

Hughes also criticised Jenny Watson's selection for this key inter-national exhibition as an example of Australia's cultural orthodoxy, a clear reference to Australia Council equal opportunity policies, and a sideswipe at the multicultural agenda of the 1993 Venice Biennale as an instance of 'political correctness'. The conventional Western cultural milieu has been seriously challenged in the last several decades, and is now mourned by critics like Hughes. The entry into the international visual arts of not only women but also non-Euro-American artists, has profoundly changed the previous certainties of Western art and also signifies a profound change in the conditions of Western culture. The appearance of women and indigenous artists, the cultural perspectives of ethnic communities, and the articulation of gay and lesbian expres-sions in the visual arts, taken in conjunction, signify a faltering in the traditional confidence of European cultures and have resulted in the breakdown in the visual arts, as in other cultural arenas, of those older certainties referred to by Jean-François Lyotard as 'master narratives'. In the place of the coherent aesthetic practised by the single, coherent, universal (male) subject, there now exists a plethora of artistic forms, interests and styles.

This historical process is continuing, a long moment of fundamental change in conceptions of creativity and of the ability to pursue them. The long monopoly over expression by (white) men as the bearers of a universal subjectivity is weakening. Not all critical responses to these developments have been hostile. In the 1990s the woman artist, as an individual able and licensed to comment on personal relations or social conditions, is being accepted within Australian art practice. Yet the contemporary moment is not merely witnessing additions to the stan-dard personnel of Western art's inner sanctum. New notions of self are being invented here. What kinds of artistic subjectivities will be called into being to replace the older universal subject? New artistic practices inhabit (and give birth to) new social milieux. These include, among others, the artist as mother, the sexually desiring woman artist, the photographer playing with the possibilities of photography as a medium, the artist in community, the collaborative practitioner, the artist interacting with new technologies, the artist practising the physically decentred, allusive art of installation, even the self-consciously 'bad girls' of art, deliberately flouting social norms and expectations of political correctness (Tucker 1994 *passim*). Nor should we neglect the art forms being developed by Aboriginal women as we think about the possible future worlds artists are making.

We are living the postmodernist moment. The final problem to consider, then, is whether the advent of the postmodern era has been structured in part by women's increasing participation in public arenas including culture, and whether the changes of the postmodern era have been beneficial to women?[4] Now, as previously, only achievement sustains an artist's reputation. But how is that achievement defined? By whom? It seems that feminist (and feminine) creative action, and the evolution of new feminine modes of subjectivity, have barely begun the poignant work of making the unimaginable. In the enjoyment of changed creative possibilities, affirmative action policies in the arts since the 1980s have played a small but vital role, as the midwife at the re-birth of women as artists. But it is the remarkable contributions to Australian cultural life by the artists themselves which has accomplished the actual work of change. If women's anger at their absence from the fields of creativity—the arts, the media—spawned initial feminist action, feminist innovations have outpaced liberal equal opportunity policies, opening the floodgates of the imagination for wholesale revisions of artistic practices and institutions.

9

Keys to the musical body*

Sally Macarthur

[T]he body [is] in a state of music.

Roland Barthes

But what is there? Is it identity or fluidity, gender or sex, real or unreal, a language or Other? Is music the Other, the feminised Other? Is music a body itself?

Thomas Sear (undergraduate student, University of Sydney)

In some way, I think, I identify the music as a(nother) woman.

Suzanne Cusick

Prelude

Feminist scholarship in music has been much slower to develop than feminist scholarship in other disciplines. This is because it has had to deal with an exceedingly resistant and conservative element within malestream musicology which, even nowadays, in some quarters, is still preoccupied with a positivistic project of exercising judgments upon the canon (a 'no-woman's land', established, authorised and patrolled by men). While the masculine bias within the canon has long been recognised in literature and visual art, it has taken longer to be detected in music. As in other fields, feminist scholars in music in the 1970s and '80s sought to discover neglected and forgotten women composers, but their work was always marginalised. It was clear that the power brokers in the musicological system regarded their work with suspicion and scorn. It is notable, too, that many of these scholars are still without tenured positions (are, indeed, fortunate to have academic

* I would like to thank Elizabeth Wood, Elizabeth Grosz and Barbara Caine for their helpful comments. This essay is dedicated to Trish Pearse.

positions at all). In those early days, their work was rarely given a hearing at international conferences and was not disseminated through 'normal' musicological channels. Elizabeth Wood's 1980 landmark review essay was published not in a musicological journal but in the interdisciplinary feminist journal *Signs*.

It is only in the last five years that this has begun to change. With the development of what has been coined the 'new' musicology, scholars have begun applying feminist, poststructural and queer theories to the study of music. Even the highly prized *Journal of American Musicology* has been involved in debates contrasting feminist strategies with more traditional ways of thinking about music (e.g. van den Toorn 1991: 275–299 and Solie 1991: 399–410).

Disregarding widely held beliefs that music is independent of society and culture, and from the bodies that produce it, the 'new' musicology is challenging a discipline which, until very recently, was blind to its uncompromising attitudes and hidden agendas. The old ways of 'doing' musicology, gathering and analysing facts according to conventional (and supposedly neutral and scientific) principles, are coming under serious scrutiny. A score-driven discipline, musicology has developed analytical systems to test music for internal coherence. These focus on syntax and structure (the way the composer has put the notes together), and their findings can be presented in graphic and numerical form. The performative and experiential aspects of music as a temporal art capable of having an intimate relationship with the human body have been ignored.

The 'new' musicology is introducing different ways of thinking about music which acknowledge the body as an important agent and participant in the musical experience. Attention is now increasingly focused on the pleasurable, sensuous and even sexual nature of music. As Susan McClary, one of the most important pioneers of feminist criticism in music, noted in an interview with me, music is seductive, 'it causes the body to move. It arouses emotions. It even arouses sexual passions and imitates them' (Macarthur 1992: 9). Music and the body are intrinsically linked, for the human body—moving, vibrating, breathing, talking, shouting, whispering, clapping, singing, dancing—is always in a state of music. The human body and music are alike capable of traversing the whole sound spectrum and of moving through (linear) time—occupying time-frames, as it were. Thinking about music's intimate relationship with the body opens it up to different kinds of interpretations. With less emphasis given to the dots on the page, the 'new' musicology is at last giving back to music what it has lacked for so long, namely its body.

Grievous bodily harm

Among the many concerns of feminist theory is the subordination of women's bodies in culture. Western thought is logocentric, encapsulated in written and verbal language (discourse) that 'represents a singular and unified conceptual order . . . a system which seeks beyond signs and representation, the real and the true' (Grosz 1989:xix). Western culture, then, is founded upon a hierarchically organised structure that lends itself to oppositions. Inherent in these oppositions (binary relations) is the sanctioning of one term—and inferiorising of the (repressed) other—by defining the other through the first term's negation. Indispensable to the construction of such dualisms female/male, mind/body, subject/object and so on is the association of men with culture and reason and of women with the body and nature.

The human body to which women in Western culture are tied is analogous in physicality to music. The auditory world of music, construed as feminine because of its association with bodily functions, has been positioned as language's (repressed) 'other' because it cannot mean precisely what it means and exists only in temporal space. The visual world, to which written language belongs, takes precedence over the auditory world (including spoken language). Even within its own discourse, music has been constructed by theorists as possessing masculine and feminine properties which are applied, for example, to the description of certain rhythms, themes and cadences. In this essay, I will argue that the codification of music as feminine, the gendering of its themes, cadences and rhythms as masculine versus feminine, and the location of music in the severely dichotomised structure of Western culture, render it inferior and inflict upon it what I suggest is 'grievous bodily harm'.

The identity of the body with music and of music, in turn, with the feminised other is set up along similar lines to the rigidly dichotomised mind/body split which valorises the mind. On this view, the female sex (or, to extend the musical analogy, the 'feminine' musical body) is reduced to its body and nature, and the male body (which, in music, is beyond the material in the realm of the cerebral and the spiritual and encapsulated in the visual, masculine score) is assumed into a transcendent condition which, as Judith Butler says, becomes, 'paradoxically, the incorporeal instrument of an ostensibly radical freedom' (Butler 1990: 12). Traditional musicological practice has elevated music as transcendence, privileging its grammar, syntax and structure (its intellect) as well as its metaphysical dimension over the profusion of bodily metaphors it (re)presents, enacts, generates and multiplies. In phallogocentric culture, the musical body (along the lines of the mind/body split posited by Plato, formulated in more modern terms by Descartes and deconstructed by Derrida) resolves into binary relations such that music's syntax and structure (its grammar, semantics and formal shape) are privileged over its extramusical references (music reliant upon text and/or program); high 'art' music over pop, jazz, and rock; scored music over improvised music; modernist (complexist) music over postmodernist (simplexist) music; Western music over non-Western music, Teutonic music (from Bach through Brahms to the Second Viennese School) over all other music, and so on.

A celebrated example of the dichotomous ordering of the musical body in musicological discourse is the application of the terms masculine and feminine to themes and cadences. Marcia Citron points out that gendering in the aesthetic of the sonata (a musical structure that was fashionable during the eighteenth and nineteenth centuries) has its origins in a treatise on composition written by A. B. Marx in 1845 (Citron 1993: 120–164). In this treatise, Marx describes sonata form in terms of a masculine theme—bold, loud, strong, powerful, active, aggressive, thrusting and so on—and a feminine theme—timid, soft, weak, powerless, passive, submissive, lyrical and so on—which are repeatedly opposed until the masculine theme wins out. The gendered sonata form, founded on conflict and conquest, is therefore about relations of power. This rhetoric was still common in pedagogy and criticism at the end of the 1960s, and while musicology has by and large since repudiated it, the fact that it lasted so long is significant.

Cadences in music are strategies for ending conflict and erasing the power relations that produce it. Perfect cadences, the strongest of all the types available in tonal music, are used to reinforce the tonic (home) key, forcefully bringing the work to closure on its final two chords (V–I), which sound on a weak followed by a strong beat. In the *Harvard Dictionary of Music* this procedure is described as follows:

> **Masculine, feminine cadence**. A cadence or ending is called 'masculine' if the final chord of a phrase or section occurs on the strong beat and 'feminine' if it is postponed to fall on the weak beat. The masculine ending must be considered the normal one, while the feminine is preferred in more romantic styles. (Apel 1970: 506)

In her book *Feminine Endings,* Susan McClary describes how Chopin (a 'romantic' composer) is reprimanded by the contemporary American composer, theorist and critic Edward T. Cone for the 'incorrigibly feminine endings' which proliferate in his piano scores (McClary 1991: 10). These are a performer's nightmare, according to Cone, and must be made to sound masculine if they are to sound at least halfway decent. If Cone's advice is followed, however, these second (weak) beat resolutions, which create deliberate cross-rhythmic effects, are destroyed. Such rigid and gendered oppositional terms, of which one is always valued over the other, rationalise and abstract music so that its transcendental nature becomes the territorial province of the mind (man). The notion of music as transcending 'beyond itself, beyond its formal systems', as referring only to 'the soul or spirit, to the very essence of the divine or the human mind' (Engh 1993: 73) is particularly prevalent in the writings of nineteenth-century humanist philosophers.

In his influential work *The Beautiful in Music*, Eduard Hanslick argues that the beauty of music is derived from the objective properties of the music itself, not from the emotional states it can induce (1854: 98). Listening to music in a spontaneous manner is no better than taking drugs, for it 'loosens the feet or the heart just as wine loosens the tongue' (1854: 93), thus degrading the listener. This kind of (dangerous) listening 'may prevent the development of that strength of will and power of intellect which man is capable of' (1854: 94). According to Hanslick, there is only one proper way to engage with music, and very few people have the capacity for such sustained concentration:

> Without mental activity no aesthetic enjoyment is possible. But the kind of mental activity alluded to is quite peculiar to music, because its products, instead of being fixed and presented to the mind at once in their completeness, develop gradually and thus do not permit the listener to linger at any point or to interrupt his train of thought. It demands, in fact, the keenest watching and the most untiring attention. (Hanslick 1854: 98)

The phrase 'keenest watching' may seem an odd choice of metaphor for the listening experience, but it helps explain why that component of music which is visual, namely the musical score, is sanctioned over the 'sound' (performance) of music.

There has been much heated argument over music's abstract nature: whether music has meanings only in and on its own terms and is thus 'free of the taint of ideology and politics' (Wood 1993–94: 11) or whether, like all other signifying systems, it is very much a part of and implicated in its culture and history. This debate, too, is set up in binary terms and remains unresolved. But it is significant that the conservative elements in musicology, which Wood characterises as 'a self-styled "academic priesthood" of formalists and positivists' (Wood 1993–

94: 11), closely guard that domain known as 'abstract music', presuming that such music is non-metaphoric, neutral and objective and that any music can only be analysed in self-relating terms.

It comes as no surprise, then, that traditional analytical methods in music focus on the score (that is, the written rather than the auditory document of music). The highly technical systems devised by analysts, which are dressed up as being pseudo-scientific and therefore neutral, are aimed at establishing the true nature of 'greatness' in the musical work. This, in turn, gives birth to the 'genius' and the 'masterwork' (sic), a construction of the nineteenth century which retains currency even today. Analysts tend to reproduce what they 'read' as important in the musical score (namely, its pitch organisation) in another representational system (graphs, number grids etc.). Schenker (whose system was designed for music from Bach to the end of the nineteenth century) and Forte (the 'numbers' man, whose mathematical 'sets' were put to work on the pre-serial, atonal music of the early twentieth century)— the 'Schenker and Sets' systems—account for music (and its 'greatness') in this manner.

These systems are designed to test for internal coherence. But they ignore the fact that music's aural qualities have a significant influence on the parameters (such as pitch and rhythm) that musicologists choose to analyse. Significant differences over the location of a climax, for example, can arise from the different possible speeds at which a musical work is played by different performers or performing groups. It is by no means clear that a bar-counting analysis (that is, an analysis which is concerned with the score) will place a climax at the same point as it appears in performance.

There are other ways to conceptualise the relations between the subject, the musical score and the performance than those which privilege certain abstract (mathematical) relations between the mind and music. Music as a physical (material) presence has been largely ignored in theoretical discourses on Western art music. When the (material) body is keyed into music, the possibilities become limitless. Sexed bodies and subjectivities are crucial to thinking about the relations of domination and subordination in music.

Together with this, I should like to explore the power of subversiveness for inserting an alternative positioning into the predominantly dichotomous musical system. I shall then play out the themes that emerge on particular instances of women's musical texts. If the interpreter allows a two-way interaction to occur between (her)self and the music (in its scored particularities and its performative potentialities), then this experience will itself create theories which serve to to elucidate and interpret music meaningfully. I have often bemoaned the fact that formalist methods which claim to be impersonal and neutral are just as experience-dependent as the approach I am proposing here. As Elizabeth Wood reminds us, 'Our perceptions in the work of forms, configurations, meanings, gestures, symbols, are always already mediated by verbal formulas, as on a broader scale by ideology and culture' (Wood 1993–94: 11).

Keying in the body

In 'Who's playing whose tune?', Elizabeth Wood declares that it is high time new insights and intuitions were brought to the study of music. It is time, says Wood, to

> begin to unpack what it is we generally repress in thinking about our own experience of music: our emotional attachments to music, our needs met by music, our accommodations to society through music, our voices, our bodies. It matters . . . that our differing experiences of ethnicity and race, class, gender and sexuality differently inflect upon our subjectivities. It matters, in other words, who is who, especially in terms of the identities, representations, and roles we perform in our musical work. (Wood 1993–94: 11)

It matters, then, that bodies and sexual positionings of all kinds mediate the musical experience. The literary critic Roland Barthes illustrates this with the simple insight that 'music's referent is the body . . . [because] music is a field of signifying [significance] and not a system of signs, the referent . . . is the body. The body passes into music without any relay but the signifier' (Barthes 1985: 312 cited in Engh 1993: 73). On that basis alone, music needs to be affirmed as a 'body' experience so that we can, as Wood puts it, reclaim 'the sense of the physical force, the sheer sound of music', thus restoring music's body to music criticism. The enjoyment and pleasure of music need to be keyed into our critical work.

The temptation, as Wood implies, is to authenticate the purely individual, subjective experience. As Lawrence Kramer points out, the whole problematic nature of interpretation is fed by the paradox that 'while bad interpretations may be manifestly false, good interpretations can never be manifestly true'(Wood 1993–94: 12). To be responsible interpreters should declare their position, 'one that lays claims to a self but simultaneously problematises the self as the site of representation and as subject' (Wood 1993–94: 12).

Effectively following this suggestion, Suzanne Cusick, who declares a lesbian position, undertakes to demonstrate that music structures a 'power/pleasure/intimacy triad'. 'Being "lesbian"', she says, 'is a way of organising the force field of power, pleasure and intimacy that refuses the simple binary opposition male and female' (Cusick 1994: 73) because 'lesbianism' is a behaviour, not an essence. Elaborating on the complexity of the relationships involved between music—(a)nother woman—and herself, she asks:

> How do relationships in the power/pleasure/intimacy triad exist with music? Music is, after all, a thing, not a person, isn't it? And most of us form our intimate relationships with other people, don't we?
>
> If music be, for some of us, or for all of us sometimes, in the position sometimes called 'significant other', then one might look for scrambling and shifting roles within it, for funny power relations with it, moments when it is the lover—that is, the active, pleasure-giving partner—and moments when it is the partner who somehow receives pleasure or empowerment. And one might find oneself to be acting out all sorts of 'sexual' behaviours with this 'lover'/'beloved'. (Cusick 1994: 73–74)

Cusick's theoretical strategies involve dissecting musical texts as (re)presentations of the complex models of the mind–body relationship. Her primary concern, however, is to reinstate the (physical) body as a valuable and significant constituent of music.

Another strategy which can be usefully deployed to reinstate music as 'body' is to take up theories which analyse the body's transgressive potentialities. Mary Douglas provides a vivid demonstration.

> Any structure of ideas is vulnerable at its margins. We should expect the orifices of the body to symbolise its specifically vulnerable points. Matter issuing from them is marginal stuff of the most obvious kind. Spittle, blood, milk, urine, faeces or tears by simply issuing forth have traversed the boundary of the body. (Nead 1992: 5)

Derrida has argued that the frame at its extreme limits (both inside and outside) is a crucial site for meaning, a site at which the inclusion/exclusion dichotomy teeters. Lynda Nead takes this idea further to show how the female nude has been constrained in Western art and represented in an ideal state. She points to the potential for breaking out of the frame, suggesting that when the body does so it evokes awe and fear. This is why Western art has traditionally represented the (female) nude in an 'ideal' state, that is, in a state of being sealed up.

The boundary-breaking potentials of the female nude, the 'leaking' (female) body, is dangerous. Coded female/feminine, music—a dangerously leaking body which is always threatening to escape its limitations—is subversive and deviant. Taking up the image of music's deviancy, its agency 'of moral ambiguity in danger of bestowing deviant status on its practitioners', Philip Brett (1994: 11) suggests that Western society's ambivalence towards it can be explained using post-Lacanian psychoanalytic theories that link auditory pleasure to the primordial experience of the mother.

> Nonverbal, even when linked to words, physically arousing in its function as initiator of dance, and resisting attempts to endow it with, or discern in it precise meaning, it represents that part of our culture which is constructed as feminine and therefore dangerous. (Brett 1994: 12)

The potentially slippery, deviant, transgressive body of music, like that of the female nude in its picture frames, is paradoxically always captured in time frames which enclose it in linear time and acoustic space. Music's frames are set in a background of cultural silence (noise). This noise (for there is no such thing as pure silence) is chaotic, destructive and violent (see, for example, Attali 1985). Noise (culture) is ostensibly 'outside' music's time frames, yet I want to argue that the very blurring of the boundaries between noise (culture) and music implicates music in its transgressivity.

Women, already positioned between inside and outside spaces, close to edges, borders, margins, are strategically placed to make significant 'differences' precisely in the manner in which they emerge from their frames (musical texts).

In *A Thousand Plateaus* (1987: 299–309), Deleuze and Guattari deploy 'disruptive' metaphors to read music's narrativity as being in a constant state of becoming. Ian Andrews summarises it as:

> a becoming woman, a becoming child, a becoming animal, a deterritorialisation of the socius, producing dangerous pleasures in a multiplication of the senses, veering towards destruction, breakage and dislocation. Through the cultural constructs of melodic and harmonic coordinates, music reterritorialises upon itself. (Andrews 1990: 20–23)

Music is both separated from and contained within the socius. There is constant fluidity of movement between culture (noise/silence) and the musical composition which, in a sense, is itself in a constant process of varying the (cultural) theme while simultaneously appropriating from it—which, in turn, becomes a musical variation. Every musical text is a variation of another musical text (culture). Everything contained inside the framing contours of one musical text is both a variation of every piece of music which has ever been written and a variation upon its own particular theme. The territory of culture folds onto the musical text, which in turn folds back onto its own musical territory when the theme embarks on myriad variations. In the act of becoming deterritorialised, the theme (music) sets up the possibility, once again, of becoming reterritorialised, and so on. Music, the female/feminine, is in a constant state of becoming. It is never a finished product enclosed in time frames. Constantly becoming, constantly shifting, unable to be pinned down, it ruptures its (the) system. With their commitment to dismantling enclosing structures and displacing systemic boundaries, Deleuze and Guattari, I think, have opened up a space in which to locate women as powerful agents in their musical texts.

Come, play (with) me

In this section I intend to 'play' the theories I have mentioned onto four musical texts by Australian women composers. I will demonstrate that when the body becomes the major determinant for thinking the relations between analyst, score and performance, women composers—as bodies represented in their scores and performances—can become sites for celebration. In other words, by transgressing 'normal' musical analytical practice, it becomes possible first to admit women into a discursive practice from which they would otherwise be excluded and, second, to produce positive images for these women in defiance of the dominant constructions of femininity in Western art-musical culture.

The first work I pinned down to a feminist analysis was Australian composer Moya Henderson's *Sacred Site*, for grand organ and tape (Macarthur 1991: 29–34, 47). Composed in 1983 for the tenth anniversary of the opening of the Sydney Opera House, *Sacred Site* was potentially a grand piece for a grand occasion. Henderson takes on a commission featuring one of the most revered instruments of patriarchal music, but her interaction with the organ is always ambiguous. She marvels at it and pokes fun at it. She writes against the paradigms of the complex counterpoint tradition for the instrument and sends up the pomp and circumstance associated with it by introducing emu eggs, didgeridoo and clap sticks from the Australian bush as well as Jew's harps from European folk music. She makes these sound just as imposing and mystical as the organ itself by recording herself performing on them (and also the sounds of car horns and tram bells) and amplifying the results electronically. The tape, an integral part of the overall conception, adds a multiple presence to the work, exploring Australian culture across a 40 000-year time span. All the incongruities of the components—ancient Aboriginal myths; the tram bells and car horns of industrialised, white, Western society; Western art music's forms and traditions; two of its composers, Prokofiev and Janáček; and even the most sacred of Australian icons, the Sydney Opera House and all its touristic associations—are thrown into relief in this extraordinary musical narrative by repeated shifts from single to split focus.

Henderson's feminism is here translated into a music with hitherto unsuspected democracies. She takes all her sound sources—the digeridoo, Jew's harps, clap sticks, grand organ and so on—back to the same starting line. All have an equal opportunity to participate in the discourse; none is advantaged over others. *Sacred Site* is in six periods, its material generated by a steady stream of gestural syntax. The work relies on interventionist strategies which constantly head it off in ever-changing directions. Henderson's discursive, improvisatory style plays humorously and cleverly with all her disparate sound sources. The work opens with an assertive, chromatic, embellished, earth-bound melody which is set against a transparent, linear counterpoint. At the half-closure, Henderson intervenes with a symbolic gestural reference to Aboriginal culture (the sound of the digeridoo is heard), calling a temporary halt to the live performance only just begun. Then she introduces a cyclic pattern, a swirling, repetitive ostinato.

This is how the whole first episode unravels. The progress of the opening theme is constantly foiled by gestural occurrences: interventions of cyclic patterns, Aboriginal sounds, excessive speed and dynamic (loud/soft) changes, pauses and so on. Indeed, these gestures predominate throughout the entire work. Even potential climaxes are avoided. The fast and furious toccata-like sections subvert traditional notions of climax by resisting the temptation to provide an ascending bass line (a rising bass line is used conventionally as a powerful device for building musical climaxes). Instead, Henderson opts for static tonal plateaus: the music feels as if it is 'rising' (going 'somewhere') but it remains firmly rooted in its static tonal site. These kinds of patterns recur throughout the piece. Henderson quotes a brief Prokofiev theme in three parts of the work but in one section, it is smartly honked out of the way by a volley of car horns. While the devices she uses are the same ones men use (for example, repeated and cyclic patterns, appropriated and parodied music etc.), she adopts them here, I believe, to destabilise the prevailing patriarchal orthodoxy of organ composition.

Another composer who identifies with 'other' cultures, in this case, Eastern ones (particularly those of Indonesia, Korea, China and Japan) is Anne Boyd, Professor of Music at the University of Sydney. The folding of culture upon culture in Boyd's music (the Western on the Eastern and the Eastern on the Western and so on); its becoming one (culture) but not being one, its becoming the 'other' (culture) but not being the 'other'—its being neither the one nor the other—dislodges the sense of her music's 'is-ness' and defies rigid categorisation. With a preponderance of gestural syntax which belongs neither in this culture nor that culture but in both cultures, Boyd's music exudes a profusion of ambiguities. In this sense, it encapsulates the essence of Deleuze and Guattari's notion of being in a constant 'becoming music' state.

Cycle of Love, composed in 1981 is a demonstration of this effect (Macarthur 1993: 32–36). The internal and external dimensions of this work (which is built entirely upon a Korean melody), and its textualities and intertextualities, produce a heteroglossic text, that is, a text that speaks/sounds in mutiple voices. It is a setting of five aphoristic poems by anonymous Korean women, in all probability concubines, from the fifteenth century, and translated into English by the Korean-born Australian writer Don'o Kim. Boyd says the texts 'explore the nature of womanly love from personal and historical perspectives with which I felt a real empathy' (Boyd, forthcoming).

The translation of the texts for this work have been mediated through a male body who is of an 'other' culture; Boyd's 'feminising' of them is further extended by her deliberate instrumental and voice setting for countertenor (a man who sings 'like a woman'), alto flute, cello and piano. I read this voice and instrumental setting as being significant, for it produces what I call a cross-voicing effect. This effect is produced not just by the voice—the 'freakish'-sounding voice of a man singing in a woman's range—but also by the instruments (the 'curvaceous' cello in its high and sometimes its low, gravelly register, and the alto flute, with its erect shape, producing high-pitched sounds). There is a blurring, as it were, of sexual identities, a kind of hermaphroditic effect, and this is borne out in the texts, for although they offer no clear sense of sexual identity (the 'I', the 'you', the 'few' could be male or female), we intuitively identify them as being female.

Like Henderson, Boyd does not aim for a traditional positioning of her climax (Henderson has two climaxes which are not really climaxes and the material is weighted to the first half of the work). Boyd adopts something of an arc structure, positioning the third song as a climactic high point near the centre. Traditionally (in male music), major climaxes tend to be located at the golden section (that is, approximately two-thirds of the way through a work). A central climax, as in Boyd's work, is traditionally regarded as not working very well structurally, for it prolongs the 'afterplay'. In this instance, where there is no 'foreplay' or 'afterplay', its positioning is exceedingly effective. Externally and internally, *Cycle of Love* is shaped by cyclic and circular patterns produced by its heterophonic textures and an abundance of ostinato patterns and tonal centres which run parallel to the overall cyclical structure of the work. Eluding any sense of closure, *Cycle of Love* comes full circle, as it were, ending where it began.

Two Australian composers who deliberately break out of music's framing contours are Elena Kats-Chernin and Kirsty Beilharz. Kats-Chernin's piano piece *Tast-En* (1991), in a postmodern style, deliberately sets up a tonic/dominant dichotomy (that is, a dichotomy between the two most crucial key relationships in tonal music) in order to dissolve it. Grounded on these two chords (and other subsequent tonic/dominants that emerge as the piece unfolds), the work is concerned with undermining the constraint that this obdurate dichotomy imposes. Since the dominant always wants to resolve to the tonic (it is a very powerful penultimate to the tonic), Kats-Chernin constantly subverts this mechanism by allowing her dominants to escape to 'other' tonal places (some of which seem illogical). Yet the very irrationality of these musical moves provides her with strategies for sending up the musical tonal system—it becomes something of a joke—with her dominant chords eliding correct closing tactics as they slip constantly outside their rigidly imposed frameworks. Moreover, the whole piece concludes on the dominant chord (to the tonic which began the piece) and is left to die away in its own time. Closure is thus avoided. The frame on the end of this horizontal axis is left gaping and open.

Similarly, Beilharz creates a sense of the broken frame in her piece *Nuances*, for piano trio (1993). By taking the instruments to the extremes of their registers, traversing the whole sonic spectrum and threatening to go way beyond the lowest and highest notes usually playable on them, the music challenges the vertical axes of its frame. As Beilharz herself has noted (1993: 36–38), *Nuances* is an exploration of extremes: of register (pitch), dynamics, timbre, texture and tempo. It sets up dichotomies (as does Kats-Chernin's work) in order to undermine them. Successions of rapid changes operate to destabilise each prevailing time-frame. With a number of climaxes (not just one important one)—creating an effect, perhaps, of muliple orgasms—

Nuances similarly defies the conventions of the traditional climax and thus subverts the musical system.

There are many more works by women to be read 'against the grain'. The ramifications for a feminist analysis along the lines I have proposed are enormous, for not only do they destabilise prevailing (male) structures in music but they reintroduce into music both its 'body' and the possibility for women to reclaim female/feminine desire.

10

Writing/Eroticism/Transgression: Gertrude Stein and the experience of the other

Anna Gibbs

To transgress is to cross a border beyond which everything changes. In colloquial usage it is to commit a crime. But in his essay 'Preface to Transgression', Michel Foucault characterises transgression as profanation (defilement, violation, degradation) 'in a world *which no longer recognises any positive meaning in the sacred*' (1977: 30, my emphasis); in other words, something like crime in a world without law. The meaning of the law or 'limit' in a post-Christian world is addressed, according to Foucault, by a 'philosophy of eroticism' opened up in the space left empty by the death of God and delineated in the writings—fictional as well as philosophical—of a group of French men: Sade, Bataille, Blanchot, Klossowski. In such a world, Foucault claims, sexuality provides the primary locus of transgression, because, in the West at least, we have carried sexuality to its limits: to 'the limit of consciousness, because it ultimately dictates the only possible reading of our unconscious; the limit of the law, since it seems the sole substance of universal taboos; the limit of language, since it traces that line of foam showing just how far speech may advance upon the sands of silence'. Foucault credits these four transgressive writers with having made certain 'extreme forms of language' (forms related to the writing of eroticism) both their 'home' and the 'summits of thought' (Foucault 1977: 30).

What, then, is the relationship of women writers to these lofty peaks (inhabited, it seems, exclusively by men) and to transgression? I intend to use a reading of Gertrude Stein's *The Autobiography of Alice B. Toklas* to question the particular notion of the erotic in play here and to suggest that, historically, women writers have had to negotiate very particular constraints on their attempts to write at 'the limit of the law' insofar as doing this involves an attempt to write the erotic.

For Foucault, the writing of transgression marks the precise point of the subject's disappearance, the signs of which can be deciphered in Bataille's work as the 'I' of his narratives disperses itself through various fictional devices such as 'temporal disengagements' (e.g. the use of retrospection) and 'shifts in the distance separating a speaker from his words' produced by the embedding of different genres ('diary, notebooks, poems, stories, meditations, or discourses intended for demonstration') within each of his texts. We can speak of the disappearance of the subject here, then, because the 'I' in such writing can no longer be read as straightforwardly authorial, nor as authentic. Foucault reads this disappearance of the subject as representing the encounter of the writer with death (Foucault 1977: 51). Now it may be that to privilege a meeting with death in this way is the mark of a particular masculine economy in which sex and death are closely linked. Certainly the writing of Gertrude Stein suggests an alternative mode, one in which the subject's disappearance entails an encounter not with death but with the other. Sexuality is still central to this encounter, but its textual inscription is very different from that described by Foucault in the work of the writers he discusses. In Stein's case, I think, what he has called 'the limit' is better described as a threshold, and transgression can be reconceived as an act of profanation which has the capacity to produce new modes of (subjectless) individuation. In this view, transgression becomes a source of renewal in and through writing, and I want to show here how this might be.

I have chosen to talk about *The Autobiography* rather than about Stein's more obviously erotic writings for a number of reasons. It is regarded by readers as the most transparent and accessible of her texts and hence is probably the most widely read, although Stein herself regarded it as 'identity' writing and therefore less serious than her other work, which she termed 'entity' writing. 'Identity' writing, according to Stein, concerned itself too closely with the expectations of an audience, but I want to argue that this concern is precisely the strength of some of *The Autobiography*'s calculated moves. Through her strategic engagement with the expectations solicited by the genre of autobiography, and her simultaneous foiling of these, she shows how to produce a text as singular and as 'embodied' as a fingerprint without ever saying 'I' (at least in her own name). This may be a provocation to theoretical writing which is currently investigating the consequences of a recognition of its own textuality—its own dependence on metaphor and other rhetorical strategies which distinguish it less sharply than it would like from literature. It is just this 'textual condition' of theoretical writing that has opened up a space for feminist interventions which argue for—and sometimes demonstrate—the possibility of an embodied theoretical writing which challenges certain kinds of disciplinary authority and which is sometimes (particularly in the fields of literary and cultural studies) called 'ficto-critical' (see Chapter 2). It is not so much that the textual strategies of *The Autobiography* provide an iterable model for such writing, but rather that, like all good ficto-criticism (which is not so much a genre as a tactic), it is an invention which responds to a very particular set of discursive and historical constraints, in this case those surrounding the freedom of women writers to tackle the topic of sexuality within the genre of autobiography. To remember this historical and discursive specificity is also to hesitate before characterising the work of contemporary writers like Kathy Acker, Eurudice, or Mary Fallon as inherently subversive simply by virtue of its explicit attention to writing the erotic. It is also to reject the rash of recent feminist readings of Stein's work which reduce the erotics of textuality to a simulation of copulation between reader and text. My most immediate reason for choosing to write about *The Autobiography*, however, is that it is here that the disappearance of the subject and the construction of a new arrangement for speaking (Stein's construction of 'Alice' as narrator for the purposes of her own authoring of Toklas' 'autobiography') to stage the encounter with the other can be seen with particular clarity, in spite of—or perhaps because of—the supposed focus of the autobiographical genre on the construction of the subject.

The Autobiography, then, effects a new discursive disposition (the enunciative arrangement or arrangement for speaking described above) in which what I will call the double-bind machinery of the confessional apparatus (which structures autobiographical writing, especially as it deals with sex and sexuality) is jammed, and the structure of what Anne Freadman has termed the 'muse discourse' (which divides speakers from those spoken for) is transformed (Freadman 1979). In the 'muse discourse', Freadman explains, the poet is normatively masculine. The muse may enable his speech—but her speech only comes into being through his words. In other words, the muse is aligned not with the *énonciation* (the speaking), but with the *énoncé* (the spoken). She is not the speaker, but the spoken for, and these positions (at least for the duration of the speaking) are mutually exclusive (Freadman 1979).

It is indeed impossible to say who speaks in Stein's new arrangement, but this is not to say that Stein achieves a non-gendered speaking position. (We know there can be no such thing, since apparent gender-neutrality merely heralds the covert return of the masculine and in any case the gender of the author's name at least partially determines the frame of reading.) Rather, in the process of shedding her author-ity

Stein enables a critique of the implicit assumptions of the genre of autobiography and opens up the possibility of a discourse which resists recuperation by the confessional mode and its obverse (the injunction to feminine reticence). In so doing, she ensures that lesbianism is neither offered to a voyeuristic and moralising public scrutiny (as any attempt to speak its truth always risks), nor concealed. For to construct lesbianism as the unspoken secret of the text would be both to solicit its excavation and to render it constitutive of Stein's subjectivity: the key by which she could be seized and (carnally) known. In order to understand Stein's achievement here, we need first to examine the generic conditions of possibility of autobiography itself, its seizure by the masculine and the consequences of such a seizure for women writers of autobiography.

Genre and gender

Philippe Lejeune's well-known definition of autobiography as 'the retrospective narrative in prose that someone makes of his [sic] own existence, when he [sic] places the main emphasis on his [sic] individual life, in particular on the history of his [sic] personality' (Lejeune 1971) both exemplifies the masculine seizure of critical discourse in its use of the so-called 'generic pronoun', symptomatic of men's access to a non-gendered discourse by which they can represent themselves as the model of the human from which women can only deviate, and reinscribes, by its refusal to recognise gender at work in the apparently neutral categories of 'narrative', 'individual' and 'personality', the masculine capture of the genre itself. Lejeune's indifference to questions of difference, however, provides a point of departure for Nancy Miller's question: 'Is there a specificity to a female retrospective, and where will it make itself felt?' (Miller 1980). Miller follows Lejeune in arguing that 'the disastrous frankness' of Rousseau's *Confessions* sets a precedent with which all subsequent autobiography written in French must come to terms. How, then, do women writers negotiate this inheritance? In her readings of the work of George Sand, Daniel Stern (Marie D'Agoult) and Simone de Beauvoir, Miller argues that all these writers demonstrate an acute awareness of the fact that they are read as *women* rather than simply as writers, and that both their sexual behaviour and their speech about it are subjected to a double standard. Although Rousseau may not have been such an important reference point for Stein (since, among other things, she wrote in English), he is certainly still a crucial point of reference for her readers, and the reception of Stein's work will still be marked by the generic expectations shaped by Rousseau and by subsequent writers responding to his example. As Nancy Miller suggests, one of the advantages of Lejeune's most recent writing on autobiography, in which he insists on its status as a 'contractual genre', is to place it, as she says, 'within the problematics of reader response' (Miller 1980: 271).

Clearly, then, the double bind enjoining women writers of autobiography, especially when they are public figures, to revelation on the one hand and discretion on the other, is operative for Stein's readers, and will shape readings of her work, as the most cursory survey of critical writings on *The Autobiography* confirms. Stein is castigated by some feminist readers for attempting to disguise the nature of her relationship with Toklas (Marie-Claire Pasquier speaks of Stein's 'effacement' of lesbianism, to cite just one example). She is criticised by other readers—especially those of her contemporaries who became her subjects—for her garrulousness and her gossip (Pasquier 1981). Braque accuses Stein of reducing the artistic movement of cubism to 'personalities', claiming that for 'one who poses as an authority on the epoch it is safe to say that she never went beyond the stage of the tourist' (Simon 1977), while Tristan Tzara dismisses *The Autobiography* as a collection of 'sordid anecdotes' which would have been better kept 'in the family circle between two maiden ladies' (Simon 1977: 152).

Confessional discourse has historically been central to a feminist identity politics and autobiography has been a privileged genre within such an enterprise. Here, however, the feminist desire to uncover an authentic self existing prior to or outside patriarchy is redoubled by the patriarchal desire to force 'truth' from women, and this presents acute difficulties for female writers in a genre in which confession has been constitutive.

The confessional imperative and how to avoid it

It is confession that is continually wrung from all texts signed by women, as if the texts were women, as if women—even when writing fiction—were capable of producing nothing but autobiography conceived of as a simple transmutation of self, of life (cf. Morris 1979). Dominant readings of women's writing commonly produce a kind of carnal knowledge in which the workings of power can be clearly seen through the familiar metaphors: jungles are to be penetrated and dark continents illuminated (and colonised) by maps. (See, for example, Norman Weinstein's comments on *Tender Buttons*, in which he makes reference to 'the dark continent of deepest Stein'—passages in her work which resist scrutiny by the light of interpretive reason.) Once again a confessional technology becomes the site of production of female sexuality as the constitutive secret of female subjectivity.

Sexuality is not only a privileged site of profanation, but also a privileged subject of confession in Western culture. This is of course one of the reasons why it is said that sexuality is 'repressed' by our culture. In fact, though, as Foucault (1988) demonstrates, repression is only one of many techniques of power, and sexuality in particular is most often subject to the technique of incitement. Women are enjoined to talk about sexuality (under certain conditions, including those set by the feminist practice of consciousness-raising) as a privileged site of self-knowledge, as Foucault's examination of the Catholic practice of confession and his critique of the Freudian 'talking cure' make clear. Foucault maintains that it is not knowledge of our sexuality that gives us power over ourselves (as Freud's work might suggest) but our will to establish power over our sexuality that incites our search for self-knowledge (Foucault 1981). Or, a feminist might add, it is men's will to establish power over women's sexuality that incites their search for knowledge about women, for it is female sexuality above all that must be subject to intensive investigation, must be policed with the most minute scrutiny.

Here again, the female autobiographer faces special difficulties—difficulties which for some contemporary women writers may indeed have been exacerbated rather than alleviated by feminist projects. For feminist identity politics has also been centrally concerned with the production of authentic selfhood and with the 'liberation' of its expression. Literary works—especially autobiographical texts—have been a particularly important site for telling the truth of the self, and this has been especially the case where illicit sexuality—notably lesbianism—has been concerned. Clearly this can have an important political function in the creation of precedents for possibilities currently under prohibition. But this positive potential coexists with one of the central preoccupations of Western culture: a cultivation or 'care' of the self (Foucault 1988) that also constitutes the self (and particularly, perhaps, the body) as a target for certain technologies of power.

Confession not only facilitates surveillance by another, but also self-surveillance, since the subject must constantly scrutinise thoughts and actions for matters to confess. Confession constitutes, as Foucault says, an incitement to discourse, and self-knowledge must thus be seen as an injunction of power. It cannot therefore be the task of feminism to seek self-knowledge (except perhaps locally and tactically, and with a wary eye on the functioning of the procedures of scrutiny). Rather, the problem for feminism must be to trace the ways in which formations of power–knowledge produce different kinds of selves and hence possible modes of resistance to the policing of identities. Here autobiography merits close examination, given its centrality to feminist literary and critical practice and its foundations in the practice of confession.

Autobiography must be considered as a special form of confessional practice that enables the self-cultivation of writer and reader alike. It is a site for action upon the self, for effecting transformations of the self and its relations with the world. It is concerned not so much with representation of the past, however 'subjective', as with performance in the present (or with representation as performance). Of course, there is a sense in which this is true of any literary genre, but autobiography is perhaps the most heavily policed of literary spaces, since it demands (normatively, at least) that the protagonist, the narrator and the author all be identical, that the author be what Philippe Lejeune terms 'a legal entity', and that the 'facts' referred to (dates, places, etc.) be, if not correct (since the vagaries of memory must be allowed for) then at least verifiable (Lejeune 1975; Bruss 1976). Of course we know, since Foucault, that an author is a function, not a person, and that the narrating 'I' can never be identical with the narrated 'me'. The author of an autobiography is, by this definition, someone who can be called to account for their version of the past; and autobiography is hence a genre which posits the necessity of reference. Conventionally, autobiography takes the form of an attempted reconciliation with the world from which the subject is violently alienated, and is often provoked by a crisis which sets the narrative in motion.

However, no reconciliation is ever possible for, as Gertrude Stein says, 'you are never yourself' (Stein 1985): subjectivity depends upon entering into—subjecting yourself to—a system of signification that precedes the subject, a system which constrains subjectivity at the same time as it enables it. This very impossibility at the heart of the autobiographical enterprise, the impossibility of being 'yourself' pure and simple, may even be said to be autobiography's generic condition of possibility. It is this differing of self from self—which we might term 'desire'—that the narrative/enunciative strategy of *The Autobiography* figures: the text itself is an emblem of the self-estrangement which is brought about by writing, and which at the same time enables it. It dooms to failure the successful fulfilment of the 'autobiographical contract' which specifies the 'identity' of author, narrator and protagonist, and which Lejeune maintains is definitive of the genre (Lejeune 1975). (Here the importance of Rousseau as precursor is reinscribed, for he was, of course, the philosopher of the contract.) The contract may or may not be explicitly stated (it is always implicit in the term 'autobiography'), and consists in a promise by the writer to attempt sincerity in his or her account of the past. (For Lejeune, the failure to try to be sincere disqualifies a work as autobiography, though failure itself does not.) What is emphasised by this notion of a 'contract', however—even if the contract is unfulfillable—is that autobiography is essentially performative: it must be considered, as Elizabeth Bruss has pointed out, as an act (Bruss 1976).

Some contemporary readers of *The Autobiography of Alice B. Toklas* were so enraged by what they saw as Stein's self-serving version of events that they collaborated on the publication of a refutation in which Matisse, for example, described the book as like 'a harlequin's costume whose different pieces, having been more or less invented by herself, have been sewn together without taste and without relation to reality' (Matisse et al. 1935). Similar responses still abound: to cite just one instance, Lynn Z. Bloom argues that Stein's use of Toklas as narrator 'mitigates the egotism of the consistent first-person usage that is otherwise inevitable in conventional autobiography. This is an extraordinarily clever way to eliminate a plethora of I's; "I" here refers to Alice B. Toklas and her persona uses it sparingly' (Bloom 1978). However, it is also the case, according to Bloom, that:

> the removal of the first-person pronoun from the real subject of the autobiography permits Stein to be even more conspicuously egotistical than she might appear if she used the first person consistently. By putting references to herself in the third person instead of the first, Gertrude Stein as autobiographer gives herself the advantage of allowing Alice B. Toklas' persona to perform the egotistical function of referring to Gertrude Stein by her proper name many more times than are necessary for either clarity, emphasis, or stylistic grace. (Bloom 1978: 83)

Bloom also points out (1978: 83) that the sheer number of references to 'Gertrude Stein' (rather than simply to 'Gertrude') performs an 'honorific function' (and breaks with the convention 'that has persisted in women's biographies throughout the centuries, of addressing women subjects by their first names, regardless of their age, rank, or social status'). Along with this formality, though, goes a certain distancing of Stein from the reader. Bloom terms this 'objectivity', and argues that it enables Stein 'to avoid the confessional mode common to autobiography':

She doesn't tell anything she doesn't want to, and because of Toklas as the intermediary persona, the reader doesn't expect Stein to be more revealing than she is: she leaves finances, personal conflicts (such as her estrangement from her brother Leo), and griefs vague, and never discusses her own sexuality, spinsterhood, or loves— except for dogs. (Bloom 1978: 88)

Bloom thus reads *The Autobiography* as if its real subject was Stein (rather than Toklas, as the title promises), and treats the 'substitution' of Toklas for Stein as narrator (Stein's wilful rupture of the autobiographical contract) as a strategy for Stein's self-aggrandisement on the one hand, and self-concealment on the other. Indeed, this reading, so different from the contemporary popular reception of the text, at least in the US is now almost universal among academic commentators, feminist or otherwise. (Neil Schmitz [1988] is perhaps an exception.) What is felt so strongly, then, is the effect of *The Autobiography* on its readers—or, at least, what the readers suspect was the intended effect, for the transparency of the presumed strategy is also its failure. If Gertrude Stein had to go to such lengths to assert her own genius, then perhaps the claim is a false one. What such a reading presupposes is a certain earnestness: it is a 'literal' reading of the text that excludes the possibility of a deliberately provocative, that is to say ironic, treatment of either the category 'genius' or its composition. It is the privileging of biographical, psychologising readings of Stein, especially in feminist work, that has facilitated the literal rather than the ironic reading of *The Autobiography*, because these readings tend to link what they see as Stein's simple self-promotion, and her merciless exploitation of Alice Toklas in the service of this enterprise, with a desire to hide the truth of her sexual relationship with Toklas. A close examination of the construction of the category 'genius', though, might enable another, more ironic, reading of the text.

Early in the narrative, Toklas as narrator is made to recount her meetings with and instant recognition of three 'geniuses' (Picasso, Whitehead and Stein) and her subsequent attachment to Stein ('In this way my new full life began'). This passage marks the end of the extremely short introductory section ('Before I came to Paris') which begins with a sketch of Toklas's early years in America and introduces her persona, closing with her decision to go to Paris and her meeting there with Stein. It is a propos of this passage that Marie-Claire Pasquier argues that the Stein–Toklas relationship is legitimated (and lesbianism effaced) because the term 'genius' has 'no gender, no sex': it 'is not to a woman that she [Toklas] attaches herself, but to a genius'

(Pasquier 1981). This same manoeuvre allows Stein another benefit that overlays what is either 'deliberate provocation (since it's Stein who is dictating the narrative)' or an 'intolerable, even laughable vanity' (Pasquier 1981): she need make no arrogant claim of her own to genius, because the infallible 'Alice', who has recognised Picasso and White-head, has also recognised her.

The numerical predominance of men's names in the category of genius does not of itself suffice to make the category masculine. Moreover, 'genius' is set in opposition not to womanhood but to wifehood. 'Toklas', herself the wife of a genius, must occupy other wives while 'Stein' converses with other geniuses, and a strict separation between the two series is maintained as if they are mutually exclusive. However, they each move in and out of a third category, the 'real' as opposed to the pseudo, or the inauthentic:

> Before I decided to write this book my twenty-five years with Gertrude Stein, I had often said that I would write, the wives of geniuses I have sat with. I have sat with so many. I have sat with wives who were not wives, of geniuses who were real geniuses. I have sat with real wives of geniuses who were not real geniuses. I have sat with wives of near-geniuses, of would be geniuses, in short I have sat very often and very long with many wives and wives of many geniuses. (Stein 1966: 18)

Although Stein seems to be anomalous, an interloper in the category 'genius', the category itself is not defined by the masculinity of its constituents, even if men are in the majority here. Nevertheless, 'Alice's' situation of her in this series rather than in that of wives (at least at this point in the text) has been read as Stein's characterisation of herself in masculine terms. There are two problems here. One is the assumption that 'Alice' as fictional narrator is a simple mouthpiece for Gertrude Stein, but, as I will argue later, this is not the case. To begin with, such a view is not consonant with the text's construction of character, since *The Autobiography* does not attempt a realistic mode of characterisation and rigorously eschews all construction of psychological interiority. The immediate effect of this is to render problematic the conventional notion of self-portraiture in autobiography, especially as it is taken to mean intimate disclosure or minute psychological self-scrutiny. We will examine the functioning of proper names in the text more closely later: for now, suffice it to say that the name 'Stein' does not merely refer to an extratextual, empirical person, but also designates a perpetually shifting set of relations, a textual ensemble rather than a completed 'character' whose reality the text must then re-present. 'Stein' is therefore a changing effect produced by her function in the patchwork of 'Toklas's' anecdotal narrative.

The second—and related—problem concerns the distinction between language and discourse. Stein's 'self-portraiture' here has been linked—especially in biographical readings of her work—with her use elsewhere of apparently masculine terms to refer to herself. 'Husband', 'caesar', and 'admiral' all recur in her writings, and it is simply assumed in these instances that 'admiral', for example, denotes the masculine, as if it were not the case that it does so only by a convention of discourse (which can be subverted or transformed) and not by a universal 'semantic rule' in a 'man-made' linguistic system (Black and Coward 1983). Moreover, this use of putatively masculine designations of herself is frequently seen as the gesture which authorises Stein to write, to engage in what she is said to posit as the essentially masculine activity of artistic creation. Catharine Stimpson, for example, comments that 'despite her sexual preferences, Stein never ceased to believe in bourgeois heterosexuality: its decencies, norms, and families'. As a consequence, Stimpson argues, Stein 'equated the mind, especially that of genius, with masculinity' (Stimpson 1986). But focusing on the riotous taxonomic procedures of the text may enable another reading, in which the alignment of masculinity and genius is further weakened.

The Autobiography mocks the conventional/'official' construction of the figure of the artist as a man by way of an anecdote which the narrator claims pleased Gertrude Stein immensely: the printer Pierre Bonnard complains 'about the lack of recognition of himself and his friends':

> Duret looked at him kindly, my friend, he said, there are two kinds of art, never forget this, there is art and there is official art. Just look at yourself. Supposing an important personage came to France, and wanted to meet the representative painters and have his portrait painted. My dear young friend, just look at yourself, the very sight of you would terrify him. You are a nice young man, gentle and intelligent, but to the important personage you would not seem so, you would be terrible. No they need as representative painter a medium-sized, slightly stout man, not too well dressed but dressed in the fashion of his class, neither bald or well brushed hair and a respectful bow with it. (Stein 1966)

More importantly Stein, though fascinated by classificatory systems, plays with them in *The Autobiography* in such a way as to produce an ironised version and hence a critique of the alignment of the categories of gender and genius.

Just as the category of genius is not exclusively constituted by men, the category of wifehood may not be exclusively constituted by women. The series are not only reversible in unexpected ways, they are also internally unstable, that is to say, heterogeneous. Take, for instance, the anecdote involving 'Alice's correspondence with T.S. Eliot's secretary:

> Then began a long correspondence, not between Gertrude Stein and T.S. Eliot, but between T.S. Eliot's secretary and myself. We each addressed the other as Sir, I signing myself A.B. Toklas and she signing initials. It was only considerably afterwards that I found out that his secretary was not a young man. I don't know whether she ever found out that I was not. (Stein 1966: 218)

'Alice', who has already classified herself as a 'wife', here sets up a symmetry between herself and 'Stein' on the one hand, and 'Eliot' and his secretary on the other, thereby suggesting that she too may thus be classified, even if she is a he, as 'Alice' at first assumes. That the opposite should be the case, that he should be a she, as 'Alice' is a she and not a he, is ostensibly to redouble the symmetry, covering the heterogeneity that fractures the structure at another level. This is the essence of Stein's humour. Moreover, if sitting with 'Alice' defines someone as a wife—and, conversely, wives must sit with 'Alice'—then Tristan Tzara turns out, unexpectedly, to belong in this category, for he comes to the house with Picabia and sits with Alice:

> I have always found it very difficult to understand the stories of his violence and his wickedness, at least I found it difficult then because Tzara when he came to the house sat beside me at the tea table and talked to me like a pleasant and not very exciting cousin. (Stein 1966: 212)

Now, if Stein can't show the women who are wives—of one kind or another—(e.g. Fernande and Mme Matisse) of geniuses, real or otherwise, she can at least show Picasso and Matisse as husbands. And this she does, to devastating effect, in rather unflattering portraits of Matisse the egoist and Picasso the womaniser. Here, as Neil Schmitz points out, Gertrude Stein has escaped from her position as the muse of Picasso's famous portrait of her and turned the tables—though not by making him her muse (cf. Schmitz 1978).

Stein plays with the possibility of Alice Toklas as muse: early in the text she has Alice the narrator characterise herself by a fondness for needlework. Now Anne Freadman maintains that 'to put a spindle in the hands of a muse figure is to say very clearly that she's a "woman" and not a "poet"', since spinning is one of a number of activities 'in the stereotyped discourse opposing "women's work" and "men's work", firmly established as the opposite of intellectual pursuits' (Freadman 1989). We might turn this around a little and say that to put a spindle in the hands of a woman is to establish her as a muse and not a poet. Stein takes the parody of this muse discourse even further by having 'Alice' embroider her motifs ('rose is a rose is a rose') on the household linen. But in fact the entire enunciative arrangement of the text is to make the maintenance of the opposition between muse and poet—like the absolute opposition between wife and genius—untenable. In the event, as we now know, it is Stein who writes *The Autobiography of Alice B. Toklas*. But as ghost writer of Toklas's autobiography, she has dissolved the opposition between wife and genius, for the genius becomes, in the punch line of a long joke on the reader, no more than the wife's amanuensis.

Finally, the ubiquitous free indirect speech of the text effects a fluctuating distribution of discourse between the poles of narrator and characters, the proportions of which are not fixable unless we invoke the authority of authorship to establish an origin for the text. *The Autobiography* seeks to stave off this gesture, perhaps even to prevent it altogether. It consists of nothing but anecdote or gossip: so-called feminine speech, a speech without a singular attributable origin, or, to paraphrase Derrida, a ruse in which the origin of the work is at stake between the author who reads, and the first reader (Alice) who dictates (Derrida 1987). In the new enunciative arrangement the text constructs, the unitary subject has disappeared, but not into a void. Rather than a confrontation with death, *The Autobiography*'s staging of writing as gossip, as a collective mode of enunciation, has its *raison d'être* in the encounter with the other. At the limit, it is this encounter which enables writing.

11

Of spanners and cyborgs: 'De-homogenising' feminist thinking on technology

Zoë Sofia

Technologies mediate human actions and perceptions; they are social processes of making and doing that could be described as 'languages of action' (Benston 1988: 18) in which power may be expressed through its potential to harness materials, exercise skill and force, and alter patterns of perception and social organisation. Power relations are also involved in the regulation and distribution of 'speech' and 'silence' within the actional 'grammars' of particular technological systems. The outcomes of these regulative and distributional powers have been of concern to feminists investigating gender biases in technologies and technical training in Western(ised) societies, of which studies Sue Curry Jansen makes the following critique:

> Current, laudable concerns within social science and education for reforming gender-based educational practices, gender inequities in access to information technologies, gender-based segmentation of technical skills, and gendered mentoring systems in science and engineering deal only with symptoms. These concerns seldom adequately grasp or treat the causes of these inequities. (Jansen 1989: 205)

Jansen surveys the resources available to feminists who want to rethink questions of 'technologies, gender, information, epistemology, and communication' in relation to theoretical developments centring on recognition of 'the embodiment and situational and linguistic embeddedness of knowledge' and 'the irreducible differences and radical multiplicity of local cultures' (pp. 206–208). To get beyond merely cataloguing symptoms of gender inequity, Jansen suggests, feminist studies of contemporary technological culture might draw on interpretive methods from semiotics, feminist and psychoanalytic philosophy, deconstruction, cultural theory, etc. to develop a more nuanced

147

understanding of the many 'variables'—not all of them statistically measurable—that shape the terrains of contemporary technological cultures and position people differentially within them.

Increased attention to particularity and rejection of 'homogenised' general concepts from earlier rounds of feminist inquiry are recurrent themes in contemporary feminist theorising (see Chapters 13 and 15). This essay is concerned with 'de-homogenising' some concepts of technology found in feminist writings on the topic, particularly those with a cultural-studies bent. (In feminist social science and historical studies of technology, by contrast, particularism is already de rigueur; here the task of critical theory may be to (re)situate the particular within broader contextual analyses.)

Some problematic homogenisations and over-generalisations in discussions of technology include:

- the representation of a particular technology as a synecdoche of technology in general
- the homogenisation of all technology as phallic, masculine, and/or deathly, whereby interpretations of an industrial, environmentally exploitative, war-based and male-dominated Western technological configuration are extended to technology in general
- the typically Western homogenisation of technology with 'high technology', so that statements about technology are made which only make sense within Westernised contexts featuring large-scale systematic production of technologies in close relation to exact sciences and specialised expert knowledges
- over-simplification of the *relationships* people have to technologies, examples of which include the reduction of relational possibilities to the technophobia/technophilia binary; the assumption that enthusiasm about equipment is equivalent to competence in its use; or accounts of cyborg phenomena and politics that don't pay attention to the specific features of particular relations between humans and various kinds of high technologies.

In this essay, I want to draw on the philosophy of technology, psychoanalytic thought, and feminist theory to outline ways of 'de-homogenising' some of these concepts of technology. The following section, an unpacking of the implications of the slogan 'Give a girl a spanner', addresses the first two concerns listed above, while the final section deals mainly with the last two, and focuses on the interpretation of cyborg states (different kinds of human–technology fusion).

'Give a girl a spanner'

I encountered this slogan and its variant 'Hand a girl a spanner' on posters and bumper stickers in Western Australia in the late 1980s. One of its mainstream cultural references is to a television advertisement for Sidchrome tools in which a Scots-accented male voice proclaimed, 'Ye canna hand a man a grander spanner.'

Political slogans usually imply an analysis of a situation, an evaluation of it, and a program of intervention: in this case, that the girl is spannerless, that she ought not be, and that her lack should be remedied. The slogan is aligned with feminist grass-roots and official efforts to break down gendered occupational segregation by encouraging women to train in non-traditional areas, such as mechanical and technical trades. The 'spanner' is presented as a synecdoche for these trades, and possibly a stand-in for technology in general. To give a girl a spanner is to encourage her to share the power men have hitherto enjoyed from having privileged access to a wider range of better-paid jobs, and to experience the pleasures of exercising skill and mastery with associated equipment. The slogan's implied strategy is to encourage changes in individual attitudes to counter the gender stereotyping that perpetuates traditional gendered divisions of labour: it expresses the hope that by playing with spanners (and not just dolls) girls will develop more positive feelings towards technology in general, and so be more likely to make non-traditional career choices in future.

The tendency to generalise from a particular technology to fields of technical practice (e.g. from the spanner to the manual trades), or to technology in general, does not arise merely as an error of thinking, but is in a sense 'built in' to technologies themselves. In his analysis of everyday human being as a form of involvement with the nearby material world, the philosopher Martin Heidegger proposes that particular tools are inseparable from their context: there is no such thing as 'an equipment', rather, there are ensembles of equipment and domains of equipmentality (Heidegger 1962: 97). The spanner is usually found in the context of a workshop containing an array of tools and materials for use in particular tasks (e.g. pliers, hammers, nuts and bolts, wire, pipes, etc.): to be a mechanic a girl needs a workshop, or at least a tool-box; a spanner by itself won't do.

A 'domain of equipmentality' can also be understood more generally as the technological framework of which any particular tool is a part, as in Heidegger's later writings on technology, where the emphasis shifts from tools in the craftsman's workshop to technology as a worldwide system of stockpiled equipment (Dreyfus 1992). As a metal hand tool, the spanner refers both to a premodern craft age and to an industrial age of drop-forged chrome alloy tools, furnaces and foundries, a 'heavy metal' age whose 'defining technology' was the railway and whose primary energy sources were coal and steam (Bolter 1984: 29–32). It is part of the history of many Western industrial technologies (including those exported to developing nations) that equipment designs, standard load sizes, and practices of using (or not using) load-bearing aids have been established in relation to (euro)masculine physical norms (for example, see Cockburn 1985; Benston 1988). The spanner is one of many tools designed for manual operation and dependent on upper-body strength, whereas women tend to be stronger in the lower body. (A point worth remembering when changing car tyres: it's often easier for women to start and finish using leg power on the tyre spanner.) Biases like this creep into the design of tools and workshops to make them less readily appropriable by women: facilitating access to a particular tool does not in itself redress problems in the design of technologies and technological ensembles.

Rather than giving girls spanners and admitting them as individuals into otherwise all-male equipmental domains, perhaps we need to 'Give a team of girls a workshop' where they can decorate, play, design and explore according to their own social, technical and aesthetic preferences. Not equal access, but differentially privileged access—for example, girl-only classes in maths, science and computing—might be a more effective antidote to a history in which men have controlled not only tools themselves, but the spaces for inventing and using them.

On the one hand, Heidegger's concept of 'domains of equipmentality' validates thinking of a particular tool as a signifier of a whole technological domain. On the other hand, it shows up the flaws in arguments that attempt to decontextualise particular technologies from their equipmental and cultural fields. For example, Sherry Turkle begins an article on the social psychology of 'computational reticence' in young women with the statement: 'The computer has no inherent gender bias. But the computer culture is not equally neutral' (Turkle 1988: 41). Her misleading presupposition is that the computer could somehow be encountered and mastered separately from its cultural (and hence also its gendered) contexts. The computer does not shed its broader cultural connotations when it enters the classroom, despite the equal opportunity principles which might apply there. These connotations include those of male-oriented high-tech mythology elaborated through special-effects films, advertising, and computer and video games with militaristic, futuristic and extraterrestrial themes. Boys who use classroom computers not only have the advantage of extra technical competence gained, for example, in video-game parlours, they can also find their egos supported through the illusion of exercising command and control over a futuristic 'Star Wars' world to which they securely belong and in which only token women are usually included (Edwards 1990; Wajcman 1991: Chapter 6). Within this mythic context, girls' negative attitudes to computers are interpretable as forms of conscientious resistance to the militaristic values and adolescent masculine escape fantasies associated with the equipment (Sofia 1993: 110).

The Western feminist idea that technologies (or technology generally) are 'phallic' is perhaps less a diagnosis than an effect of masculine supremacist ideology in a capitalist context, which insists on men's control over all kinds of power and knowledge by labelling many areas of practice as masculine, phallic, and hence inappropriate for (and inappropriable by) women. The slogan both reiterates and defies this notion, calling on the addressee to give a girl a tool which not only bears the masculine connotations of mechanical and metal trades ('Ye canna hand a man a grander spanner'), but whose typical length and graspability evokes the male genital. Three conflicting positions may be discerned here. First, that the spanner is phallic and masculine, in which case women who grab it might be seen as envious and castrating attackers of masculinity, at risk of losing their own femininity. Second, that the spanner is phallic but nevertheless appropriable by women. While this interpretation can accord with recent feminist theorisations of gender performance and transgression (e.g. Butler 1993: 159–164), it doesn't sit well with earlier feminist/psychoanalytic theories of sexual difference (e.g. Mulvey 1975) to the effect that women cannot possess but can only lack or be the phallus (i.e. they either are spanners—objects available for men's use—or are spannerless). The third interpretive position is to deny the spanner's phallic significance and insist on its 'gender neutrality'. This position suits liberal feminist political rhetoric and resonates with the popular (mis)conception that technologies are neutral, good or bad according to the uses to which they are put.

Insistence on the 'gender neutrality' of technologies can be tactically useful for feminists. It serves as a corrective to disempowering views of technology as masculine, or women as 'technophobic', and proposes that once questions of equal access have been addressed, women can become proficient technicians. It recognises the somewhat arbitrary and unstable character of relations between certain technologies and particular genders (or ethnicities): 'masculine' technical fields can become routinised, downgraded in status and allocated to a lower paid female (or ethnic) workforce.

But despite its tactical convenience, the 'technology is (gender) neutral' line is not ultimately sustainable from a perspective informed by deeper-going interpretations of technology. For if tools are always part of a domain of equipmentality, they might be ambiguous (Feenberg 1990), not always specifiable in function (e.g. a spanner can be used in a burglary or a fight), and polysemic in their associations with gender and mythology, but they can never be neutral. A tool will always carry reference to its equipmental context and to the specific networks of distributed powers, knowledges, myths and resources that sustain it. Moreover, as the philosopher of technology Don Ihde points out, so coextensive are tools and technological ensembles with culture that the question of how we might 'gain control' over (a) technology is really a question of how we might 'control' an entire culture (Ihde 1990: 140). From a feminist—and, for that matter, environmentalist—perspective, more salient questions might be: What are the principles and structures according to which we might piece together different technological contexts and configurations? How can we effect cultural changes to develop the libertarian rather than authoritarian tendencies of techno-logical innovations?

In posing the spanner as a representative of 'technology', the fem-inist slogan exhibits a tendency observable among some thinkers to assume that the prototype 'tool' is something like a 'probe' (McLuhan *passim*; Innis 1984: 75–76), that is, a stick-like graspable object of phallic proportions. Lewis Mumford reminds, us however, that the emergence of civilisation out of agricultural settlements in neolithic times was closely associated with the development of container, shelter and storage technologies, including urns, pots, granaries, housing, and other utilities (e.g. irrigation), whose anatomical prototypes are not probing penises but female organs like breasts, vaginas and wombs (Mumford 1966: 139–141). Judy Horacek's cartoon about a woman and a man madly 'inventing' to produce a hot water bottle (or urn?) and a sword (or missile?) respectively reminds us that technological inven-tions may be inspired by different anatomical prototypes and libidinal interests.

One possible counterpart to the spanner slogan would be: 'Give a boy a bowl'—a container technology connected with domestic labour and techniques of nurturance (e.g. cooking), a gift that symbolically makes good the male's lack of a 'fertile hole'. Now although men in Western technological configurations might be anatomically wombless, and bowl-less on the domestic front, in general they are not lacking tools to intervene in, control and emulate female fertility and 'storage', for example in new and imagined reproductive technologies and technoscientific efforts to create or mimic life without the aid of women (as in the Frankenstein myth), and through extensive systems of stock-piled resources (Heidegger's *Bestand*, standing-reserve or resource-well; 1977: 17). From this perspective, the problematic gender asymmetry with respect to Western technology is not that men have it and women don't, but that women were allotted provenance mainly over domestic and nurturant technologies and discouraged from sym-bolically supplementing their anatomical 'lack' with phallic tools at the same time as men have increased their control over women's reproduc-tion (Sofia 1992b: 384–385).

Psychoanalytic interpretations of technology need not lead into the dreaded 'sin' of biological essentialism, so long as we remember not to conflate psychoanalytic categories of desire and subject position with sociological and political categories of gender (Rose 1986: 83–103), and so long as we recognise that the body of which tools are extensions and metaphors is not the 'objective' anatomical body but a polymor-phously perverse fantasy body that can possess combinations of organs not found in nature. A vulgar psychoanalysis that assumes spanners, skyscrapers and cars are phallic may be correct insofar as such tech-nologies are perceived to be under men's control (phallic in a 'political' sense) or to look somewhat phallic (or more accurately, penile). How-ever, closer consideration of a tool's function often reveals other organ connotations: the graspable spanner is, after all, an extension of the fingers and hand; the erect skyscraper functions primarily as a shelter technology, a womb with a view; the thrusting, mobile car is also a comfortable womb (an association made explicit in a controversial 1993–94 Toyota advertisement which compared a pregnant woman with a 'wide-bodied' Camry car).

Instead of entrenching phallocentric and essentialist ideas about technology, the investigation of organ-metaphors and erotic meanings could help to unravel them. At a feminist seminar I attended in 1993, a cordless microphone was quickly dubbed 'the phallus', an interpre-tation obviously suggested by its size, shape, and graspability. It possessed two operating buttons, which befuddled many users, who assumed it was difficult to operate. Functionally, though, the micro-phone is an extension of the ear and voice, a potentially enabling technology for women speaking in public (McKay 1988). Thinking of the microphone as a friendly ear–mouth instead of an alien penis could help some women feel more comfortable with it. However, thinking of such tools as phalluses could also be enabling if such organs were understood as belonging to an imaginary morphology that was not collapsible onto anatomy or gender.

The girl goes cyborg

In a famous discussion on the difference between a tool and a thing, Heidegger draws attention to the way hand tools such as the hammer (or spanner) 'withdraw' from conscious attention when being used on the job; they are only perceived as 'things' in themselves when they are missing or break down. But even though the tool may be experienced as a more or less 'transparent' extension of the body, it is still distinguishable from it: you can leave it on the workbench and take a tea break. The spanner refers to technological configurations where differences between bodies and tools, users and equipment, can be reliably discerned. Such distinctions become hazy in the world of postmodern technics, where life becomes subject to technological intervention in its innermost recesses (e.g. gene splicing, IVF) and where electronic technologies involve us in human–technology interfaces of indeterminate reality (e.g. computer writing, Poster 1990).

The possibilities for feminist empowerment in this rather scary but also enticing technological configuration are explored by the US feminist theorist Donna Haraway in an influential essay commonly known as 'The Cyborg Manifesto' (Haraway 1991: 149–181). Here Haraway points out that even if the overall logic of the postmodern technological configuration is the trajectory she calls 'the informatics of domination', this configuration not only allows for 'top-down' powers of control, command, negation and repression; it also provides opportunities for perversion, resistance, productivity and pleasure. Instead of critiquing technology from a feminist position miraculously 'outside' the (post)modern world or nostalgically harking back to an agricultural 'golden age' of maternal fertility goddesses, she urges feminists to concede our complicity with the current world systems and begin taking more responsibility for our actions within them. Haraway argues that the goals of feminist political and technological empowerment might be better served by myths and metaphors from the information age, such as the figure of the cyborg, a term condensed from 'cybernetic organism' and typically defined as an entity comprising organic as well as machinic parts and information circuits. The term is now used loosely to refer to many kinds of human–technology interface. Cyborg entities can include people with heart pacemakers, people wired up to biomonitors (electrocardiographs, CAT scanners, etc.), and deep-sea divers.

Many of Haraway's readers are tempted to interpret the cyborg's contraventions of traditional dualisms (organism versus machine, self and other) as signs of inherent political subversiveness. But Haraway suggests that cyborgs as feminist metaphors are only as subversive as the theories and political interventions they inspire:

> Cyborg gender is a local possibility taking a global vengeance . . . There is a myth system waiting to become a political language to ground one way of looking at science and technology and challeng-ing the informatics of domination—in order to act potently. (Haraway 1991: 181)

Nevertheless, the kinds of category confusions and interactions cyborgs generate are worthy of further attention by feminist sociologists, phi-losophers, artists, cultural critics and political theorists interested in assessing the potentials of electronic culture. In discussions of high-tech phenomena, homogenisation of different kinds of cyborg states can readily occur: one kind of body–technology intimacy is equated with others. The remainder of this essay focuses on the domain I call 'cyborg technics'—the human–technology–world relationships associated with postmodern, especially information, technologies—and aims to provide some categorical signposts. The preliminary coordinates are taken from Don Ihde, a philosopher concerned with perceptual experiences of and relationships to technologies and the lifeworld of which they are part. Ihde's 'program in the phenomenology of technics' (1990, Chapter 5) outlines this four-part classification of basic genres of human–technol-ogy–world relations:

Embodiment relations (technology as body/prosthesis): Here the tool is an extension of our organs or senses through which we perceive and act on the world (the hammer or spanner as an extension of the arm; the blind person's cane as a tactile prosthesis). The tool 'withdraws' from our awareness as we use it, becoming a more or less transparent mediator to the world.

Hermeneutic relations (technology as sign or text): The perceptual focus is on a technology that is read or interpreted, a text through which a state of the world or technical system is inferred. The map is a hermeneutic technology, as are dials and gauges, and computerised airline booking systems; the prototypical example is reading/writing.

Alterity relations (technology as second self): The technology here is encountered as a thing in itself; we may have passionate love/hate relations to it as to a quasi-human entity. The self-contained, linguistic and logical qualities of computers, their abilities to be programmed to individual specifications, as well as myths of artificially created life, foster the experience of the computer or program as a 'second self', a technological rival. Alterity relations are typically favoured by 'computer nerds', whereas many girls prefer treating the computer as a hermeneutic (communications) medium or as 'just a tool' (a variety of embodiment relations) (Sofia 1992a; 1993: Chapter 4.)

Background relations (technology as world): The prototypes here are container and shelter technologies, including clothing and housing (whose anatomical prototypes are in turn female organs). Technology is experienced as an integral part of the world, or as the world itself (e.g. the background hum of domestic machines; 'technological cocoons' such as environmentally controlled buildings, space stations).

Specific technologies may favour certain kinds of relations: tools of the craft era favour embodiment relations, while those of the information age favour hermeneutic and alterity relations. Alternatively, different aspects of the same technology may be experienced in different ways: in driving a car, for example, we are in embodiment relations when we identify our body with the car's body, making allowances for its proportions as though they were our own. When reading the speedometer and fuel gauges, we are in hermeneutic relations. When we give our car an affectionate nickname, or kick and swear at it when it breaks down, we are in alterity relations. Background relations are experienced in both macro and micro dimensions: when we inhabit the vehicle as a comfortable, womb-like shelter technology, and when we live in 'car culture', experiencing the technological assemblage of automobile production, roads, petrol stations, traffic authorities, urban landscapes with poor public transport, and so on as part of our world.

Now the phenomena of 'cyborg technics' do not neatly fit these categories, but are mainly what Ihde calls 'horizonal instances', limit cases where the very terms of the relationships break down and it becomes hard to differentiate between the human and the technology, the technology and the world, or the human and the world. Since the genres of technics themselves begin to blur—e.g. horizonal instances of embodiment and alterity relations may be identical—any efforts to taxonomise 'horizonal' phenomena can only be partial and by no means definitive.

The limits of embodiment

Some commonly recognised forms of cyborg technics appear at the limits of embodiment, where the body/tool distinction breaks down. In bionic technologies like tooth crowns, heart pacemakers, or robotic limbs, and in edible technologies like steroids and contraceptive pills, the body is implanted with, invaded by, or incorporates technologies and becomes continuous with them. In another trajectory, linked to background relations (technology as container), the body remains intact but inhabits or is implanted into the technology, extending its powers through interface with it. An illustration is Ripley's battle with the Alien Queen in the film *Aliens*, which she wages from within the 'Powerloader' (a partly robotic device for moving heavy objects), that resembles a gigantic exoskeleton and amplifies Ripley's strength and size to match those of her monstrous opponent.

A more complex example of cyborg embodiment is afforded by virtual reality (VR) set-ups, in which users wear 'data gloves' and body suits that transmit data about physical movements via fibre-optic cable to a computer. In response, the computer generates representations of analogous movements in the form of computer/video graphics of 'virtual' bodies within a computer-simulated environment (Rheingold 1993; Heim 1991; Helsel & Roth eds. 1991). Such devices expand the human–computer interface to allow operation by whole-body movements and gestural languages, inspiring fantasies of 'teledildonics', long-distance computer-mediated 'virtual sex' (Rheingold 1991: 345–353). VR could as well be discussed as a limit case of the other relational genres: hermeneutic (the body rendered as information, as computer-generated image), alterity (confused ontological status of actual and virtual bodies; of self and 'second self'), and background relations (the data suit as a kind of 'technological cocoon', the virtual environment as a 'microworld'). VR could even be interpreted as a technics of 'disembodiment' that plays out masculinist fantasies of transcending the messy gravity-bound material body and becoming a luminous ethereal being in a fully programmed irreal world (Sofia 1992a; Grosz 1992–93)

The experiences of leaky boundaries between body and world, and of invasion of the body by 'others', including obstetric and gynaecological technologies, are aspects of women's ordinary experience that have defied definition in the Western philosophical tradition, which has centred around an image of the male body as a smooth, impenetrable and controllable whole. As Catherine Waldby notes in her discussion of Iris Young's work (Chapter 2), pregnancy has served as 'the very emblem of embodiment' yet it defies traditional (masculinist) phenomenological assumptions about the embodied state. Experiences of transgressed body bounds have been encoded in women's visions of technoscience from Mary Shelley's *Frankenstein* to the cyborg visions of feminist science fiction since the 1970s. But these same experiences can also motivate women's efforts to guard against further invasion, and to explore the possibilities for inhabiting and using, rather than being inhabited and used by, technologies: putting the body into the machine rather than the other way around. In postmodern technics, however, the male body is also 'feminised', and cyberpunk visions exploit the novelty value of a male body that has become so intent on communing with technologies that its borders now break down and leak, a body now subject to rupture from without and within, and capable of harbouring the other—the foetus, the virus, the body-altering hormones—within it. One possible cyborg identity available to postmodern subjects irrespective of gender—though perhaps especially attractive to those who feel themselves to be 'outside' or on the margins of dominant technological orders—is that of the virus, a tiny 'other' that can invade, and proliferate in the interstices of, the informatics of domination. The Australian 'cyberfeminist' art group VNS Matrix imaginatively explore viral and other metaphors in artworks on the theme of a computer game in which the data banks of 'Big Daddy Mainframe' are invaded by players aligned with a polymorphous feminine entity, All New Gen (described variously as a virus, a slime, an intelligent mist), and her henchwomen, the DNA Sluts. VNS Matrix calls on women to challenge the rationales of male-centred technological visions by rupturing them 'from within' and, in statements like 'the clitoris is a direct line to the matrix', insists on the possibility of relating to information technologies without abandoning the erotic body (Flynn, 1994).

In the technics of cyborg embodiment, technology is not necessarily something cold, inflexible, and alien to our bodies, but something to which we may be most intimately related. Where the body–technology distinction is disrupted, so are the conventional alignments that place man and machine, mind and culture on one side and woman and organism, body and nature on the other. If 'technology' can go over to the side of 'body', it can also go over to the feminine side; anatomy need no longer constrain what a body might become or do once it is united with its technological prostheses. The ability to represent oneself—if only virtually—as another kind of body may be liberatory for those who have been traditionally defined only as feminine and natural bodies. The potential for technological refashioning of the feminine body is taken to one extreme by the French performance artist Olan, who is giving her body a technological make-over in a documented series of medical art events in which she directs the 'performance' of plastic surgery upon her body, itself an 'artwork'—or an experiment?—in process.

Limits of hermeneutic technics

Cyborg phenomena are also found at the limits of hermeneutic relations. As Heidegger has described it, twentieth-century technoscientific systems proceed by the principle of 'challenging forth' the world to 'report itself' as measurable data, a calculable coherence of forces and materials available for further ordering and mobilisation (Heidegger 1977: 14–24). As the world is rendered as retrievable information, the distinction between a hermeneutic technology and the world on which it reports breaks down. The fragmented info-bits may then be rejoined into new formations, producing 'texts' that are encompassing and world-like (e.g. VR, flight simulators). Hermeneutic technologies may thus no longer merely *represent* a world: in postmodern culture they simulate it, producing 'maps' that take precedence over the 'territory' in 'the generation by models of a real without origin or reality: a hyperreal' (Baudrillard 1983: 2). The real is made over into a simulation of itself, as when tourist-oriented towns reconstruct buildings and facades in 'more authentic' versions according to some idealised view of history. And reality is transformed to suit the image: American military raids are often timed to coincide with the nightly news, and filmed to resemble special-effects films and 'Star Wars'-type computer games.

Perhaps of more direct interest to feminists are examples of cyborg hermeneutics in which the human–text distinction is eroded. Writing is a conventional hermeneutic technology that disrupts the contiguity of person and text, allowing for playful forms of self-representation (e.g. pen names). Computer-mediated social interactions amplify these disjunctive possibilities by permitting informal real-time interactions between people who may never see or speak to each other. One's identity in a computer network is an 'address' from which one can send or receive 'mail' and interact with any number of others, using names that may be aliases. Here, 'self' becomes reduced to 'text'—pixels of light on a screen—but that reduction also opens other possibilities, including the possibility that the text is 'reporting' not on an 'actual' system or person but on a fictional one. Allucquère Rosanne Stone refers to the now legendary case of 'Julie', a multiply disabled older woman who was for several years an active and popular identity on an American computer network, and who was subsequently tracked down by one of her fans and disclosed to be an able-bodied, middle-aged male psychiatrist. Stone writes:

On the nets, where *warranting*, or grounding, a persona in the physical body, is meaningless, men routinely use female personae whenever they choose, and vice versa . . . Gendered modes of communication themselves have remained relatively stable, but who uses which of the two socially recognised modes has become more plastic. A woman who has appropriated a male conversational style may be simply assumed to be male at that place and time, so that his/her on-line persona takes on a kind of quasi life of its own, separate from the person's embodied life in the 'real' world. (Stone 1991: 84)

New genders are not necessarily invented on the nets, and the subversive potential for gender-bending in computer communication is probably overrated. Of potentially greater political and social significance than the occasional instances of gender masquerade are the consequences of increased access to many kinds of information and research data, and the enhanced possibilities for forming new alliances and pathways of interaction among new constituencies of computer users.

Computer-age science fiction explores extremes of cyborg hermeneutics: William Gibson's visions of cyberspace are of world-as-data, information-as-landscape; his novels include figures of self-become-data such as the Dixie Flatline, a former 'console cowboy' who died in cyberspace, survives as a package of computer memory, and asks to be destroyed after consenting to help on a major hacking operation (*Neuromancer*). The idea of data-becoming-self is played out in many science fiction android fantasies, for example in the *Star Trek: The Next Generation* character Data, an android who wants to be human. The android's programming is a 'text' made real as it generates a 'self' that interacts with others in the world. Here the limits of hermeneutic relations shade into those of alterity relations.

The limits of alterity

The cyborg possibilities of self-becoming-text and text-becoming-self are grounded in the character of information technology. Computers and robots are programmable tools into which are 'downloaded' certain logical and linguistic operations that allow them to function as partly autonomous 'intelligent' systems: bits of mind externalised as computer code; electronic 'second selves' that seem to have minds of their own. In alterity relations, 'smart' technologies can be anthropomorphised and become a focus of narcissistic identification. Automated and robotic technologies are situated on a trajectory whose science fiction extensions include androids and other artificial life forms (e.g. the robot

Maria in *Metropolis*, and the replicants and cyborgs of countless other science-fiction films). Besides relating to technologies as though they were human, there is the possibility of de-anthropomorphising oneself, and entering into a machine–machine relationship or even identifying with that quintessential element of the computer age: information. In the computer hackers' slogan 'Information wants to be free', the human's subjectivity and the anarchist's desire for freedom, including freedom of information ('I want information to be freely available') have been deleted from the syntax and 'information' is anthropomorphised: information now becomes the subject who wants to be free. Further possibilities include relating to machines (and other anthropomorphised entities, for that matter) as truly alien intelligences. Alternatively, as Sadie Plant suggests, feminists might claim machines as allies that share our emergent powers to evade total control (Plant 1994).

Limits of background relations

The cyborg limits of background relations involve disturbances in the relations of the 'shelter' and the world, and in relations between the self and the world. Ihde notes that northern cultures' shelter technologies already tend to the limits of background relations, creating total cocoons to defend against the natural environment rather than enhancing experience of it. Further along this trajectory is the notion of the 'wired house', where a life of work, consumption, entertainment, education, and social interaction is conducted almost entirely from within the home by means of electronic communication. Here, the 'world' implodes into the domestic shelter technology, a prospect which may be appealing for women in certain periods of a working life (e.g. after having a baby) but is not universally welcomed by those who seek to escape their imprisoning domestic confines for the world of public life and social interaction in shops and workplaces (Huws 1985).

As the lifeworld of people living in affluent industrialised society becomes replete with technological gadgetry, and especially since computerisation, people find themselves spending more time and attention interacting with or via technologies, which themselves become taken as the 'world' and make it easy to forget that most people in the 'real' world have extremely restricted access to water and electricity, let alone the fancy tools of the information age. Computer-assisted design, virtual-reality systems, game playing, network interactions, and other electronically mediated experiences involve participants in what may be a highly seductive irreal 'microworld' (e.g. the program or computer game) or in a globe-spanning space of electronic data storage and communication, now commonly referred to as 'cyberspace' (Benedikt ed. 1991).

Breakdowns in the distinction between the self and the technoworld it inhabits comprise another class of limit cases. Not only has the world been remade as a 'technoworld', that technoworld can become more and more 'human': soft-drink dispensing machines start thanking us for using them, electronic tellers ask us to donate blood to the Red Cross. A highly commodified postmodern culture offers many opportunities for people to develop relationships of love and identification with things in their environment. Particular brands of shoes or sunglasses become totems which replace the heroes and spirit beings of traditional cultures as axes of identify-formation, especially among youth. The psychiatric concept of psychaesthenia, the inability to distinguish oneself from one's surroundings, becomes a relevant term for discussing human–world relationships in postmodern and electronic culture (Olalquiaga 1992; Grosz 1992–93). Take, for example, the statement from William Gibson's cyberpunk fiction: 'The street finds its uses for things.' This statement refers to the way people living in the cracks of the corporate matrix are bricoleurs who appropriate whatever technologies come their way for their own purposes. Here 'the street' is a metonymy for the humans on it, and the statement's linguistic effect is one of erasing both human agency and the distinction between the humans and their environment: it is the street, not the human, which uses technologies.

Psychaesthenic relations may also be explored in more positive ways. Many women artists, for example, are interested in exploring the human–environment relation in installations that redeploy surveillance and other technologies to create interactive and responsive environments—art works that do things when you go near or enter them. The German artist Ulrike Gabriel's installation 'Breath', exhibited at TISEA, required visitors to strap a device around their waist: 'the belt monitored the viewer's breathing through a computer interface creating real-time animations and sounds' (Conomos 1993: 58) thus blurring the body–environment distinction. More recently Sydney artist Sarah Waterson has explored how bodies are mapped in space, and the (im)possibilities of technologically simulating erotic responses, in 'Mapping E-motion', an installation featuring suspended perspex panels on which are mounted latex casts of breasts whose nipples pump up and down at rates and intensities determined by the movements of gallery visitors as detected by surveillance technologies.

This essay has outlined a number of issues in the complex, wide-ranging and open-ended field of women and technology, a field that includes concerns with the nitty gritty of job training and opportunity, philosophical and psychoanalytic questions about the character of different kinds of technologies, and fictional and artistic experiments with technologies. The convenient notion that technologies are 'gender neutral' is of limited tactical effectiveness in the long term; instead, I proposed that we pay more careful analytic attention to the erotic meanings and organ symbolism of technologies. I have tried to show how feminists might enrich our understandings by drawing more extensively on ideas in the philosophy of technology that deal with questions of context and help us specify different kinds of human–technology–world relations and their limit cases. By 'de-homogenising' over-generalised notions of technology, feminists may be better able to identify both the possibilities and limits of empowerment through current technological configurations. We may come up with better strategies for changing the gendered relations of technologies, based on the recognition that efforts to secure equal access to technologies are not adequate in themselves, since technologies are coextensive with the whole cultural field, a field that extends beyond the microcontexts of the workplace or classroom and includes the domains of myth, art and fantasy.

12

Reclaiming social policy*

Sophie Watson

Feminism and social policy have had rather an uneasy relationship since the late 1960s which in many ways parallels feminism's relation to the state (see Watson 1990). On the one hand feminist activists have been ambivalent about what kinds and forms of social policies would most benefit women. On the other, feminist academics have attempted to enter and subvert a debate which was inevitably already constructed in masculinist terms. The social policy arena has been a crucial site in feminist struggles for change, particularly in the earlier years. At least three of the six demands of the early Women's Liberation Movement—24-hour child care, abortion on demand, and equal pay for equal work—involved demands on the state for policies and provisions directed to women specifically. Issues of representation did not feature. Some of the earliest politicising forces for feminism derived from women's involvements in campaigns for refuges for battered women, for child care, for women's health centres, for equal employment opportunities. Many of the campaigns were so successful that the provisions and services which resulted are now taken for granted as necessary forms of social welfare. All of these campaigns involved complex debates about the role of the state, women's autonomy, co-option, the relation between equality and difference, and definitions of need. Tensions arose around the question of whether it was better to be autonomous and independently financed via donations, charities or unpaid work or to accept government funding even if it implied forms of control, a dilution of radical possibilities, and the cooption of the workers involved. There were also fierce arguments as to whether policies should support women in their domestic responsibilities—at

* I should like to acknowledge joint work with Rosemary Pringle in this area and to thank her for detailed editorial comment on this piece; my thanks also to Paddy Hillyard for earlier discussions of this material.

least in the short term—or whether it was better to demand policies which released women from the domestic arena and enabled more equal participation in paid employment.

Feminist demands for welfare provision were linked to more academic debates about the relation between distinctions of public and private, home and work, production and reproduction, and the precise meaning of the slogan 'the personal is political'. Demands for welfare implied shifting the boundaries between public and private, often with some confusion as to the implications. While the discourses deployed were often unclearly articulated, the politics and language of welfare have been crucial in repositioning women as subjects over the last two decades.

Since the 1970s, the shifts in feminist theory and practice towards cultural issues and psychoanalysis have relegated social policy to a more marginal position, and the shifts which have taken place in the political-economic terrain have had similar effects. Feminist social policy sat more comfortably in a period during which Marxist theory, with its emphasis on the role of the state in preserving dominant class relations, was in the ascendancy and Keynesian economics underpinned government policies. In this essay I want to reassert the importance of feminist strategies and interventions in the domain of the social, and more particularly, in social policy arenas and consider these in the light of the current political climate. In doing so, I suggest that feminist and poststructuralist theories offer important critiques of the ways in which need has hitherto been theorised and deployed strategically.

Needs discourses

In feminist, socialist and social democratic struggles for public services and provisions, the concept of need has been routinely deployed yet rarely specified or clearly defined. In social policy, it is the organising term for the subject's relation to scarce resources and their distribution. Short of a utopian society in which no one has less than anyone else, public goods and services must be allocated according to some explicit or implicit notion of need. The proliferation of needs discourses has been closely linked to the growth of the welfare state and the public sector in capitalist countries since the Second World War. Although important in earlier political and philosophical texts, not least Marx's writings, it is in the context of the welfare state that needs discourse has been more actively deployed as a strategic tool for material and political ends. Feminists have not been shy to enter the terrain, arguing that women should have at least equal amounts, and possibly more, of the cake, and deploying explicitly or implicitly a discourse of need.

Need is an area which is constantly contested, and how needs are defined is a central concern for feminists. The state attempts to regulate and intervene in the aspects of the everyday life of selected members of a social community via discourses of need; and needs discourses are used to legitimate claims for the distribution of resources and benefits. Need is central to the operations of power and resistance at the points where government intersects with people's daily life.

In the 1970s, feminists made demands on the state for the provision of services, benefits and goods which, it was argued, women lacked as a result of their domestic and child-rearing responsibilities and their marginal position in the labour market. Women's perceived powerlessness in relation to men, at a physical and economic level, precipitated other demands. At the time, the countries where feminism was strong had relatively robust economies, viable public sectors, a commitment to welfare provision, and strong social democratic parties. The debates about the funding and control of feminist services, forms of welfare provision, community participation, employment policies and the role of feminist bureaucrats that took place during the Whitlam years, for example, marked a political and economic climate very different from that of the 1990s (Watson 1990).

Given the reliance on a discourse of needs there has been surprisingly little theoretical-feminist interrogation of the concept in social policy arenas. Social policy feminists have worked with concepts developed mostly by Marxists and Fabians who have paid little attention to gender. Doyal and Gough (1982, 1992), for example, writing in the Marxist tradition, emphasise the universality and objectivity of human needs, with survival/physical health and autonomy being the most fundamental. The Fabian social policy analysts (mainly British) have tried to sidestep the problems of treating needs as objectively existing or as absolute by introducing the notion of relative needs. Peter Townsend argues for a relative definition of the notion of poverty, which varies cross-nationally, cross-culturally and historically. But he is still searching for

. . . objective measurements of poverty: to measure all the public and private resources which are unequally distributed in society and which contribute towards actual standards of living. And to define the standard of living which is agreed or approved in a particular society and find the point in the distribution of resources below which families find it difficult to share in the customs, diets, and activities central to that society's life style'. (1979: 54–60)

In this context the members of a household may be impoverished if they have no television when everyone else around them has one. Despite this emphasis on the relative in Townsend's work, the search is still on for the 'best' ways to measure quantifiable and objective attributes which exist autonomously from discursive construction.

Marxists and Fabians share notions of universal needs and a humanistic notion of needs satisfaction as intrinsic to social organisation. Even those theories which have criticised essentialism usually retain untheorised essentialist components, and the association of 'need' with some non-discursive reality has been strong. The existence of need is taken as unproblematic. The assumption is made that it can be defined and measured and a solution found. Cartesian rationality has characterised all social policy thinking. The objective throughout has been to seek the truth about people's (men's) needs and develop scientifically based solutions to these needs. Marxist and Fabian texts rely on the rational disembodied but implicitly masculine individual. Difference is ignored. There is little or no inquiry into who are the subjects who speak the discourse or make and establish the accepted or operational definitions of needs, or how they are inscribed with power or an authoritative speaking position. As Nancy Fraser (1989) points out, there is little recognition that the authorised forms of public discourse available for interpreting needs are skewed towards a specific group. There is no scrutiny of the processes of need definition, of the institutions which develop need discourses, or the relations of power which exist between those who provide the authoritative definitions. These are questions of crucial significance to women and central to feminist debate as well as policy formulation.

One attempt to shift from a purely quantitative approach was made by Bradshaw (1972). Along with the various measures of expressed need, the judgments of experts and the comparison of the requirements of individuals or groups, he identified perceived or 'felt need' as an important indicator. To assess the levels of felt need for a service, one simply asks people if they need it. This approach is limited by its reliance on the perceptions of the individual and dependent on their knowledge of the services. It can lead to gross underestimates of need levels, and estimates are likely to be fluid. But it does give people agency. From a gendered perspective, such an approach is attractive in that it gives women space to define their own needs rather than defining their needs for them. It does not, however, address their potential reluctance to ask for a service, the dependence or stigma that may be implied, or the lack of knowledge that may result from marginality. Neither does it look at how subjective needs are constructed or problematise the unitary rational subjects who know what they want and what they need.

Needs rethought

An alternative approach is suggested by the work of Foucault and Donzelot. Rather than defining and attempting to quantify needs, establishing universal claims, and considering how they can best be satisfied, they ask what notions of power, control, normalisation and self-regulation are involved in producing the concept. Once the social is understood as the site where needs become politicised, contested and interpreted, then what is important is the processes by which certain needs are politicised and others are not. Needs can no longer be taken as given and simply waiting to be expressed and satisfied. Before considering these questions, I shall look in more detail at how the term has been deployed within specifically feminist interventions in social policy.

In the domain of needs, feminists have generally argued that women should be treated differently from men in order to make up a 'deficit'. This approach is based on the assumption that once women's needs (for child care, health, refuges and so on) are met they can enter the terrain of demands for equal treatment in the labour market or 'public' life. It situates women's needs perilously in the more private domains of life. Needs discourse has been strategically deployed by feminists to win gains from the public purse, but women's needs have always in some sense been marginal to the main game. In many cases women are constituted as victims or as 'lacking'.

Housing need provides a good illustration. In Australia the principal form of housing provision is home ownership (approximately 70 per cent), which is both heavily subsidised and widely perceived to represent social and economic success. Households defined as in housing need are those whose members have no shelter or are in temporary shelter, those paying over 30 per cent of their income in housing costs (the level shifts), and those in very insecure or overcrowded accommodation. Whatever measures are used to define housing need, and there are many, households headed by women constitute an overwhelming majority of those in need. And what is provided for those in need, if they are lucky, is public or cooperative housing. Approximately one-quarter of female single parents live in public housing compared to one-twentieth of male single parents (Watson 1988). I am not arguing here that public housing is a bad thing, far from it. But in the Australian context, it is a marginal sector, and discourses of need reinforce rather than challenge that positioning.

Social policy is a highly normative discipline which constructs ideal models of society based on notions of social justice. These models disguise the hard realities of power, and more specifically gender, relations, which operate subtly through the constitution of specific subjects: the single parent, the battered wife, the girl in moral danger. These subjects become the focus of a whole range of practices wherein the modern forms of domination and repression are to be found. This is not to deny that there are women bringing up kids on their own, nor that some women are battered. But feminists have sometimes been unaware of the way in which these subjects are constituted as having built-in attributes and defects, and as requiring certain kinds of intervention or surveillance. The social practices which are directed at these subjects stem directly from the discourses which have created them in the first place.

Need is located within discourses of the private–public interface while at the same time producing these private–public distinctions. Thus it is deemed that elderly people cared for at home by women for free do not have needs, while those cared for in the public domain do. Women's need to be protected from violence is more clearly established and recognised in the public arena. This lack of protection actually in part constitutes the domestic for women.

No claims for provisions and services based on need can have a neutral effect. By claiming that they need special treatment as embodied subjects who bear and support children, who are vulnerable to men physically and so on, women may further disadvantage themselves in terrains designated as public and mainstream. Needs discourse has operated to provide women with all sorts of benefits and to shift back the boundaries of the domestic. But it has also confirmed women as lacking, marginal and powerless, as subjects to be regulated.

How can this be subverted? It is important to shift from the business of identifying and measuring needs to the politics of needs interpretation. Nancy Fraser (1989: 162) suggests that the discourse of needs is actually 'a medium for making and contesting political claims: it is an idiom in which political conflict is played out and through which inequalities are symbolically elaborated and challenged'. The positing of needs creates a space in which contemporary meanings of the state are negotiated. As Nicholas Rose puts it:

> the state can be seen as a way of dividing a "political" sphere, with its particular characteristics of rule, from other "non-political" spheres to which it must be related. The vocabulary of the state thus functions as an historically variable linguistic device for conceptualising and articulating rule—or, as in present demands to "roll back the State", as a means of contesting the nature and limits of political power. (1993: 288–289)

In public policy arenas, need is defined according to bureaucratic procedures and regulations which define some people—those who are deemed to be deserving—as 'in', and other people—the undeserving—as 'out'. A social-pathology discourse is invoked to imply that some individuals are to blame for their own predicament and are therefore not worthy of assistance and not in need. The dichotomy between the deserving and the undeserving leaves it up to experts, or gatekeepers, ultimately to decide whose needs will be met and whose will not. The UK Housing (Homeless Person's) Act of 1979 takes this dichotomising process to its ultimate extreme by making an absurd distinction between the intentionally homeless and the unintentionally homeless. Women who have left their residence because of domestic violence have often been termed intentionally homeless because they supposedly had a home to return to. Where resources are scarce, definitions of need are restricted in this way. Where resources are more plentiful, definitions of need may expand and bureaucratic restrictions on allocation and provision be removed.

The family has been the depoliticised terrain of needs while at the same time being the target of certain needs discourses, thereby legitimating state intervention. Donzelot (1979) has traced the change in the family from an autonomous institution to a site of intervention for the growing plethora of health, social and psychiatric professionals. In Britain the attachment of a means test to benefits meant that one pattern of relationships and responsibilities was sanctioned while others were condemned (Squires 1990: 139). Fraser (1989) shows how the imposition of a 'social' sphere repositions the political, economic, and domestic spheres of life. The 'family' is defined as outside of the political sphere. It is supposed to satisfy its own needs internally yet, at the same time, it is the site of regulatory practices. Feminism has succeeded in politicising needs which were previously invisible or ignored because of their location in the domestic/familial. But, Fraser asks, do these shifts in the domestic represent an extension of modes of the political sphere or, in the light of Donzelot's argument, a colonisation of that domain by newer modes of power and social control?

Feminists have long been aware that women need to occupy certain arenas to have their voices heard, to influence debate, to define policies for themselves. In order to participate fully in needs interpretation, women need certain discursive resources and linguistic skills. In Australia the femocrats have played a key role in creating alternative needs discourse and thereby winning resources such as child care provision (Franzway, Court and Connell 1989; Watson 1990), which are not matched in the UK or US. In Britain the absence of senior women from the civil service has made it more difficult for feminists to offer alternative interpretations of needs except at the local level, where they are more strategically placed (Watson 1992).

The implication of this analysis is that feminists engaged in social policy must sharpen their awareness of the discursive strategies of need articulation and their effects. Rather than assuming that women's needs are a given, this implies a more fluid approach which recognises that needs are not fixed in the 'real' but are discursively constructed and will always be politically contested. It requires being alert to the ways in which activities defined as marginal, pathological or deviant articulate needs. It means being aware of the arenas in which needs are established, and the alliances and power–knowledge relations that are in play. Who are the subjects of these shifting discourses, and what subjectivities are being produced within specific social policies?

Social policy had its heyday in the postwar Keynesian consensus which dominated politics and government. Feminist social policy theories and interventions also originated in this period. In a climate of political and economic privatisation, where needs, however defined, are being met less and less from the public purse the discursive strategies deployed are all the more limited. Feminist social policy analysts and practitioners must seriously rethink the strategies and discourses of the last two decades and devise new approaches appropriate to the individualised, privatised, regulated, and divided world we inhabit. The shift of interest in feminism to culture, representation, deconstruction and psychoanalysis should not mean that the social, or our interventions therein, become a thing of the past.

13

Beyond patriarchy and capitalism: Reflections on political subjectivity*

J. K. Gibson-Graham

Feminists are currently rethinking conceptions of power and the visions of change they enable or preclude. The focus of this essay is upon different representations of women as acting subjects, that is on the vexed issue of women and political subjectivity.[1] How do we conceive of women as subjects involved in action, particularly around dimensions of antagonism present in social relations?[2] Are women 'powerless' or 'powerful' in relation to the rest of society? How do women become 'empowered' to effect social change? What power is invested in questions such as these and the answers to which they might give rise?

The following discussion of politics and women in coal mining communities explores the problems and possibilities for feminism invested in two quite different conceptions of power and political subjectivity, the first associated with structural Marxist theory and socialist feminism, the second with poststructuralist theory and postmodern feminism.[3] My argument is that these different conceptions enable quite different strategic interventions, practical effects and visions of social change. This essay presents an illustration of these differences in a reading of political events in Australian coal mining communities.

Representations of mining-town women and their partners have played a significant role in illustrating structural Marxist conceptions of society and power, which are associated with well-established models of political organisation and emancipatory visions of change. In the sociological and socialist imaginations the coal miner appears

* I would like to thank Barbara Caine, Liz Grosz, Rosemary Pringle and participants in the Summer School on Feminist Theory and Women's Studies in the 1990s held at the Humanities Research Centre, Australian National University in February 1994 for their helpful comments on a first draft of this essay. Thanks also must go to the Faculty of Arts, Monash University for the fellowship that supported Julie Graham while this paper was written.

manly and strong, grim and grimy-faced as the archetypal proletarian and political activist (Campbell 1993; Gibson-Graham 1994). On the one hand he is endowed with moral power by his contribution of honest physical labour to the dangerous production of a commodity crucial to the functioning of industrial capitalism and modern life; on the other, he is situated in a dominated subject position prey to the excesses of capitalist exploitation, forced to risk his life as his surplus labour is appropriated by the owners of capital who oppress him. So visibly and dramatically caught in the capitalist dialectic of class power, the coal miner has traditionally figured as an icon of the working class. And because of his clear-cut location in this landscape of class, he has similarly been figured as the iconic conscious agent of working-class struggle. In countless films, folk songs, novels and news reports the coal miner appears in the guise of working-class warrior, politically mobilised, armed with real industrial muscle, ready to man barricades in the class war. Indeed, if the structural conception of social, economic and political power relations could have a human face, it might well be that of the defiant yet necessarily supplicant coal miner.

Of course, this visage is gendered. And while it might nobly represent the person of the structurally dominated within capitalism, it rather ignobly represents the figure of the structural dominator within patriarchy.[4] That coal miners are almost exclusively men reflects a history of active exclusion of women from the coal industry and an ongoing process of gender discrimination.[5] Thus the male miner is represented as occupying two rather different identities/subject positions: on the one hand as subjected within the capitalist class structure, on the other as oppressor within the patriarchal structure of gender.

Behind the face of the coal miner is that of another, the miner's wife. She is a shadowy figure living, for the most part, in the background, providing the backstage labour that enables her husband to strut in the limelight, on the discursive stage of economic, if not world, history. In this role she is portrayed as supportive, obedient, rather conservative and apolitical, family centred, parochial and oppressed. Structurally positioned within capitalism as a member of the working class (by virtue of her relationship to her husband), and structurally positioned within patriarchy as a subordinated woman, the miner's wife experiences the double dose of exploitation and oppression.

The political implications of the dual and different subject positions occupied by miners and their wives are complex. While miners are seen as having individual power (over their wives)[6] in the structure of patriarchy, they are individually powerless within the structure of capitalism and can only claim power through collective organisation.

Miners' wives are seen as powerless in both structures. But they are also politically ambiguous in that they seem to slide in and out of structurally defined subject positions and the appropriate forms of consciousness and agency that these positions denote. In remarkable and relatively short-lived periods of social upheaval, these women are catapulted out of the wings and onto centre stage, into a leading role in the drama of social and political change. In this 'part', the miner's wife is portrayed as fiery, committed, intensely political and clear-headed, often more so than her husband. Usually the narrative in which she is called upon to play this role is that of a prolonged strike or the threatened closure of a mine. In this dramatic conjuncture, the miner's wife, while locally identified, is often the spokesperson who makes links across communities, nationally and internationally.

In such situations of accentuated conflict, miners' wives are seen to throw off the chains of gender oppression to become conscious working-class agents fighting alongside their husbands. Women become empowered with respect to men by joining with men against capitalism. This structural representation offers a very simple notion of power as coercion or domination, something which the powerful have and exercise in negative ways. Political subjectivities are constituted through a process of conscious alignment of subjects with a social structure. When two structures are involved they are seen to be engaged in a metaphoric battle for dominance over the alignment of 'their' subjects.

The bodies, actions and political subjectivities of miners' wives are sites of this discursive battle at its most virulent.[7] Indeed, no group of women has more often been found in situations (usually when playing a leading role in a prolonged strike) where their actions have been so intensely scrutinised as litmus indicators of the relative power of class and gender structures in constituting agency (acting political subjects). When mining town women become participants in public political activities it is asked, 'Is this because, as women, they are throwing off the chains of gender oppression, or is it as true members of the working class that they are rallying forth?' Which social structure is subordinate to which? How does one triumph over the other? How does each work to reproduce the other?

The structural Marxist view of power and political subjectivity seems anachronistic when presented in such bald terms, and yet this model has been central to most of the emancipatory movements of modern times (the socialist, the feminist, gay and lesbian movements).[8] Foregrounded in this model is (true) consciousness of the individual's place in a social structure and the means of translating this insight into progressive change via collective action. Politics is conflictual, power is coercive/oppressive and identity is structured by a hierarchy in which one subject position is seen to be dominant over the other(s). The question arises: If this model has been successful enough to inspire the trade union movement and the feminist movement (to name just two), why abandon or question it? One answer is that this model is tied to a vision of revolutionary change in the structures of capitalism and patriarchy that precludes more local, partial and ongoing visions of social change (Gibson-Graham 1993; see also Chapter 15). Another is that this model can lead to political disappointment and exhaustion and to invidious judgments about the truth or falsity of the consciousnesses of individuals.[9] In the remainder of this essay I would like to illustrate the difference an (existing) alternative vision of power and political subjectivity can make to the feminist project of social change.[10]

Reading political subjectivity

Restructuring in the Australian coal industry has recently highlighted some local differences in the political subjectivities of women in coal mining communities. Telling the tale of these differences from two different theoretical perspectives will illustrate what I see to be the greater political attractions of a poststructuralist rather than a structuralist feminist orientation.

Miners usually work some form of shift work, which means that the lives of women and children in the home are expected to fit in with the abnormal sleep patterns, meal times and leisure time of the miner. The arrangement of shift work patterns became an important point of conflict for coal miners and their wives in Australia around 1988, when a new industry award was introduced as part of a process of industry rationalisation.[11] In the move towards greater 'flexibility' (for the companies), plans to improve productivity involved maximising production through the introduction of a new work schedule called the seven-day roster. This regime allowed continuous coal production around the clock, week and year, without an increase in employment levels. Productivity increases were bought by the companies at the cost of higher wages. But in return for more money, miners were required to rearrange their shifts so that the bulk of their days off were mid-week. In fact, the seven-day roster allows for only one consecutive Saturday and Sunday off a month.[12]

Understandably, many women in the coal mining communities of Central Queensland and the Hunter Valley of New South Wales, where it was clear that the coal companies were keen to institute the new award immediately, greeted the seven-day roster with alarm. The separation of men's working schedules from the regularities of the Monday to Friday or Saturday working week meant significant changes in the life of the family and in the work of the miner's wife. For the purposes of this discussion of subjectivity and politics, what was interesting was the differential involvement of women from different communities in this debate and struggle over industry work practices. A different politics of action was constructed in each place and very different outcomes emerged.

In the new mining region of Central Queensland, coal miners and their families live in single industry towns some 200 kilometres from the coastal towns of Rockhampton, Mackay and Bowen. Opportunities for women's employment are severely limited in these relatively remote towns. For many, living in 'outback suburbia' (Brealey and Newton 1978) is compensated for only by the extremely high levels of income that can be achieved. Queensland coal miners have, since the 1960s, fought for and won huge increases in wages from their multinational employers.[13] Money has been the major attraction for new recruits to the industry. Many families move to the relatively remote coal towns as part of a savings or family plan—they intend to 'do it' for five or ten years, 'while the kids are little', or 'until we save up for a house'.[14]

In most Central Queensland localities the miners, excited by the prospect of wage increases of from $10 000 to $30 000 a year, were happy to accept the new roster system and easily dismissed the misgivings expressed by their partners.[15] Women in these communities watched in collective silence as major changes in their own and their husbands' lives were implemented.

By contrast, in the Hunter Valley women opposed the introduction of what quickly became known as the 'divorce roster' and successfully organised opposition to its institution. In this valley some 100 kilometres north of Sydney, coal mining dates from convict days. The coal communities of the Lower Hunter Valley and Cessnock have a rich and militant labour history (Gollan 1963; Metcalfe 1988; Ross 1970). The new open-cut mines that opened in the Upper Hunter during the 1970s drew a large proportion of their workforce from the coal-mining families of the older Newcastle and Cessnock fields. Although more rural and further from the coast than the older mines, the new mines are in no way remote, unlike their counterparts in Central Queensland. Mining families live in the established rural centres of Singleton and Muswellbrook, and opportunities for female employment are reasonably plentiful and diverse. When the seven-day roster was first talked about, miners and their families became alarmed and decided to oppose it.

After a seven-week dispute led by the miners' union at the Howick open-cut mine, the employees were forced to return to work by the local coal authority while the dispute was arbitrated. In the mean time BP Coal, the company concerned, proceeded to take the issue to the Supreme Court to sue for damages. In this climate of extreme class hostility, and under a writ forbidding further strike action or media exposure by the miners themselves, a group of miners' wives mobilised a campaign to oppose the new roster system on the ground of its impact on family and community life. They made industrial history by becoming the first group of women (and non-coal miners) to present a submission to the Coal Industry Tribunal (the industrial court for the Australian coal industry). After their impassioned and personalised submission, and while the tribunal was considering its judgment, BP Coal and the Combined Mining Unions struck an out-of-court deal to settle on another, more sociable roster system. The seven-day roster was successfully opposed and the women were celebrated as true working-class heroines (Robinson 1989: 6–7).

Southern militance, northern apathy

From the perspective of structural conceptions of power and political identity, the struggle in the Hunter Valley was a political victory in which men and women, structurally positioned within capitalism as members of the working class, and miners' wives, structurally positioned within patriarchy as subordinated females, threw off their chains of class exploitation and gender oppression to become conscious agents of resistance and change. The Hunter Valley miners and miners' wives became imbued with political agency, loudly proclaiming their existence as powerful beings whose political identities are subjectively realised but structurally ordained.

By contrast, their Central Queensland comrades and sisters were devoid of political energy; their structurally defined political identities were quiescent, their potentially militant voices unheard. As employees and producers of surplus value for the coal companies, the Central Queensland miners were working-class men whose political consciousness had been 'bought off' by economic gain.[16] Their 'false' consciousness was in part attributable to their wives, constituted in this formulation as a politically conservative working-class element—consumers and family managers who are primarily interested in money.

As women, they are also implicitly viewed as relatively powerless, occupying a subordinate position with respect to their menfolk, quietly accepting the burden of greater domestic responsibilities (for example, over the weekends) and keeping out of industrial political debates.

In this structural reading, the Hunter Valley is represented as politicised and active while the Central Queensland communities are apolitical and apathetic. In order to explain why the 'falsely conscious' Queenslanders failed to act in their own structually defined interests, we usually resort to arguments about the particularities or contingencies of geography, history and political culture. Essentialist arguments about the inherent nature of 'Queensland', the state that functions as the backward 'other' in discourses of Australian nationalism, spring to mind to account for the different awareness of and resistance to the identity-defining experiences of class exploitation and gender oppression that have developed in the northern coal communities.

Such a discourse has many effects, one of which is the overriding sense of disappointment and political pessimism it can engender. A sequel to the Hunter Valley tale might illustrate this point.

Flushed with the success of their action to oppose the introduction of the seven-day roster, the main organisers of the Hunter Valley women decided to form an Upper Hunter branch of the Miners' Women's Auxiliary and carry on with their activity around industrial issues.[17] When, in 1991, they became active on the issues of sackings and pay cuts and threatened to repeat their strategy of presenting a case before the local coal authority, they began to experience significant opposition from men and the union. Harassment of their husbands and themselves forced them to retreat from their campaign. The Hunter Valley women believe that their actions were too great an embarrassment to the politically lethargic local union branch. Somehow they had overstepped an invisible line. In 1989, as spokespeople for their silenced working-class husbands, it had been acceptable for women to lead the campaign against the seven-day roster, but in 1991, as alternative spokespeople, more outspoken than the men, their leadership could not be condoned.

In the structural reading, gender oppression undermines the possibility of lasting working-class success, and patriarchy becomes the brake upon an effective challenge to capitalist hegemony. While in a certain kind of 'political' moment subjects can resist or modify aspects of 'the social structure', these moments will only ever produce transitory change.[18] Capitalism and patriarchy figure as obdurate structures of unchanging power. In the face of the disappointments associated with this discourse (we look for political subjectivity and find a

structural subject position, we expect change and get unchanging structure), it is easy to become politically alienated and disaffected.

Tales of potentiality

In hegemonic popular discourses of society, gender and, to some extent,
class are represented as stable and central constituents of personal
identity. The discursive constructs 'men' and 'women', 'capitalist' and
'worker' have become naturalised fictions within which we all work
and live (Butler 1990). Socialist feminism has ossified these subject
positions, cementing them in place as expressions of dominant social
structures (capitalism and patriarchy).[19] Thus we are not at all surprised
by descriptions of, for example, mining communities as 'working class'
or as places of gender polarisation where 'men harbour animus against
women' (Campbell 1993: 16).

In both the popular and the socialist feminist discourses of subjectivity, there is no room for multiple gender or class identities (Connell
1987). Within the 'miner's wife discourse', for example, we are not
permitted to conceive of non-traditional gender identities for women,
or non-capitalist class identities for mining town residents, and our
understanding of political subjectivity is thereby impoverished and
restricted. It is not possible to see the political subjectivity of mining
town women as constituted by multiple and possibly contradictory
discourses, discourses that locate women in a variety of subject positions each with its own powers of action and capacity (Yeatman
1994: 20).

How might we think, or rethink, political subjectivity in poststructural terms? This would involve theorising the diversity of discourses and
narratives that could constitute a decentred and shifting subjectivity.
For an example, we can take another look at the discourses of class
and gender to see the diversity both within and between subjects that
differing narratives may engender.

Some two years after the introduction of the seven-day roster in
Central Queensland mines, the expected benefit of increased productivity had not been realised. While production disruption from strikes
and slowdowns had not increased, the rate of absenteeism and number
of sick days being taken by coal miners had risen. In households, the
personal strain of the new work regime was beginning to be felt. It
was becoming clear that any increase in coal production was being
gained at the expense of the intensification of domestic labour by
women. In their capacity as producers of surplus labour in the

household sexual division of labour, women were dependent upon the support, reliable help and relief of husbands at certain times of the day or week. When this was no longer forthcoming because of the disruption caused by the new roster, some women responded by walking out (hence the designation the 'divorce roster') while others encouraged their husbands in absenteeism and taking sickies (Gibson 1992). Participation in a non-capitalist class process in the household (the production by women of surplus labour and its distribution to their husbands and children) in which their labour was being intensified produced reactions in women which constituted them as political actors in the so-called 'personal sphere'. And individual 'acting up' in the household produced a cumulative effect on class relations at the mine. In this alternative discourse of class, one can see the accumulation of household struggles over work having industry-wide impacts.[20]

Other non-capitalist class processes that are part of life in a remote mining community can also be seen as important conditions of political subjectivity. In Central Queensland many of the 'working-class' miners are also self-employed. While this class position, and its contribution to identity, is recognised in popular discourse when it is held by a shopkeeper or small businessman (petit bourgeois), whose primary occupation is as a self-employed worker, its effects are generally ignored when it is held in addition to the position of full-time paid worker. Many Central Queensland miners have used their high wages to buy up local properties and take up farming, or to buy shooting and refrigeration equipment and take up commercial pig shooting. Some own real estate on the coast and have become landlords. Given the financial commitments entailed in these investments, the additional wages offered by the new roster were doubly attractive. What might be seen as false consciousness with respect to a working-class structural location—that is, the miners' acceptance of the new award and their willing submission to capitalist exploitation—could instead be seen as an overdetermined effect of their participation in self-employment. In the light of this alternative discourse of class, what might be construed as political quiescence—from a structural perspective that sees only one (capitalist) class process and a stable and single class identity for each subject—could be seen as activism on the part of an individual with a complex and shifting experience of class.

The picture of political 'apathy' among Central Queensland miners and their wives becomes, in this poststructuralist discourse of multiple and contradictory class identity, a complex representation of agency and power; events relating to the new award and roster changes can be read as a social narrative in which all actors 'have power' and use it to effect. Yet recognition of the capacity of this power may well be undeveloped, especially in the social world of the mining community where power is so uniformly portrayed in reductive structural terms. In this environment, the discourse of working-class politics easily eclipses alternative discourses of class and of political action based around class exploitation.[21]

Gender identity is similarly constrained by the hegemony of patriarchal discourses of binary and mutually exclusive gender roles. But in a poststructural rethinking of political subjectivity we can see many different constituents of gender identity and their influence in constituting political subjects. The three women who led the Upper Hunter Valley opposition to the seven-day roster were, as well as being wives, sisters and daughters of coal miners, a part-time clerk, a casual teacher and a community worker. Like many women in their region, they were balancing domestic labour and responsibilities with part-time or casual jobs in the paid workforce. Their identities as women were not solely confined to their roles as carers, domestic workers and miners' wives; they also had a sense of themselves as intellectually and economically independent and powerful. As subjects partially constituted by the discourse of 'working mother', they had negotiated with their partners complex arrangements concerning child care and domestic labour. It was these arrangements (and the gender identities they enabled) that the new roster system threatened.

The political strategies developed by the women harnessed many non-traditional notions of gender identity. The struggle produced moments of identification and solidarity between women who wanted careers and needed from their partners regular assistance with child care, and men who wanted to be carers and needed to be free on weekends to keep up their access rights to children from former marriages.

Two of the three women who were the prime organisers of the struggle were constituted in relation to another discourse of personal trauma and courage. They had each lost a child to cot death and were involved in the Sudden Instant Death Syndrome (SIDS) fund-raising and educational movement. This very personal political involvement fed into and fanned their commitment to the struggle against moves towards industry rationalisation. Rather than a consciousness of themselves as 'working class', it was the emotional strength they had gained from having 'survived the worst thing that can ever happen' (that is, their shared subject position within a discourse of survival) that gave them the capacity to invade the industrial political arena.

The 'militance' of the Hunter Valley miners' wives can now be seen as the rather unexpected, or indeterminate, outcome of political subjectivities constituted by, among a possible infinity of influences, psychological and emotional discourses of personal loss and survival and alternative social discourses of gender identity. It is not necessary to place these women on some pedestal of 'true' political (read feminist) sensibility over and above their Queensland sisters, with all the attendant moral judgment that such an analysis implies. Nor is it necessary to portray these women as a unified bloc, solidly identified as 'miners' wives' and imbued with working-class politics by virtue of their structural location. Their story illustrates the power that can be liberated as multiple and differing subject positions—posited within a variety of narratives and discourses—interact within an individual subject and combine in a group to produce a moment of affinity and partial identification.

From the foregoing discussion it might be evident that poststructural analysis presents a very different view of political subjectivity. Women catch a transitory glimpse of themselves as individuals with power in many different ways. Different discourses and narratives offer women different roles as political agents, and the momentary performative fixing of any of these roles by or upon an individual subject is itself a constitution of power.[22] In this way, political subjectivity is continually made and remade.

Political subjectivity is crucial to the feminist project, to the extent that feminism involves empowering (female) subjects to enact a drama of social change. But the ways in which power is engendered and distributed among political subjects is a vexed theoretical question the different answers to which are themselves influential constituents of political possibilities and interventions (Metcalfe 1994). A structural vision sees power as originating in the social structure, and the subject as a conduit of power who is structurally aligned. A poststructural perspective understands power as a ubiquitous and fluid substance that is discursively as well as non-discursively constituted and is never absent from a social site or agent. To fix women within a structural discourse is to reduce their political potential by essentialising their identities around a structurally defined core. To fix their identities in a poststructural context is a momentary process, a temporary halting of the discursive flux; it involves inhabiting a location within discourse that coexists with multiple other locations (places of performance or action) at one moment and over time. To view women's actions in poststructural terms is therefore to liberate a multitude of political subjectivities and to make visible a wide variety of possible interventions.

14

Rethinking prostitution*

Barbara Sullivan

Prostitution occupies a significant position at the intersection of feminist debates about the relationship between power, sex, sexuality and work. In this essay I examine first and second-wave feminist accounts of prostitution. These often situated prostitution in pervasive patterns of sexual economics and on a continuum with both other types of 'women's work' and other relationships like marriage. I then explore several recent feminist texts which argue against this continuum approach and which advance specific grounds for a principled feminist opposition to prostitution. My conclusion is that existing feminist accounts of prostitution are inadequate. I argue that we need new types of theories which avoid universal and essentialist claims about prostitution, which pay attention to the effects of feminists adopting an anti-prostitution stance and which contest dominant cultural discourses about sexuality.

Feminist theory and prostitution

Many 'first-wave' feminist accounts of prostitution focused on issues of sexual economics, stressing the connections between sexual and economic practices. They argued that women were vulnerable to a 'fall' into prostitution because of the inadequate wages paid to women, because of their economic dependence on men as a result of marriage and childbearing, and because of a male demand for sex without love or responsibility (see Allen 1988). Most feminists argued that prostitution was both exploitative and demeaning for women. Consequently,

---

* I would like to thank Felicity Grace and Kylie Stephen for their comments and discussion.

while engaging in the 'rescue' and 'protection' of sex workers, they also usually looked to the abolition of the prostitution industry.

Through this focus on sexual economics, many first-wave feminists drew significant continuities between the position of prostitutes and the position of all women. They emphasised the relationship between prostitution and other 'women's work' as well as between prostitution and other relationships involving sexual–economic exchange, including marriage. As Emma Goldman argued in 1911:

> Nowhere is woman treated according to the merit of her work, but rather as a sex . . . it is merely a question of degree whether she sells herself to one man, in or out of marriage, or to many men. (1969: 179)

The argument that prostitution exists on a continuum of sexual–economic exchange was also taken up by 'second-wave' feminists in the 1970s. They argued that in all areas of society women were forced into sexualised roles and into the (sexual/domestic) servicing of men in order to sustain themselves. From this perspective, it was simply the degree of overtness which separated the prostitute from other women. Some feminists like Jocelynne Scutt (1979) argued that marriage was a form of prostitution in which women received poor recompense for their work, were more vulnerable to violence (from their husbands), and had less control over their daily lives than sex workers.

Feminists like Jocelyn Scutt and, more recently, Christine Overall (1992) have insisted that many of the arguments commonly used to condemn prostitution are without foundation and that prostitution cannot easily be distinguished from other types of sexual–economic exchange. As we shall see, however, Overall does suggest that there are some specific grounds on which feminists can condemn prostitution. While prostitution has been seen as problematic because it involves particular dangers for women, such as disease, indignity, physical and psychological abuse and emotional pain, Overall argues that danger and injury cannot be considered essential elements of sex work. Women are frequently subjected to disease, injury and psychological abuse in other workplaces such as offices and factories as well as in their own homes. Moreover, as Roberta Perkins (1991) has recently demonstrated in the Australian context, these factors may be absent altogether in sex work. When they are present they may be a specific consequence of the illegality of most prostitution-related activities. What needs then to be recognised is that sex work occurs under a wide range of conditions and circumstances—some better, some worse than others.

Overall also examined the view that sex work was wrong because women were coerced into it. She concluded that all workers face an absence of choice in relation to their work and that the presence of coercion and the absence of consent were features of many women's activities under capitalism and male dominance. Thus, there is a need to acknowledge both the presence of (economic) coercion in paid work generally and the agency which some women exercise in relation to sex work. While some sex workers have very little choice about their work, others quite deliberately choose prostitution.

Finally, Overall examines the claim that sex work should be condemned because of its lack of reciprocity. It is often argued that intimate personal acts should not be sold on the market but should be exchanged between equals in a respectful relationship. But as Overall points out, the retailing of intimacy is a common feature of modern life and of other paid work like therapy and massage (1992: 715). In the case of both therapy and massage, equality and reciprocity are not usually features of the professional relationship. Moreover, it is only in the last few decades that these values have been seen as desirable in 'normal' intimate relations. It is clear, too, that the enormous differences between men and women, particularly in terms of economic, social and political resources, means that equality and reciprocity are rarely real features of contemporary relationships between adult men and women. If fairness, kindness, and respect were also acknowledged as important values—in the marketplace as well as in intimate relations (professional and personal)—then there would be no reason why prostitution would continue to suffer a definitional exclusion from the realm of morally acceptable work.

The continuum approach and feminist politics

Feminist approaches which situate prostitution on a continuum of sexual–economic relationships and which question popular accounts of prostitution tend to facilitate a broad feminist support for prostitute women. They 'cut across' dominant cultural meanings of prostitution by refusing to regard prostitutes as 'bad' women or prostitution as a sexual–economic exchange which is somehow radically different from other sorts of sexual–economic exchange held to be more 'normal'.

In the 1970s Australian feminists used the continuum approach extensively. Anne Summers (1975) argued that prostitution played a central role in Australian history. This was because many of our non-Aboriginal 'founding mothers', the convict women transported to the Australian colonies between 1788 and 1867, were casual prostitutes in Britain. The organisation of convict settlements in Australia also meant that all women (particularly convict women but at a later point also free immigrant and Aboriginal women) were subjected to an 'enforced whoredom': in order to survive they were forced to trade sexual services for food, clothing and shelter. According to Summers, this situation shifted in the colonial period, when women were increasingly divided into 'good' and 'bad', either 'damned whores' or 'god's police'. It became the assigned role of 'good' women (a category that included married women, celibate spinsters and early feminists) to discipline and divert 'bad' women from their evil ways. The overall effect of this process was to divide and classify women as either 'maternal figures who are not . . . sexual or as whores who are exclusively sexual'. Summers argued that these stereotypes functioned to discipline all women, for they ignored or actively repressed 'good' women's sexual needs ('good' women were seen to be asexual) and treated all sexually active women as 'bad' like prostitutes. It was in the interests of all women for these stereotypes to be broken down. Summers thought that one way this could be achieved was for 'good' women to refuse their traditional policing functions and for feminists publicly to identify themselves with those who were designated as 'bad': prostitutes, lesbians and prisoners.

In the 1980s Summers' arguments were utilised by feminists like Jackson and Otto (1984) to argue that the dichotomy between prostitutes and other women was 'a form of social control of female sexuality' which 'makes the support of prostitutes by other women a matter of self-interest rather than moral imperative'. However, this approach was seen to involve a significant 'dilemma' for feminists. How could they provide effective support for prostitutes in the short term without compromising a feminist opposition to prostitution in the long term? Jackson and Otto regarded prostitution as the most blatant form of sexual exploitation, but similar patterns were seen in other areas of the paid workforce and in relationships like marriage. There were additional problems which had to do with the rights of all women to bodily self-determination. If the laws controlling prostitution were indeed 'laws on property, forbidding women to sell something (their bodies) that can only belong to men' (Bacon 1976–77), then feminists could not adopt a stance which advocated the legal suppression of prostitution despite what was regarded as its *inherent* sexual exploitation.

Several Australian feminists argued that the resolution of this 'dilemma' could be achieved by a focus on prostitution as 'sex work' (Aitkin 1978; Jackson and Otto 1984). Feminist support could then be confined to areas of immediate concern to prostitute women, such as wages and working conditions. Feminists could lobby for the decriminalisation of prostitution as a necessary precondition for improvements in the working conditions of sex workers without abandoning their long-term goal of abolition of the sex industry. It is notable that this approach did not mean an abandonment of a feminist opposition to prostitution or of the long-term goal of abolition of the sex industry. These issues were simply 'set aside'. This approach gave an important impetus to the formation of political alliances between feminists and sex workers. In Australia during the late 1970s and early 1980s feminists and feminist organisations (such as the Women's Electoral Lobby) actively campaigned for the decriminalisation of prostitution. Consequently, feminist arguments were used to support law reform initiatives in several states, most notably NSW (where street soliciting was decriminalised in 1979) and Victoria (where brothel prostitution was decriminalised in 1984).

Since the mid-1980s, however, feminist support for the decriminalisation of prostitution would appear to have declined. In part, this relates to the tensions inherent in an approach which regards prostitution as fundamentally about sexual exploitation but which advocates decriminalisation as a short-term strategy. Feminists remain in substantial conflict about the sexual economics of prostitution, the moral status of the prostitution industry and the strategy of decriminalisation. In both Queensland and South Australia some feminists have argued that the law should be used to protect women and girls from exploitation within the sex industry and to dissuade men from participating in prostitution as clients. They have lobbied against measures—such as the decriminalisation and licensing of brothels—which were seen to offer state endorsement of the sex industry. Other feminists have lobbied for decriminalisation but remain in substantial disagreement about the form and extent of this process. In Victoria, the feminist law academic Marcia Neave—who conducted the government's *Inquiry into Prostitution* (1985)—argued in favour of a limited decriminalisation of street and brothel prostitution. However, the sense that there is something inherently wrong with the prostitution transaction was evident in her proposed new restrictions on prostitution advertising as part of an overall strategy designed to reduce the demand for prostitution.

Feminist arguments against prostitution

During the 1980s some feminist theorists rejected the whole idea of a continuum between prostitution and other aspects of women's sexual and economic lives. Carol Pateman (1988), for example, contended that prostitution was not like other work because the prostitution contract was not like other employment contracts. It should be kept in mind here that the main focus of Pateman's work is not prostitution but a critique of contractarianism within liberal theory. She is predominantly concerned about the way that concepts like 'freedom' and 'consent' are used in modern-day relations (for example, in employment, marriage and prostitution 'contracts') to oppress women. Like Overall, Pateman emphasises the coercive nature of all paid employment under capitalism. But she also argues that the position of prostitutes is different from that of other workers both because of the particular dangers involved in sex work (for example, the fact that prostitutes are often sought out by serial killers) and because of the nature of the work itself. In her view, the 'embodied' nature of prostitution means that it is not like other paid work. This is because, economically or otherwise, vulnerable women are coerced into 'selling sexual access to their bodies'. In our culture and time such 'sale of sexual access' is regarded as 'sale of self'. According to Pateman, this means that prostitution looks less like an employment contract for sexual services and more like sexual slavery which, of course, is to be condemned.

Pateman does not argue that prostitution *is* sexual slavery, only that, in our culture and time, it *appears* like this (and consequently is usually experienced as such). The issue here is as much about discourses of sexuality and their effects on individuals as about prostitution contracts. Those who reject the argument that prostitution is the 'sale of bodies' (and, therefore, sexual slavery) often contend that prostitutes sell only sexual services or the illusion of sexual intimacy. This position is often adopted by sex workers themselves. But it is difficult, if not impossible, to 'step outside' cultural meanings. For the community at large, sex work is regarded as a profound sale of self. This is, I think, why sex workers are disparaged and abused (by clients, the community, the judicial system and often too, feminists).

Pateman is concerned with the political relationship between the sex industry and the maintenance of male dominance. In her view, the fact that men can purchase sexual access to women via the sex industry is intimately connected to the establishment of their public and private power over women. As she sees it, masculinity and femininity are sexual identities which are confirmed in sexual activity and, in particular, via heterosexual intercourse. Men create and maintain their sense of themselves—both as men and as women's civil masters—in heterosexual intercourse. But it is the public nature of the sex industry which makes it particularly problematic:

> When women's bodies are on sale as commodities in the capitalist market, the terms of the original contract (which is about men's civil power) cannot be forgotten; the law of male sex-right is publicly affirmed, and men gain public acknowledgement as women's sexual masters. (Pateman 1988: 208)

Pateman's point about a general relationship in our culture between heterosexuality and men's power is quite convincing. But the problem she identifies is clearly about heterosexual identity (for men) and its cultural and political meanings rather than about prostitution per se. The power associated with men's heterosexual identity is produced and affirmed in a range of public institutions, the most obvious and visible of which is the institution of marriage. While the sex industry is neither invisible nor irrelevant, it cannot claim the power and legitimacy of these more 'normal' public institutions which affirm male dominance. Although Pateman is opposed to both marriage and prostitution contracts, she is explicit in her condemnation of prostitution and considerably less forthright about the institution of marriage.

Pateman correctly draws attention to dominant cultural meanings of prostitution and their effects on prostitute women. But ultimately she reinforces these cultural meanings by treating them as fixed and given. If prostitution is problematic because of contingent, culturally based assumptions about the bodily submission involved in sex work, then a feminist condemnation of sex work based on its conceptualisation as always 'sexual slavery' is simply repeating and reinforcing these cultural assumptions. Different cultural understandings of prostitution can and do exist in the Australian community. In popular culture as well as in some feminist history and fiction, prostitute women are often represented not as sexual slaves but as rebels and resistors of male power and as women who are cleverly seeking to maximise their conditions and opportunities in a problematic environment (see for example Daniels 1984; Horn and Pringle 1984). Feminist efforts to intervene in and change the present practice of prostitution could place their emphasis on contesting dominant cultural meanings of prostitution (as 'sale of self') and bringing marginalised discourses, about prostitutes as rebels and empowered women, into the mainstream.

Two other recent texts, very different from Pateman's, have also attempted to elaborate the foundation for a principled feminist opposition to prostitution. Like Pateman, Christine Overall (1992) and Laurie Shrage (1989) reject the continuum argument and stress that there are clear differences between prostitution and other types of sexual economic exchange. Overall concludes that 'sex work differs in a crucial way from other forms of women's labour', because it is not 'reversible'. Nothing about the service, nurturing and domestic work that is presently done by women for men would prevent its being done by men for women, by men for men, or by women for women in an ideal (postcapitalist and postpatriarchal) world. She also contends that:

> the value of office workers, sales clerks, cooks, cleaners and child care workers has a value independent of the (present) conditions of sexual and economic inequality under which it is done, and much of it would still be socially necessary in a postcapitalist, postpatriarchal world. (1992: 718)

By contrast, sex work, argues Overall, is not inherently valuable or 'reversible' because it involves a commoditisation of sex (which could not exist in a postcapitalist world) and because prostitution is essentially premised on conditions of sexual and economic inequality (which would disappear in a postpatriarchal society).

In a similar vein, Laurie Shrage has argued that commercial sex, unlike marriage, is not 'reformable'. She suggests that 'because marriage can be founded on principles which do not involve the subordination of women, we can challenge oppressive aspects of this institution without radically altering it' (1989: 360). The sex industry is not similarly situated and feminists are therefore justified in adopting a principled opposition to prostitution.

But there is probably no inherent reason why sex work should not also be regarded as 'reversible' or 'reformable', unless one adopts fixed notions about the essential nature of male and female sexuality. There is also no basis for assuming that in a postcapitalist, postpatriarchal world, sex work would not be valued. In a world where sex and power were connected (or not connected) in quite different ways from our own, the knowledge which professional sex workers have could well be of use to men and women in the simple pursuit of sexual recreation and pleasure. In this case a desire to acquire specialist and expert knowledge would be the main reason for visiting a sex worker, in the same way that (even in a postpatriarchal world) one might visit a doctor for specialist medical advice. Of course, an approach like this is premised on an acceptance of the validity of a wide range of different sorts of sexual relationships. Sex is not inherently 'sacred' or meaningful. Some might consider it to be so, particularly in the context of a monogamous partnership. However, sex might also be a valid part of non-monogamous, non-romantic relationships focused on pleasure, play, companionship and earning a living.

Even at present, there are clear grounds on which feminists could argue for a re-evaluation of the work prostitutes do. Many sex workers have specific knowledge and skills—for example, about the problems involved in recommended regimes for 'safe sex'—which are of value to the wider community. This knowledge has already been utilised by researchers and by state health authorities in Australia in the planning of AIDS prevention programs designed for the whole community. This does not mean that the prostitution industry—as it is presently consti-tuted—is without major problems. Prostitutes face a number of signif-icant hazards—including violence from clients, legal discrimination, health problems and a cultural stigmatisation of their work. I am also not suggesting that prostitution is inherently empowering for women. Perkins has recently argued that a feminist re-evaluation of prostitution is needed because 'female prostitution is a social situation in which women have more power over sexual interactions than in any other circumstance involving both sexes interacting' (1991: 389). She says that because prostitutes can set limits on the work they do, because they acquire economic power and 'knowledge of true male sexuality' in their working lives, they are 'a far cry from the common feminist assumption of prostitutes as the most explicit example of female oppression' (p. 349).

Perkins's empirical investigation of a group of sex workers in Sydney does provide a valuable corrective to feminist accounts of prostitution which represent prostitutes as special victims of patriarchy. As she suggests, there is also a need for a feminist re-evaluation of prostitution. Her research indicates that prostitutes are like other, 'normal', women and their clients are like other 'normal' men. Many prostitutes do assert a significant amount of control over their working lives and, like other employees (even under capitalism), can often *feel* empowered by their work. Perkins found that most of the women in her sample had not been arrested, raped or subjected to other assaults at work and that the vast majority did not take drugs or, alternatively, did not increase their drug usage as a result of engaging in sex work. Moreover, they were more likely than other women to be orgasmic in their private lives.

O'Leary (1992) has criticised Perkins's study on several grounds. She says that Perkins's sample is concentrated on the upper echelons of the prostitute workforce—brothel workers and call girls—and does not include ex-workers. Consequently, her results tend to be more favourable and to 'gloss over' the dangers sex workers face. This would appear to be a valid argument. But O'Leary is also critical of Perkins's view that prostitution inherently empowers women. She says that prostitutes can be empowered and empowering only within pre-existing patriarchal confines and that this means they cannot do what is necessary, which is to mount an overall challenge to patriarchy. This sort of feminist approach glosses over the ways in which prostitutes are empowered—at least economically—particularly in relation to other women workers. It also fails to establish any specific grounds on which to condemn prostitution. As Elizabeth Grosz argues (1994), our 'struggles are inherently *impure*' and always bound up with what we struggle against. For Grosz this means that feminists need to refuse 'the fantasy of a position safe or insulated from what it criticises', for it is impossible to engage in any work, political or sexual activity and not be to some degree complicit in the perpetuation of existing structures of power. Of course, non-engagement is equally impossible. This does not mean that all activities and relationships are equally worthy; some may 'stretch' and challenge (rather than totally subvert) dominant paradigms, while others will not take issue with the status quo. But it is not clear to me that many prostitutes (as well as many married women, mothers and lesbians) do not already challenge and stretch dominant paradigms in their personal and working lives. Judgments about the degree of challenge and complicity need to be specific and contextual.

It is probably impossible, then, to describe prostitution as either inherently empowering or disempowering for women. There are many problems in the sex industry as it is presently constituted. However, the sex industry is not unique in this regard. To varying degress, sexual oppression is a problem right across the board in Australian public life—for example in work and parliamentary politics—as well as in private institutions like marriage and the family. Clearly, some workplaces and families are better than others; and some types of prostitution are less problematic than others. Perhaps what feminists need to emphasise is that the power relayed in the sex industry—as well as elsewhere—is both contingent and contestable.

Rethinking feminist approaches to prostitution

There are several grounds for suggesting that existing accounts of prostitution, including some feminist ones, are inadequate. First, if we make 'big' arguments or construct universal theories about the essential 'wrongness' of prostitution, we may be unable to locate and deal with specific differences and problems. There are obvious differences, for example, between prostitution in Thailand and in Australia. Thailand's developing economy means that there is a shortage of alternative forms of paid work for women and an absence of public welfare. Even in the Australian context there are important differences between working in an 'upmarket' legal brothel in Melbourne and being a drug-addicted street prostitute in Kings Cross. Sex workers in these environments will share some problems (like the cultural stigmatisation of their work) but will also have a number of different concerns and problems. What we need are more careful and nuanced accounts of prostitution which are able to both specify differences and problems (for example, the legal harassment faced by street prostitutes in Australian cities) and point to strategies for solving problems. Such strategies might include a broader feminist support for the decriminalisation of street prostitution as well as discursive approaches designed to reduce the cultural stigma faced by prostitute women (for example, refraining from making principled statements of opposition to prostitution).

Second, arguments about the inherent 'wrongness' of prostitution lead inevitably to arguments about the 'wrongness' of sex workers. This tends to affirm dominant cultural and legal discourses about the essentially corrupt nature of prostitute women. It also undermines the possibility of productive alliances between feminists and sex workers, alliances which are an important part of reform processes. Elsewhere (Sullivan 1991), I have argued that prostitute women have been marked out in Australian legal and political culture over the last century as essentially bad and deviant women. This is a trend which has accelerated (and which has started to similarly mark out male clients) over the last 30 years. As social ideals of equality and mutuality between men and women have become widespread, prostitution has increasingly been designated as the dark underside of 'normal' sexual relations. With the advent of new public concerns about HIV and AIDS, the prostitution industry has also been singled out as a particular threat to the health of the community.

These changes have had ongoing effects for prostitutes including, most notably, increased legal harassment and cultural stigmatisation. Despite the fact that male clients constitute the largest single group within the sex industry and that prostitution laws are now written in 'gender neutral' language, women remain the vast majority of those arrested and gaoled for prostitution offences throughout Australia. The cultural stigmatisation of sex work also makes prostitutes a particular target for male violence. At the same time, their recourse to legal redress is significantly reduced; prostitutes who have been raped are even less likely than other women to receive fair treatment in the judicial system.

As I have noted above, feminists have often struggled to support prostitutes while maintaining an opposition to prostitution. They have argued that it is possible to condemn prostitution without condemning those who perform sex work. But this is a difficult—possibly incoherent—position to maintain. Moreover, some recent feminist accounts of prostitution do specifically condemn prostitutes. Shrage (1989), for example, argues that prostitutes are complicit with the patriarchal domination of all women. Overall (1992) argues that prostitutes perpetuate rather than challenge patriarchy, although she concludes that it 'makes sense to defend prostitutes' entitlement to do their work but not to defend prostitution itself as a practice under patriarchy'.

In my view, this position does not make sense. If the sex industry is particularly responsible for the subordination of women, then it is not logical for feminists to defend prostitutes' right to do sex work. But, as I have argued above, it is problematic for feminists to argue that sex workers are particularly complicit in the patriarchal domination of women. If feminist arguments about the inherent 'wrongness' of prostitution tend to slide into and collude with dominant discourse about the inherent 'badness' of sex workers, then feminists must position themselves much more carefully if they wish to avoid endangering the lives and livelihoods of prostitute women. Feminist arguments against prostitution do have the capacity to reinforce the stigmatisation of sex workers, thus increasing prostitutes' vulnerability to violence and decreasing their ability to negotiate, on favourable terms, with clients, the owners of sex businesses, and public authorities. These sorts of problems—which are related to the effects of particular feminist discursive practices and theoretical positions—cannot be simply set aside as irrelevant or unimportant. They are also not 'solved' by feminist approaches which emphasise the need to refocus analysis on male clients and 'the problem of demand' (Carpenter 1994).

My third reason for suggesting the need for new approaches to prostitution is based on the general need for feminists to contest rather than confirm dominant cultural discourses about sexuality. In our culture sexual difference is usually talked about via notions of (men's) bodily integrity and (women's) bodily submission. Women's bodies are marked out as vulnerable, violable and possessable. In heterosexual intercourse, women's bodies are said to be 'entered' or 'penetrated' by men's bodies. Young women are said to 'lose' their virginity while prostitutes are seen to 'sell themselves'. This means that women are perceived to have a 'normal' lack of bodily integrity and, thus, bodily autonomy. In our culture and time this 'lack' is akin to a deficiency of selfhood (see Marcus 1992).

All women are disempowered by these ways of thinking and talking about sexual difference. However, for some women—prostitutes and victims of sexual assault are an obvious example—these discourses are particularly burdensome. They mark out prostitutes and rape victims as particularly damaged and violated, as 'fallen' and shameful women who lack, lose or sell their bodily integrity (and, thus, themselves).

Sharon Marcus has argued that rape can be both contested and prevented by attention to the discursive construction of 'rape scripts'. She points out that in our culture the most common ways of talking and thinking about rape, sexuality and gendered violence invite women to position themselves as endangered, violable and fearful; men are invited to position themselves as legitimately violent and entitled to women's sexual services (1992: 390). This language situates women as inherently rapable and structures the experience of rape for both male perpetrators (who feel empowered) and female victims (who feel violated, invaded and humiliated). This is what poststructuralist theorists like Marcus mean by the discursive construction of 'experience'; rape victims are subjected to real physical acts, but the cultural *meaning* assigned to these acts largely (but not completely) determines how they will be experienced and 'embodied' by women.

Marcus proposes that feminist anti-rape strategies could usefully be focused on disrupting and eradicating rape scripts. This involves displacing the emphasis on what existing rape scripts promote—men's power and capacity to rape—and putting into discourse what is presently stultified and excluded, that is, women's will, agency, and capacity for violence. The idea is to transform dominant ways of talking about women, female sexuality and rape as a way of both preventing rape and transforming the destructive experience of rape for women.

This sort of approach points to new feminist strategies in relation to prostitution. In our culture prostitutes are marked out as women who are bad, who sell themselves and are different from other women. I have already suggested that feminist arguments which stress the continuities between prostitution and other forms of sexual–economic exchange 'cut across' these dominant cultural discourses. I have also suggested that feminist positions which refuse this continuum approach and which posit both essentialist and universal accounts of prostitution fail to contest dominant cultural discourses about sexuality and prostitution.

At a minimum, feminists need to refrain from making principled statements of opposition to prostitution. But this is unlikely to be enough. What we need are feminist accounts of prostitution which assert the will and agency of prostitutes, which emphasise their capacity to resist male violence, which refuse the notion that women sell themselves in prostitution, and which reconfigure prostitution transactions. This sort of discursive strategy would change the often destructive discourses which prostitute women are presently forced to embody. It would also change the experience of being a male client, challenging men to embody new forms of sexuality. This sort of discursive strategy would also contribute to a broader feminist project which is addressed to the reconfiguration of 'normal' ways of talking about women, sexual difference and sexuality.

15

Destabilising patriarchy[*]

Rosemary Pringle

> If patriarchy is a symbolic universe, then no one better than Lacan expressed its surreal qualities.
>
> Nye 1989: 141

> Few can summon up Dworkin's fevered pitch, her vampire imagery, but the sentiment is there, diluted, palatable, draped in loose words like 'patriarchy'.
>
> Roife 1993: 46

The concept of patriarchy, so central to feminist political agendas of the 1970s, has fallen into disuse. Radical feminists invoke it, albeit with rhetorical rather than explanatory purpose, to proclaim the universality of male dominance deeply rooted in male consciousness. Others have quietly dropped it from their repertoire or permit it only a hazy, faraway existence as a referent. But there remains some tension around its usage that replicates some of the old conflicts between Marxist and radical feminism.

To the existing string of 'posts' within contemporary feminism could be added 'post-Marxist feminist' and 'post-radical feminist'. The first is concentrated among social scientists and historians concerned with gender relations in the domain of the social—in commonsense terms, the 'real world'. Drawing on Foucault and others labelled 'post-Marxist', scholars like Rosalind Coward (1983), Carol Smart (1989) and Geraldine Pratt (1993) have questioned the strategic value of treating patriarchy as a social system and emphasised the more fluid and local contexts in which power and gender operate. The second approach, associated with philosophy, cultural studies and deconstruc-

---

[*] My thanks to Barbara Caine, John Fletcher, Liz Grosz and Sophie Watson for critical comments on an earlier draft.

tion, shares something with radical feminism in that it takes the existence of patriarchy for granted. In the mode of Derrida, Irigaray and the 'post-Lacanians', the object here is the 'texts of patriarchy' and the world of the symbolic. Elizabeth Grosz understands feminist theory as a series of strategic interventions into patriarchal texts which render them unable to function. Feminists, she says, 'resort to forms of intellectual guerilla warfare, striking out at the points of patriarchy's greatest weakness, its blindspots. The grounds and terrain upon which patriarchy develops its arguments reveals their partial and partisan instead of universal or representative position' (1986: 197). A term heard frequently in this camp is 'phallocentrism' (or phallogocentrism for the purists), which implies a specific reference to sexuality, fantasy, representation and the constitution of the sexed body. Deconstruction is not concerned with producing 'better' understandings of the world but with reading between the lines of texts in order to unsettle existing 'truths' and open up spaces for multiple new meanings to emerge.

This paper traces the shifting approaches to patriarchy and reflects on its contemporary relevance for feminist theory. I believe we have reached a point where patriarchy, at least in its systemic sense, is more of an obstacle than an aid to understanding the specific operations of power. A term that was alive with possibility in the 1970s has become banal: critics like Katie Roife (1993) see it as little more than a swear word for male power. The alternative focus on more local, fragmented and specific relations of gender domination can look dangerously like a retreat. 'Is the story of oppression and patriarchy more persuasive than one of multiple sites of domination and meanings?' asks the geographer Geraldine Pratt, and 'does feminist theory lose its coherence and force as rhetoric if it embraces ambiguity, complexity and partiality?' (1993: 58). Only, I think, if it denies the need to identify and destabilise patriarchal residues in the world of the symbolic, in texts and in psyches.

It is not only 'patriarchy' that is problematic but the whole notion of 'the social'. As Denise Riley puts it, 'once the seemingly neutral and vacant backdrop of "the social" presents itself for scrutiny, it appears as a strange phenomenon in its own right' (1988: 49). Texts cannot merely 'reflect' the social but neither can the social be simply read from a series of chosen texts. And there is the further question of the relation between the social and the psychological. The 'texts of patriarchy' concerned with the structuring of the psyche often take it for granted that the psyche will find itself mirrored in the social. Yet it may be part of our current predicament that we retain a 'patriarchal unconscious', even though patriarchal social relations have been substantially dismantled. It is important therefore not to conflate the psychic and the social. It may always be necessary to deconstruct the patriarchal symbolic while treating gender relations in the social world as more amenable to change.

The early debates

In the early 1970s feminists brought issues of inequality between men and women dramatically to centre stage. They did this by creating a vision of patriarchy not as a residual family form but as a social system broadly equivalent to capitalism, and by converting 'gender' from a grammatical term to one which described sexual relations, arguing that they were similar to and possibly more basic than class relations. With considerable flair, Kate Millett (1972) identified the power-structured relations in which men controlled women and older men younger men. She established her case with an analysis of the portrayals of the sexual act in the writings of Henry Miller, Norman Mailer and Jean Genet, showing the importance in them of male power and female subordination and linking these individual stories to the many institutions through which consent is manufactured and male domination maintained. This was a challenge to both Marxists and liberals who had comfortably believed that gender inequalities were a relic of a past age that would fade out over time, a by-product of economic inequalities, or a personal affair outside the realm of politics. It is impossible to overstate the importance of Millett's assertion that sexual relations were political ones, that sexual inequalities were fundamental, long-standing and systemic. Patriarchy, gender and women's oppression became the key terms of the Women's Liberation Movement.

The emerging positions of radical and socialist feminism defined themselves in relation to their approaches to patriarchy. All assumed that patriarchy had an existence in the real world, separate from the terms in which it was theorised. For radical feminists, the power of men over women was taken to be an autonomous and fundamental structure of social relations. It was not a side-effect of any other structure (like capitalism or mode of production) and it was an organising principle of social life. Mary Daly, Andrea Dworkin, Susan Brownmiller, Adrienne Rich, Catherine Mackinnon and other (mostly American) radical feminists whipped up enormous anger about this totalising system. For Daly (1978) patriarchy was a planetary system which crushes women everywhere: she cited Chinese foot binding, Indian suttee, African genital mutilation and American gynaecology to illustrate the tortures that men inflict on women. Men are power-hungry necrophiliacs who want to reduce women to helpless corpses. Mackinnon (1987) thought heterosexual intercourse was inherently male dominated and regarded male power as so utterly dominant that 'women' exist only as a social construction produced by and for men. These are extreme statements, perhaps partly because American rhetorical styles use exaggeration to get attention. These theorists assumed the existence of patriarchy based on relations of domination and subordination between two fundamentally opposed categories of people, men and women.

Inevitably there was a search for the linchpin of such a system, and a variety of 'bases' have been identified in the literature. Shulamith Firestone identified reproduction as the problem, arguing that women were at a disadvantage in the biological family because children were dependent for such a long period. The French sociologist Christine Delphy took over some Marxist concepts to suggest that patriarchy was based on a domestic mode of production in which husbands as a class exploited their wives through controlling their labour. For Adrienne Rich it was compulsory heterosexuality which drove women into relations of subordination. Nancy Chodorow argued that women's responsibility for mothering systematically reproduced gender inequalities through the formation of masculine and feminine core selves.

For many feminists of both tendencies, the question of the interrelationship between capitalism and patriarchy was central. The problem seemed to be resolved when Heidi Hartmann (1981) formulated a way of thinking about patriarchy and capitalism as 'dual systems' with separate sets of material relations. This had the advantage of treating patriarchy as a specific set of relations rather than an overarching system. In practice it was impossible to distinguish where one system ended and the other began. Instead the terms 'capitalist patriarchy' and 'patriarchal capitalism', which were little more than slogans, came to be used.

Socialist feminists identified problems with 'patriarchy' almost from the beginning. Veronica Beechey spoke for them in treating Millett's book as a description of patriarchal relationships and some of their manifestations but not a satisfactory explanation of their foundations. Michelle Barrett believed the term represented 'insuperable difficulties to an analysis that attempts to relate women's oppression to the relations of production of capitalism' (1980: 19). Sheila Rowbotham (1981) was troubled by the use of the term to distinguish sexual from class oppression, objecting on the grounds of its alleged universality and biologism. In a characteristic attempt to fit patriarchy into a Marxist analysis, McDonough and Harrison posited two separate structures of oppression but argued that class determines the extent to which women will be subjected to patriarchal structures (1978: 36). Mary McIntosh's work on the state (1978) also presumed that patriarchal relations change according to the requirements of a separate or determining economic formation.

It is not my intention to rehearse these debates at any length. What seems obvious, looking back, is the earnestness of the attempts to theorise the social totality; the emphasis on the nuclear family as the key institution of patriarchy, however defined; and the extremely formal terms in which the debate was expressed. Carol Smart draws a comparison with the domestic labour debate. Both, she suggests, are ultimately sterile but probably had to happen so that feminist theory could progress (1984: 9).

Two of the most original attempts to go beyond 'dual systems' have come from the sociologists Bob Connell (1983, 1987) and Sylvia Walby (1990), who have tried to move away from monocausal accounts and to theorise patriarchy as both less total and less coherent. Connell argued (1983: 56) that theories of patriarchy suffered from 'an excess of theoretical centralism', from the attempt to organise the whole field around some one master principle. A theory of patriarchy does not require a key, core, central relation that organises all the rest. Its unity is a composed unity, the (fleeting) product of the history of many processes, which always show some incoherence, some contradictions. Connell (1987) went on to suggest three main structures—labour, power and cathexis or emotional/sexual attachments—and discussed them in a number of institutional contexts. Not to be outdone, Walby (1990) proposed six structures which make up patriarchy as a system. Against accusations that patriarchy is biologically reductionist, essentialist, idealist and transhistorical (Barrett 1980), both writers claim that it is possible to produce accounts that are historically specific, and that recognise different modes of the operation of power.

The historical shifts within patriarchy are addressed specifically by Walby (1990), Pateman (1988), and MacCannell (1990), all of whom identify a move from 'private' to 'public' forms no longer based on the direct authority of the father. Public patriarchy, the rule of the brothers, can be seen as both an advance and a retreat for women. Male authority became more diffuse but harder to contest. The political philosopher Carole Pateman (1988) analysed the seventeenth-century debates between patriarchalists and contract theorists, showing that a sexual contract underlies the social contract; men's freedom rests on women's subjection and a new form of 'fraternal' patriarchy underlies the discursive practices of contemporary liberal democracy. This work raises many questions, however. It implies that feminists should reject all forms of contract; and it takes for granted the prior existence of men and women, assuming that a just society would be based on an autonomy that derived from sexual difference.

While such writers have continued to theorise modern patriarchy, others stopped using the term or used it in a different form. Michelle Barrett (1980) wrote of patriarchal ideology and Carol Smart (1984) of patriarchal relations and structures, hoping, by using the adjective instead of the noun, to avoid the implication that male domination was a rigid system with its own material base or mode of production. The adjective suggested something more fluid, employing a variety of mechanisms and strategies in the exercise of power. Five years later, Smart had replaced it with 'phallocentric' to refer to a 'culture which is structured to meet the needs of the masculine imperative' and which invokes 'sexuality, desire and the subconscious psychic world' (1989: 27). This was indicative of a general shift in feminist thinking away from patriarchy as a social system towards the analysis of discourse and culture—a shift that was led by the 'French feminists' and their deconstructive readings of psychoanalysis.

Psychoanalysis and patriarchy

While attempts were being made to map the contours of public patriarchy another debate unfolded which derived from psychoanalysis. Many feminists felt that socialisation theories were inadequate to explain the formation of subjectivity, the deep resistances to change and women's complicity in the patriarchal system. Juliet Mitchell's book *Psychoanalysis and Feminism* (1975) marked a movement away from the analysis of particular political or economic systems to a questioning of the symbolic construction of society itself. Patriarchy here refers not to the power of men in general but very specifically to the symbolic power of fathers and their representations. Using Levi-Strauss, Mitchell argued that the universality of patriarchy is rooted in the exchange of women by men, the necessity of which is located in the incest taboo. She defined patriarchy as ideology and argued that only by understanding how the unconscious operates is it possible to gain insight into the functioning of patriarchal culture. Patriarchy is here postulated as a universal structure which is equated with culture itself. Mitchell stressed the importance of the family as the place where the 'law of the father' was passed on in the formation of masculine and feminine subjects. Freud had thought of the patriarchal family as synonymous with human history and culture. He argued that before human society began, a dominant male controlled a group of females. In order to avoid the struggle to the death that leaves only one male the victor (as in the kangaroo world), the sons made a pact: each would abstain from sexual relations with his own female relations. The law of the father was instituted both in reparation of guilt about the murder of the father and to monitor the alliance under one authority. We inherit an unconscious understanding of our animal origins and this original relation to the father which makes the nucleus of the oedipal family invulnerable to social change. For Freud, although the family may take various forms, it is always patriarchal. Similarly, for Lacan there can be no question of the elimination of elementary kinship structures or the replacement of the phallus and the name of the father, because without these symbolisations there would be no language and therefore no human culture.

Mitchell argued, rather lamely, that each mode of production expresses the universal law of patriarchy in a different ideological form and that under capitalism, the conditions for disappearance of the incest taboo and kinship structures have finally developed. Since the capitalist economy is not organised around kin relations, there is finally a prospect of throwing off the patriarchal shackles. While most feminists at the time did think that patriarchy had been universal, a common reaction to Mitchell's book was despair. Although it purported to be an argument for an autonomous women's movement to assist the birth of non-patriarchal structures, it was hard to believe that if civilisation and patriarchy had been synonymous for millennia they could suddenly change.

Feminists have had several responses to this work. Jane Flax complained that Mitchell treats the unconscious as a disembodied structure outside both history and social relations, reducing sexual politics to 'the acquisition of patriarchal law' by each individual and the contradiction between this law and the world of work as structured by capitalism (1990: 158–59). Those working with object relations theory (Chodorow 1978) have emphasised a social dimension to family relations that is lacking in Mitchell's analysis. Mitchell was not concerned with what went on in actual families but with symbolic positions. Lacanian feminists have disagreed about whether the phallus inevitably represents the penis or whether it is an empty signifier of difference. The former position implies a linguistic determinism as strong as that of any of the earlier social or biological versions. The French theorists Irigaray and Cixous drew on Derrida to develop a new feminist 'textual practice' based on a destabilising of the self-present symbol of the phallus. While there could be no escape from the signifying chain, they claimed that it was possible to show the gaps and inconsistencies in phallocentric thought and to decentre the stability of the Father. Derrida identified the unmasking of phallic authority with femininity, but it may be argued that he replicates woman's place as the undifferentiated other to man, that it is still Man who gets the attention, even in the hour of his death (Flax 1990: 214–15). Critics of Irigaray have argued that she posits woman as a unified category in just the way she wants to reject (Moi 1985: 142). The 'deconstructive' projects necessarily affirm the structures, social, linguistic or discursive, that they seek to unsettle. Whether they also subvert by creating new meanings may depend on which texts are chosen and how powerful these texts are. As Eve Sedgwick makes clear, structures do not disappear because they have been shown to be unstable; on the contrary, an understanding of their 'irresolvable instability' may lend them discursive authority (1990: 10). Given these problems, many feminists turned away from psychoanalysis altogether towards discourse analysis.

The Foucault effect

By the early 1980s, the debates about both the social and symbolic dimensions of patriarchy had reached a hiatus. The meaning of patriarchy and its relationship to capitalism seemed to pose intractable theoretical problems. Then things shifted quite suddenly as Marxism came under scrutiny from a number of directions broadly associated with poststructuralism and postmodernism. In the early 1980s a number of social theorists were questioning the independent existence of 'the social'. Baudrillard's (1983) formulation was the most extreme: the social has collapsed or imploded and become invisible through a process analogous to that which produced the black holes of astrophysics. The implication of both Foucault's and Lyotard's work was that the social is an effect of power/knowledge relations. All three criticised social theory for its reliance on 'grand narratives', especially narratives of enlightenment and emancipation. The claim was that social reality is not a totality and that any theory necessarily provides only a partial account. Theorists who aimed to provide a total account were now judged authoritarian insofar as they silenced other groups and experiences (Cutler 1979; Laclau and Mouffe 1985).

Feminist theorists of 'patriarchy' were included in this critique. Some of the implications for feminism were articulated in the debate provoked by Donzelot's *The Policing of Families*, published in English in 1980 and very favourably reviewed by Paul Hirst (1981) a year later. Donzelot traced the emergence of the social as a distinct domain, an artefact of a variety of discourses and practices to do with social problems—health, education, poverty, housing—and crucially linked with the familial. He argued that the family had become a site of social interventions rather than a protagonist. Donzelot and Hirst rejected the view that the family was an autonomous or unified entity, or that the modern family could be seen as a part of an unchanging phenomenon of patriarchy and male oppression. The shift from government *by* the family to government *through* the family instead created new possibilities for mothers to empower themselves in alliance with the new professionals, especially doctors, social workers and teachers. The role of the father has shifted, said Hirst, from paterfamilias to being an adequate parent, a support and auxiliary to his wife. He criticised feminism for its anti-family ideology, its denial of the genuine popularity of the family with the majority of women, and its invocation of some alternative set of ideal social relations.

Feminists reacted strongly to both writers. Barrett and McIntosh (1982: 100–104) acknowledged the originality of the work but criticised its functionalism, its failure to attribute agency to the state and its romantic nostalgia for the old patriarchal family. The theory offered new strategic possibilities for feminism but at the price of rejecting any underlying system of patriarchy which constituted 'men' and 'women' as unified categories in a relation of domination and oppression. Well over a decade later, while one feels irritation with the smug superiority that both men convey, their arguments have been substantially accepted. While domestic violence remains a matter of concern, attention has otherwise shifted away from the tyranny of fathers and husbands towards more nuanced accounts of subjectivity and power.

Ironically it was Rosalind Coward, one of the fiercest critics of Donzelot and Hirst, who produced the most exhaustive critique of the concept of patriarchy. Coward (1983) points to our amnesia about the widespread use of the term in the late nineteenth century in forms that were inherited by twentieth-century Marxism, psychoanalysis and anthropology: precisely those theories that were most important for feminism. She traces these theories in considerable detail, starting with Henry Maine's 'Ancient Law' of 1861, which argued that the patriarchal family, though not a biological unit, was the fundamental and universal unit of human society. Bachofen, Engels, and later Freud and Levi-Strauss, treated marriage and family forms as the critical moment in the shift from the animal to the human and assumed men and women were radically different creatures with different interests. Coward argues that the intensification of discussion of the family and kinship in the second half of the nineteenth century created the terms and limitations under which sexual relations are still theorised. Contemporary feminism, in her view, breaks new ground not in theorising patriarchy as a sex–class system but in its efforts to deconstruct sexual identity and the notion of pre-given gender interests.

The critique of patriarchy has been powerfully reinforced by Foucault's more fluid approach to power as 'chain', 'strategy' and 'disjunction' (1980: 88–89). Power works in a capillary fashion from below rather than deriving from the figure of the father/king at the top of the pyramid. Power is not merely coercive but productive and is associated with pleasure and subjectivity. Rather than presenting a history of gender relations or of patriarchy, Foucault gives us a history of sexuality that refuses pre-given identities as men or women and forces us to look at the power/knowledge relations within which subjectivities are constituted. It is possible to be both the subject of and subjected to discursive frameworks. Women actively produce the forms of femininity through which they are also controlled: they are never merely victims.

It may be particularly difficult for women to cut off the head of the king. Patriarchal residues and images of all-powerful fathers have played an important role in most of our childhoods, probably overshadowing any actual relation with our real father. We do not need much psychoanalysis to be aware that the oedipal attachment to the father is a key to the girl child's taking her place in the symbolic order and that fathers retain a powerful hold on women's emotional lives. Rosalind Coward (1993) has suggested that women collude in the maintenance of patriarchal order—insofar as we retain the fantasy of the strong man who will take care of us, rely for our self-esteem on male approval, subtly give men the message that we do not really want them to change, stroke men's egos, and understate our own achievements—and perhaps in overestimating the systematic nature of men's power. Women may even have a vested interest in retaining a notion of 'patriarchy' as a monolithic system at once horrendous and familiar. It is too big to overthrow but we can continue to complain about it and build solidarity with other women in the process.

By overstating the coherence and stability of men's power women may project their psyches onto the social world in ways that are not always appropriate. It is important to continue testing the limits of men's power rather than assume defeat in advance. The glass ceilings may retreat if the will is there. It is also time to reconsider fathers, to stop homogenising them as 'the patriarchy' and automatically identifying the father with disembodied authority—the law, the gaze, the power that exchanges and represents women and appropriates their sexual services. Real fathers, as well as men in general, may be less certain about their powers or identities. They may, as Virginia Woolf suggested, depend on women to function as their magnifying mirrors.

The last decade has seen a turning away from attempts to integrate the monolithic structures of capitalism and patriarchy and a new sense of the need to look at concrete instances of gender domination and its interrelation with class, ethnicity, sexuality, politics and culture—all analysed in the context of their historical development. Patriarchy implies a model of power as interpersonal domination, yet many aspects of women's oppression are constructed diffusely. It is sustained by the whole construction of sexual identity and desire, not necessarily by the literal overpowering of one interest group, women, by another, men. The categories 'man' and 'woman', the building blocks of patriarchy, have come under criticism as essentialist. 'Woman', it has been argued is an unstable entity, historically and discursively constructed, that cannot be relied upon to hold a constant meaning (Riley 1988).

What were once regarded as patriarchy's key institutions, the family and the state, have undergone considerable changes and can no longer be treated as monolithic. The question is not only whether we can talk about the patriarchal family or the patriarchal state, but whether we can talk about 'family' or 'state' at all as coherent or unified entities, let alone protagonists (Pringle and Watson 1992). The modern family retains few of the features of a classic patriarchal structure. People live in a variety of family forms; their experience of family shifts and fluctuates, often incorporating complex relationships with stepchildren and relatives from previous relationships. Women's greater legal, sexual and financial autonomy makes the 'patriarchal nuclear family' an anachronism. Pratt (1993) takes feminists to task for caricaturing the family and argues that it may be a resource a well as a prison. The working-class Canadian families that she studied arrange paid employment sequentially, which gives both men and women periods of sole responsibility for the children. This implies a commonality of experience which might differentiate them less from each other than from people of other classes. To focus on gender alone may repress or marginalise the multiple and contradictory threads in an individual's identity.

My own research into women in the medical profession raises similar questions. The large-scale movement of women into medicine over the last two decades suggests that inroads are also being made into that most patriarchal of institutions. Feminists have not been comfortable with this move because it challenges widely held views that the medical control of women's bodies is a central weapon of contemporary patriarchy. Mary Daly (1978) has used gynaecology as a metaphor for global patriarchy, while feminists of all shades have argued that doctors are women's main enemy, and that they systematically displaced women healers. They have responded to recent changes either by arguing that women, because of their medical training, are just as bad as men (Daly 1978: 277) or by affirming women's subordination within medicine. One of the main researchers in this field, Judith Lorber, entitled a recent paper 'Why women physicians will never be true equals in the American medical profession' (1993). It can readily be shown that women earn less, are cut out of the most prestigious specialties, are poorly represented in powerful administrative and policy areas, and congregate in part-time jobs, locum work, and family planning and public health— areas that do not interest many men. But this is only part of the story. Some feminist historians have begun to view medicine as 'more complicated and less villainous' than previously assumed (Theriot 1993) while the sociologist Mary Ann Elston (1991) suggests that we may be on the threshold of a decline in medical dominance. My research indicates that the presence of women doctors challenges medical power and hierarchy regardless of the personal views of these women (Pringle 1993). Without ignoring continuing inequalities, I believe it is important to identify tactical successes and not imprison women in a permanent no-win situation.

Doctors supposedly embarked on a triumphal march to power from the seventeenth century onwards. But the idea that the brightest members of a generation would automatically want to study medicine is a postwar phenomenon. My older interviewees insist that subjects like classics and mathematics were held in much higher esteem in their day. While consultants retain their prestige, the tide has begun to turn. White male students are not clamouring to get into medicine in the same numbers as they were ten years ago. Critics of medicine are so mesmerised by its power and status that they often overstate them and reinforce what they wish to attack. Undoubtedly for two or three decades after the Second World War medicine reigned supreme, as it seemed finally to be able to cure as well as diagnose. From the discovery of antibiotics to the first heart transplants, medicine exuded glamour and status. Now the romance with modernity is over: medicine is seen as deeply troubled. People are cynical about its claims to cure and 'alternative' therapies have become popular, while social scientists have been busy exposing the concealed power play behind 'professionalism' (Freidson 1970). Feminist critiques both have contributed to and are part of a wider challenge to medical power.

It is unnecessary to invoke a monolithic male conspiracy to say that gender relations have profoundly structured obstetrics and gynaecology and the reproductive technologies that have become available. To portray the relation between women and their doctors as an us/them or male/female battle is far too simple. If feminists operate on the principle that 'the doctor is always wrong', it becomes difficult to establish what the criteria of evaluation are, and this enables doctors easily to dismiss criticism as feminist paranoia. David Silverman suggests that 'medical dominance' is an inappropriate model of doctor–patient relations, for power is not simply a finite quality to be fought over in battles. Both doctors and patients may speak through a variety of discourses. None is intrinsically more liberating than any other (1987: 231–232). It is always a question of the relation between discourses and the context within which they are invoked. A patient can interrupt a discourse on the virtue of high-tech births by demanding 'natural' birth. But she can also disrupt discourses of patient power by demanding advice rather than self-expression, or pain relief rather than autonomy. Similarly, a doctor might assert power by refusing pain relief, or refusing surgical intervention.

The search for overarching 'systems' or 'logics' of oppression is misplaced. Gibson-Graham (1993) has observed that 'capitalism' is still treated respectfully as a noun: global, monopoly, postindustrial or late capitalism. This reinforces the feeling that we can never change it significantly or get outside it: socialism is just capitalism's opposite, a great emptiness on the other side of a membrane. Images of putative ancient matriarchies function rather similarly to reinforce the hegemonic nature of patriarchy and to confirm its identity. If we continue to treat it as a noun we are landed with another omnipresent system that is impossible to change. As Marian Smiley suggests, rather than imposing on 'women' the identities of potential overthrowers of the patriarchal order, it is better to start with practical questions about empowerment and disempowerment. The kinds of generalisations that are appropriate 'do not begin with questions such as "Where do women fit into the system of patriarchy?"' but 'with practical questions geared to finding out how women are disempowered in particular situations' (1993: 113). Sullivan's account of prostitution and Gibson-Graham's of miners' wives in Chapters 13 and 14 develop similar points. Rather than assuming the latter's inevitable failure why not celebrate their more varied political subjectivities and open up a wider variety of possible interventions? It is not a matter of overthrowing the family or the state or the medical profession but of contesting specific instances of power.

The danger is that in our desire to be optimistic we play down very real structures of power. We have to understand the ways in which family, state and professions have moved beyond patriarchy while remaining patriarchal. This can be done, I believe, by combining a more open-ended approach to the 'social' with the insights of deconstruction. Together these approaches make possible a significant destabilisation of patriarchal categories and residues.

Notes

Introduction

1 This striking metaphor was included in an informal talk given by Elizabeth Grosz to the Humanities Research Centre Summer School on 'Feminist Theory and Women's Studies' in February 1994, where most of the papers in this volume were discussed.

Chapter 1

1 Bessie Raynor Parkes to Barbara Leigh Smith Bodichon, n.d., Bessie Raynor Parkes papers, Girton College Library, Box V, item 171. I am indebted to Jacqueline Matthews for this reference.

Chapter 5

1 On the theoretical importance of emphasising failure rather than success in communication, see Ang 1994.
2 For an historical analysis of the construction of this hegemonic masculine identity in imperial Britain, see Hall 1992.
3 While most white feminist critics have come out as Madonna enthusiasts, there are exceptions; see for example Bordo 1993.
4 See, however, Patton 1993.
5 See Kristeva 1991.
6 It should be added that 'whiteness', too, is a structurally impure position, deriving its very meaning from suppressing and othering that which is not white. But while the centre, by virtue of its being the centre, can subsequently repress the marginalised other in its sense of identity, the margin(alised) always has to live under the shadow of the centre and be constantly reminded of its own marginality.
7 For this kind of interrogation by white feminists in Britain and the US, see Ware 1992 and Frankenberg 1993.
8 I would suggest that it is for this reason that the scare campaign against

Mabo relied so much on a populist hysteria focused around 'people's backyards'.

9 For example, I have not come across any discussion about the relation between Asian and Aboriginal women.

10 In this sense, the theme of reconciliation is more important to the peace of mind of white Australians than to Aboriginal people, for whom reconciliation will never compensate for their permanent displacement from their land.

Chapter 7

1 This is an Australian Research Council-funded project being undertaken with Lyndall Ryan, and with the assistance of Barbara Baird and Kylie O'Connell, all of whom I would like to thank for their responses to this essay.

2 Convened by Lesley Johnson and Pru Black at the University of Technology Sydney, November 1991.

Chapter 8

1 Recent texts have considerably expanded knowledge of contemporary art practice by Australian women: Kirby, S. 1992 *Sight Lines: Women's Art and Feminist Perspectives in Australia* Craftsman Press, Sydney; Marsh, A. and Moore, C. 1994 *Indecent Exposures: Twenty Years of Australian Feminist Photography* Allen & Unwin, Sydney. See also Parker and Pollock 1987 (edited pp. 92–93). This contains an extensive dossier of original texts from British feminist art practice.

2 Betty Churcher, National Gallery of Australia and Paula Latos-Valier, Art Gallery of WA, both directors of their museums, are among recent female appointments to the previously masculine pinnacle of curatorship. Only three women have headed art schools in Australia, all since the 1980s: Churcher, Bea Maddock and Alwynne Mackie. Only Maddock is an artist.

3 See the following publications by the Australia Council, Sydney: NSW Women and Arts Festival Research Advisory Group, 1983 *Women in the Arts*; Throsby 1983 and 1986; Women in the Arts Committee 1987; Throsby and Mills 1989. The most recent research is Rogers et al. 1993. *Women and the Arts* 1993 (photocopied paper) Australia Council, Sydney, which identifies Council policies and achievements, and notes increases in women applying for and receiving grants in all art forms; separate figures for the visual arts are not given.

4 The classic statement of this position is Owens 1983: 57–82.

Chapter 13

1 In talking of political subjectivity I draw upon Anna Yeatman's definition of politics as the 'domain of action' (1994: 23) and confine myself to subjectivity as it is constituted in actions of some kind.

2 That is, in relation to 'the political' in the words of Chantal Mouffe (1994: 9).

3 In order to highlight the differences between these two conceptions I am consciously smoothing over the differences within each set of theories and feminisms, creating as I do so my own image of the unity of each. In this essay the term 'structural' is used to refer to those theories that argue for the existence of fundamental, more stable, social relations which underlie the day-to-day contingencies of social life. This usage bears a hereditary relation to theories of linguistic structuralism that has become looser over time. In the latter theories meaning is fixed in a relational system or structure in which the signifier and signified bear a stable and fixed relation within the sign. In poststructuralist theories, the fixity of this relation is severed and each signifier has a potential multiplicity of referents. Within social analysis, poststructuralism dispenses with the concept of fixed structures, with the idea that theory reflects reality, and with the notion that determination originates in those social relations that are 'more' fundamental (Barrett 1992).

4 Indeed, Beatrix Campbell has recently described the British coal miner as the archetypal patriarch. She writes:

> In coal communities . . . men commanded real courage. The colliers' work risked the roof falling in on life itself. The mechanics maintained machines designed to save lives. Death shadowed their everyday life . . . But they wrenched comfort and compensation from women. No group of men has been so sustained by women's self-denial. No group of men has been so cold and confident in its exclusion of women, yet so dependent on their support . . . Coal communities harboured men's animus against women. (Campbell 1993: 16, emphasis added)

Campbell's shocking portrayal is a far cry from the cosy images of closely knit, solidary communities of socialist imagination in which men and women work together against the dangers of nature and corporate control (Dennis et al. 1956). Her description is of a place in which women's oppression is peculiarly accentuated. 'That the face of the coal miner represents traditional, "hegemonic" masculinity reflects another aspect of partriarchal oppression—the culturally enforced exclusion of alternative, "subordinated" masculinities that might be tainted by "feminine" attributes and affect' (Connell 1987: 183).

5 Traditionally the history of female exclusion has been represented as a working-class victory, protecting the gentler sex from the rigours of dangerous and heavy work. More recently, feminist labour historians have documented the murky politics surrounding the liberation of women from underground coal mining work, showing how the exclusion of women allowed for increased wages for male miners and the securing of a labour market position that could not be undercut by unorganised (female) labour (Humphries 1981; John 1984; Metcalfe 1987).

6 This power is seen to be exercised physically, psychologically, emotionally and/or politically.

7 Certainly within socialist feminist discourse. See, for example, Green 1990; Kingsolver 1989; Leonard 1991; Long 1985; Stead 1987; Williams 1981.

8 See Chapter 4 for a discussion of the tense relationship between different emancipatory movements focused upon different sources of oppression.

9 A recent example of what I am talking about is presented by Beatrix Campbell's 1993 latest assessment of the aftermath of the British miners' strike of 1984–85. Her disclosure is designed partly to destabilise established left-wing wisdom about the successful gender politics of the miners' strike and to expose a continuing blind spot crucial to contemporary politics, particularly leftist or progressive politics: that much of what is considered political in the public arena is predicated upon the systematic exclusion of women and non-recognition of their real contributions.

Campbell's specific disappointment comes from the fact that 'The women's movement during the great strikes of the Seventies and Eighties gave miners an alternative welfare system and a moral authority they often seemed to squander' (1993: 16). But her deep anger appears to well from the belief that the squandering and exclusionary practices of male miners result from their 'animus against women'—the enmity or hostility toward women that, consciously or not, forms a basis for their actions. Campbell's analysis points to the structural constitution of subject positions from which political agency operates. In her view the male miner, as a more or less powerful, or 'conscious', agent of the working class, is always also a psychologically, emotionally and politically powerful agent of patriarchy.

In a defiant but resigned manner, Campbell is led by this structural analysis to argue that in the aftermath of the miners' strike, gender oppression won out over class solidarity. Miners' wives contributed the most progressive and innovative working-class actions in the class war only to be defeated in the gender struggle. Indeed, she sees changes in the oppressive gender landscape of British mining communities only now being wrought by the imperatives of capitalist restructuring as more women find themselves in paid employment in these towns than men. Her hope is that the new culture defined by this 'new majority' of women workers will be less exclusionary and oppressive than the old masculine mining culture. In the final analysis, gender relations are seen to be contained 'within' capitalism, and both patriarchy and capitalism are portrayed as entities which are impervious to the political activities of women.

10 See Gibson-Graham 1993 for a critical discussion of this conception of capitalism as a 'container' of all other social relations.

11 The new work practices legislated at that time were designed around those in operation at coal mines in the western United States which are seen to be the 'most efficient' in the world. The international discourse of industrial relations and best practice industry performance which informed this new award contributes to the constitution of another, political economic space of exploitation and oppression on a global scale.

12 This work roster involves dividing the workforce into four groups such that at any time there is one group on each of the day, afternoon, or night shifts (of eight hours in length) and one group off work. Workers labour in each shift for seven consecutive days, afternoons or nights which advance on a rotation from afternoon to day to night. Between each shift, workers have one or two days off, and at the end of the cycle four days off.

13 Today coal miners are the most highly paid 'blue-collar' workers in

Australia and their wages (which can range from $60 000 to over $100 000 a year) far exceed those of many 'white-collar' or professional occupations.

14 This plan is usually abandoned as families find that as their income increases so does their spending and consumption. In fact, the level of saving is minimal and many stay much longer than initially intended (Gibson 1991).

15 This was in the face of opposition to the new award, and all the 'flexible work practices' it introduced, by the miners' union leadership. In this situation the state officials were unable to convince the rank and file that the roster might be detrimental to health and family life.

16 They have been economically militant but not politically. In structural terms, the Central Queensland miners relinquished some portion of the political power they had gained as members of a (mainly economically) militant working-class faction in return for individual economic power (higher wages).

17 The Miners' Women's Auxiliaries are organisations which usually confine their activities to the welfare of miners and their families (particularly during protracted strikes or during and after mining disasters).

18 Revolutionary structural change is an impossibility in this discourse. See Gibson-Graham 1993.

19 See Chapter 15 for a critical discussion of this vision of patriarchy.

20 This anti-essentialist discourse of class constitutes class as a process involving the production, appropriation and distribution of surplus labour. Multiple class processes are seen to coexist and individuals participate in many different class processes (both capitalist and non-capitalist) in the course of their daily lives and lifetimes. See Resnick and Wolff 1987; Fraad et al. 1989; Gibson and Graham 1992; and Gibson 1992 for discussion of this alternative discourse of class. Fraad et al. (1989) call the traditional division of labour in the household in which women perform all the surplus labour and men appropriate it in kind in return for protection and income, among other things, the 'feudal' class process. They contrast this class process with that of the single parent (often a refugee from a traditional household in which a fedual class process was in operation) who produces, appropriates and distributes her own surplus labour, and the communal class process in which a group of people live together, collectively producing, appropriating and distributing their surplus labour. While the gender division male/female has traditionally mapped onto the division feudal appropriator/producer in this household class process, there is no necessary connection between class and gender in this anti-essentialist account. Many gay and lesbian couples may arrange their households to involve a feudal class process, and many heterosexual couples may attempt to construct communal class processes in the home.

21 My research project was partly about allowing women to catch a glimpse of themselves as 'powerful' in the industrial arena, through an elaboration of an alternative discourse of class in the household (Gibson 1992; 1993).

22 Within a poststructuralist perspective, political subjectivity is not bestowed upon the individual by a social structure which is fixed, fundamental and powerful. For some poststructuralists, social structure is dissolved into a multiplicity of discourses, each with its corresponding subject position and political subjectivity then emerges from the unique ways in which the subject is interpellated by a uniquely overdetermined set of discourses. For

others, such as Laclau and Mouffe (1985), social structure becomes those discourses which are constituted as hegemonic by political struggle in a particular time and place.

References

Aitkin, J. 1978 'The prostitute as worker' Women and Labour Conference Papers, pp. 240–248

Alberti, J. 1989 *Beyond Suffrage: Feminists in War and Peace, 1914–1928* Macmillan, London

Allen, J. 1986 'Evidence and silence: Feminism and the limits of history' in *Feminist Challenges: Social and Political Theory* eds Carole Pateman and Elizabeth Grosz, Allen & Unwin, Sydney, pp. 173–178

——1988 'Rose Scott's vision: feminism and masculinity' in *Crossing Boundaries: Feminisms and the Critique of Knowledges* eds B. Caine et al., Allen & Unwin

Andrews, I. 1990 'Music, desire and the social' *New Music Australia* no. 8

Andrews, S. 1979 *Take Your Partners. Traditional Dancing in Australia* 3rd edn, Hyland House, Melbourne

Ang, I. 1994 'In the realm of uncertainty: The global village in the age of capitalist postmodernity' in *Communication Theory Today* eds D. Crowley and D. Mitchell, Polity Press, Oxford

Annear, J. 1993 *Jenny Watson: Paintings with Veils and False Tails* Australian Exhibitions Touring Agency, Melbourne

Apel, W., ed. 1976 *Harvard Dictionary of Music* Heinemann, London

Armstrong, N. 1990 'The occidental Alice' in *Differences* vol. 2, no. 3, pp. 3–41

Arney, I.V. 1987 *Twenties Child. A Childhood Recollection* Collins Dove, Melbourne

Attali, J. 1985 *Noise: The Political Economy of Music* Manchester University Press, Manchester

Attwood, B. 1989 *The Making of the Aborigines* Allen & Unwin, Sydney

Bacon, J. 1976–77 'The real estate industry in women' *Vashti* no. 17, pp. 5–6

Ballaster, R. et al. 1991 *Women's Worlds: Ideology, Femininity and the Woman's Magazine* Macmillan, London, pp. 172–173

Barrett, M. 1980 *Women's Oppression Today* Verso, London

——1992 'Words and things: Materialism and method in contemporary feminist analysis' in *Destabilising Theory* ed. Barrett and Phillips

Barrett, M. and McIntosh, M. 1982 *The Anti-Social Family* Verso, London

Barrett, M. and Phillips, A., eds 1992 *Destabilising Theory* Polity Press, Cambridge

Barry, J. and Flitterman, S. 1980 'Textual strategies: The politics of art-making' in *Lip* 1981–82 (originally published in the British journal *Screen*)

Barthes, R. 1985 'The third meaning' in *Responsibility of Forms: Critical Essays on Music, Art and Representation* Hill and Wang, New York

Bartky, S. 1990 *Femininity and Domination: Studies in the Phenomenology of Oppression* Routledge, New York

Battersby, C. 1989 *Gender and Genius: Towards a Feminist Aesthetics* Indiana University Press, Bloomington (first published by the Women's Press, London)

Baudrillard, J. 1983 *In the Shadow of the Silent Majorities, or, The End of the Social* Semiotext(e), Columbia University Press, New York

——1983 *Simulations* Semiotext(e), New York

Beechey, V. 1979 'On patriarchy' in *Feminist Review* no. 3, pp. 66–82

Beilharz, K. 1993–94 'Is there a woman's aesthetic in musical composition?' *Sounds Australian* vol. 40

Bell, D. 1983 *Daughters of the Dreaming* Allen & Unwin, Sydney

Benedikt, M., ed. 1991 *Cyberspace: First Steps* MIT Press, Cambridge, Mass.

Bennett, R. et al. 1981 'Feminists—The degenerates of the social?' in *Politics and Power* no. 3, pp. 83–92

Benston, M.L. 1988 'Women's voices/men's voices: Technology as language' in *Technology and Women's Voices: Keeping in Touch* ed. C. Kramarae, Routledge & Kegan Paul, New York, pp. 15–28

Bhabha, H. 1991 'The third space' in *Identity: Community, Culture, Difference* ed. J. Rutherford, Lawrence & Wishart, London

Bisset, A. 1979 *Black Roots, White Flowers. A History of Jazz in Australia* Golden Press, Sydney

Black, M. and Coward, R. 1983 'Linguistic, social and sexual relations: A review of Dale Spender's man-made language' in *Screen Education* no. 39, pp. 69–85

Bloom, L.Z. 1978 'Gertrude is Alice is everybody: Innovation and point of view in Gertrude Stein's autobiographies' in *Twentieth Century Literature* vol. 24, no. 1, pp. 82–93

Bolter, J.D. 1984 *Turing's Man: Western Culture in the Computer Age* University of North Carolina Press, Chapel Hill

Bordo, S. 1993 '"Material Girl": The effacements of postmodern culture' in *The Madonna Connection*, ed. C. Schwichtenberg

Bottomley, G. et al. 1991 *Intersexions: Gender/Class/Culture/Ethnicity* Allen & Unwin, Sydney

Boyd, A. (forthcoming) 'Cycle of Love—A quest for wholeness' in Macarthur, S., ed. 'New Music Australia 1992' *Sounds Australian* Sydney

Bradshaw, J. 1972 'The concept of social need' in *New Society* 30 March

Brealey, T. and Newton, P. 1978 'Mining and new towns' CSIRO, Melbourne

Brett, P. 1994 'Musicality, essentialism and the closet' in *Queering the Pitch* eds P. Brett et al., Routledge, New York

Brunsdon, C. 1990 'Television: Aesthetics and audiences' in *Logics of Television* ed. Patricia Mellencamp, Indiana University Press, Bloomington

Bruss, E. 1976 *The Autobiographical Act: The Changing Situation of a Literary Genre* Johns Hopkins University Press, Baltimore

Bulkin, E. et al. 1984 *Yours in Struggle: Three Feminist Perspectives on Anti-Semitism and Racism* Long Haul Press, New York

Butler, J. 1990 *Gender Trouble: Feminism and the Subversion of Identity* Routledge, New York

——1992 'Contingent foundations: Feminism and the question of "postmodernisms"' in *Feminists Theorize the Political* eds J. Butler and J.W. Scott, Routledge, New York

——1992 'The lesbian phallus and the morphological imaginary' in *Differences* vol. 4, no. 1, pp. 133–171

Caine, B. 1992 *Victorian Feminists* Oxford University Press, Oxford

——1994, 'Feminism and political economy in Victorian England' in *Feminism and Political Economy in Victorian England* ed. P. Groenewegen, Edward Elgar, Aldershott

Campbell, B. 1993 'Dependable props of the Ashington pit' in *The Independent* 8 December, p. 16

Carpenter, B. 1994 'The dilemma of prostitution for feminists' in *Social Alternatives* vol. 12, no. 4, pp. 25–28

Castle, V. 1914 *Modern Dancing* Harper, New York

Chesler, P. 1972 *Women and Madness* Doubleday, New York

Chodorow, N. 1978 *The Reproduction of Mothering: Psychoanalysis and the Sociology of Gender* University of California Press, Berkeley

Chow, R. 1991 'Violence in the other country: China as crisis, spectacle, and woman' in *Third World Women and the Politics of Feminism* eds C.T. Mohanty et al., Indiana University Press, Bloomington

Citron, M.J. 1993 *Gender and the Musical Canon* Cambridge University Press, Cambridge

Cockburn, C. 1985 'The material of male power' in *The Social Shaping of Technology* eds D. McKenzie & J. Wajcman, Open University Press, Milton Keynes, pp. 125–146

Connell, R.W. 1983 'How should we theorize patriarchy?' in *Which Way is Up? Essays on Class, Sex and Culture* Allen & Unwin, Sydney, pp. 50–62

——1987 *Gender and Power: Society, the Person and Sexual Politics* Polity Press, Cambridge

Conomos, J. 1993 'Digital art' in *Artlink* vol. 13 no. 1, pp. 57–58

Corballis, M. 1983 *Human Laterality* Academic Press, New York

Cott, N. 1987 *The Grounding of Modern Feminism* Yale University Press, New Haven

Coward, R. 1983 *Patriarchal Precedents: Sexuality and Social Relations* Routledge & Kegan Paul, London

——1984 *Female Desire: Women's Sexuality Today* Collins/Paladin, London

——1993 *Our Treacherous Hearts* Faber & Faber, London

Craik, J. 1992 'Cooking up cultural studies' in *The Knowledge Explosion: Generations of Feminist Scholarship* eds C. Kramerae and D. Spender, Teachers College Press, New York, pp. 89–98

——1990 'Innovative feminism and cultural politics' in *Southern Review* vol. 23, no. 2

Curthoys, A. 1993 'Feminism, citizenship and national identity' in *Feminist Review* no. 44, pp. 19–38

Cusick, S. 1994 'On a lesbian relationship with music: A serious effort not to think straight' in *Queering the Pitch* eds P. Brett et al., Routledge, New York

Cutler, A. et al. 1977 *Marx's 'Capital' and Capitalism Today* Routledge, London

Daly, M. 1978 *Gyn/Ecology* Beacon Press, Boston

Daniels, K. ed. 1984 *So Much Hard Work: Women and Prostitution in Australian History* Fontana Collins, Sydney de Certeau, Michel 1984 *The Practice of Everyday Life* University of California Press, Berkeley

——1988 'Tools for body writing' in *Flesh* special issue of *Intervention* no. 21–22 pp. 7–11

De Lauritis, T. 1988 'Displacing hegemonic discourses: Reflections on feminist theory in the 1980s' in *Inscriptions*, no. 3–4, pp. 127–144

Deaux, K. 1985 'Sex and gender' in *Annual Review of Psychology* vol. 36, pp. 49–81

Delacoste, F. and Alexander, P. 1988 *Sex Work: Writings by Women in the Sex Industry* Virago, London

Deleuze, G. and Guattari, F. 1987 *A Thousand Plateaus: Capitalism and Schizophrenia* University of Minnesota Press, Minneapolis

Delphy, C. 1984 *Close to Home, A Materialist Analysis of Women's Oppression* Hutchinson, London

Dennis, N. et al. 1956 *Coal Is Our life* Eyre and Spottiswoode, London

Derrida, J. 1987 *The Post Card: From Socrates to Freud and Beyond* University of Chicago Press, Chicago

——1987 *The Truth in Painting* University of Chicago Press, Chicago

Donzelot, J. 1980 *The Policing of Families* Hutchinson, London

Doyal, L. and Gough, I. 1982 'Theory of human needs' in *Critical Social Policy* no. 10

——1992 *A Theory of Human Needs* Macmillan, London

Dreyfus, H. 1992 'Heidegger's history of the being of equipment' in *Heidegger: A Critical Reader* eds H. Dreyfus and H. Hall, Blackwell, Oxford, pp. 173–185

Duruz, J. 1994 'Laminex dreams: Women, suburban comfort and the negotiation of meanings' in *Meanjin* vol. 53, no. 1, pp. 99–110

Edwards, P.N. 1990 'The army and the microworld: Computers and the politics of gender identity' in *Signs* vol. 16, no. 1, pp. 102–127

Elston, M.A. 1991 'The politics of professional power: Medicine in a changing health service' in *The Sociology of the Health Service* eds J. Gabe et al. Routledge, London, pp. 58–88

Engh, B. 1993 'Loving it: Music and criticism in Roland Barthes' in *Musicology and Difference: Gender and Sexuality in Musical Scholarship* ed. R.A. Solie, University of California Press, Berkeley

Fausto-Sterling, A. 1992 *Myths of Gender: Biological Theories about Women and Men* (rev. ed.) Basic Books, New York

Feenberg, A. 1990 'Post-industrial discourses' in *Theory, Culture and Society* vol. 19, no. 6, pp. 709–737

Felski, R. 1990 'Kitsch, romance and male paranoia: Stephen King meets the Frankfurt School' in *Continuum* vol. 4, no. 1, pp. 54–70

Ferguson, K. 1993 *The Man Question: Visions of Subjectivity in Feminist Theory* University of California Press, Berkeley

Firestone, S. 1971 *The Dialectic of Sex* Bantam, New York

Fisher, L. 1990 'The 1920s cinema dancers' in *Dance Australia* August–September, pp. 37–40

Fiske, J. 1992 'Cultural studies and the culture of everyday life' in *Cultural Studies* eds L. Grossberg et al., Routledge, New York

Fitzpatrick, K. 1983 *Solid Bluestone Foundations and Other Memories of a Melbourne Girlhood 1908–1928* Macmillan, Melbourne

Flax, J. 1990 'Postmodernism and gender relations in feminist theory', *Feminism/Postmodernism* ed. L. Nicholson, Routledge, New York

——1990 *Thinking Fragments: Psychoanalysis, Feminism, and Postmodernism in the Contemporary West* University of California Press, Berkeley

Fleras, A. and Elliott, J. 1992 *The Nations Within: Aboriginal–State Relations in Canada, the United States and New Zealand* Oxford University Press, Toronto

Flexner, E. 1972 *Century of Struggle: The Women's Movement in the United States* Atheneum, New York

Flynn, B. 1994 'VNS Matrix and Virginia Barratt' Interview in *Electronic Arts in Australia* (special issue) ed. N. Zurbrugg, *Continuum* vol. 8, no. 1, pp. 419–31

Foucault, M. 1977 *Discipline and Punish: The Birth of the Prison* Allen Lane, London

——1978 *The History of Sexuality* vol. 1, Allen Lane, London

——1980 'Two lectures' in *Michel Foucault: Power/Knowledge* ed. C. Gordon, Harvester, London

——1984 'What is enlightenment?' in *The Foucault Reader* ed. P. Rabinow, Penguin, Harmondsworth

——1988 'Practicing criticism' in *Michel Foucault: Politics, Philosophy, Culture. Interviews and Other Writings 1977–1984* ed. L.D. Krtizman, Routledge, New York, pp. 152–156

——1988 'Technologies of the Self' in *Technologies of the Self: A Seminar With Michel Foucault* eds H. Luther et al., University of Massachusetts Press, Amhurst, pp. 16–49

Fraad, H. et al. 1989 'For every knight in shining armor there's a castle waiting to be cleaned: A marxist-feminist analysis of the household' in *Rethinking Marxism* vol. 2, no. 4, pp. 9–69

Frankenberg, R. 1993 *White Women, Race Matters* University of Minnesota Press, Minneapolis

Franks, A.H. 1963 *Social Dance. A Short History* Routledge, London

Franzway, S. et al. 1989 *Staking a Claim: Feminism, Bureaucracy and the State* Polity Press, London

Fraser N. 1987 'Women, welfare and the politics of need interpretation' in *Thesis Eleven* no. 17

——1989 *Unruly Practices: Power, Discourse and Gender in Contemporary Social Theory* Polity Press, Cambridge

Freadman, A. 1979 'POETA (1st. decl., n., fem.)' in *Australian Journal of French Studies* no. 16, part 2, pp. 152–165

Gallop, J. 1988 *Thinking Through the Body* Columbia University Press, New York

Gibson, K. and Graham, J. 1992 'Rethinking class in industrial geography: Creating a space for an alternative politics of class' in *Economic Geography* vol. 68, no. 2, pp. 109–127

Gibson, K.D. 1991 'Company towns and class processes: a study of Queensland's new coalfields' in *Environment and Planning D: Society and Space* vol. 9, no. 3, pp. 285–308

——1992 '"Hewers of cake and drawers of tea": Women, industrial restructuring, and class processes on the coalfields of Central Queensland' in *Rethinking Marxism* vol. 5, no. 4, pp. 29–56

——1993 'Different merry-go-rounds: Families, communities and the seven-day roster' Centre for Women's Studies and Department of Geography and Environmental Science, Monash University, Melbourne

Gibson-Graham, K.J. 1993 'Waiting for the revolution, or how to smash capitalism while working at home in your spare time' in *Rethinking Marxism* vol. 6, no. 2, pp. 10–24

——1994 '"Stuffed if I know": Reflections on postmodern feminist social research' in *Gender, Place and Culture: A Journal of Feminist Geography* vol. 1, no. 2

Gilligan, C. 1982 *In a Different Voice: Psychological Theory and Women's Development* Harvard University Press, Cambridge, Mass.

Goldman, E. 1969 (first published 1911) 'The traffic in women' in her *Anarchism and Other Essays* Dover, New York

Gollan, R. 1963 *The Coalminers of New South Wales* Melbourne University Press, Melbourne

Green, P. 1990 *The Enemy Within: Policing and Class Consciousness in the Miners' Strike* Open University Press, Milton Keynes

Grosz, E. 1986 'What is feminist theory?' in *Feminist Challenges* eds C. Pateman and E. Grosz, Allen & Unwin, Sydney

——1988 *Sexual Subversions* Allen & Unwin, Sydney

——1992–93 'Lived spatiality: Insect space/virtual sex' in *Agenda* nos 26 & 27, pp. 5–8

——1993 'Bodies and knowledges: Feminism and the crisis of reason' in *Feminist Epistemologies* eds L. Alcoff and E. Potter, Routledge, New York, pp. 187–215

——(forthcoming) 'Ontology and equivocation: Derrida's politics of sexual difference' in *Derrida and Feminism* ed. N. Holland, University of Texas Press, Houston

Gunew, S. 1988 'Home and away: Nostalgia in Australian (migrant) writing' in *Island in the Stream: Myths of Place in Australian Culture* ed. P. Foss, Pluto Press, Sydney

——1993 'Feminism and the politics of irreducible differences: Multicultural-ism/ethnicity/race' in *Feminism and the Politics of Difference* eds S. Gunew and A. Yeatman, Allen & Unwin, Sydney

——1993a, 'Multicultural multiplicities: US, Canada, Australia' in *Cultural Studies: Pluralism and Theory* ed. D. Bennett, Melbourne University Press, Melbourne

Gunew, S. and Yeatman, A. eds 1993 *Feminism and the Politics of Difference* Allen & Unwin, Sydney

Hall, C. 1992 *White, Male and Middle Class* Polity Press, Oxford

Hamilton, C. 1935 *Life Errant* London

Hanslick, E. 1854 (reprinted 1957) *The Beautiful in Music* Bobbs-Merrill, Indianapolis

Haraway, D. 1988 'Situated knowledges: The science question in feminism and the privilege of partial perspective' in *Feminist Studies* vol. 14, no. 3, pp. 575–599

——*Simians, Cyborgs and Women: The Reinvention of Nature* Routledge, New York

Hartmann, H. 1981 'The unhappy marriage of marxism and feminism: Towards a more progressive union' in *Women and Revolution* ed. L. Sargent, Pluto Press, London

Hayles, N.K. 1992 'Gender encoding in fluid mechanics: Masculine channels and feminine flows' in *Differences* vol. 4, no. 2, pp. 16–44

Heidegger, M. 1927 (reprinted 1962) 'The worldhood of the world' in *Being and Time* Harper & Row, New York, pp. 95–122

———1977 *The Question Concerning Technology and Other Essays* Harper Torchbooks, New York

Heim, M. 1992 'The erotic ontology of cyberspace' in *Cyberspace: First Steps* ed. M. Benedikt, MIT Press, Cambridge, Mass., pp. 59–80

Helsel, S.K. and Roth, J.P. eds 1991 *Virtual Reality: Theory, Practice and Promise* Meckler, London

Hewitson, G. 1994 'Rational economic man: A feminist evaluation' School of Economics Discussion Paper 1/94, La Trobe University, Melbourne

Hirst, P. 1981 'The genesis of the social' in *Politics and Power* vol. 3, pp. 67–82

Hollinshead, M. 1963 *Some Professional Dancers of, or from, Queensland and some Teachers of the Past and Present* W.R. Smith & Patterson, Brisbane

Hollway, W. 1984 'Gender difference and the production of subjectivity' in *Changing the Subject* eds J. Henriques et al. Methuen, London

hooks, b. 1984 *Feminist Theory: From Margin to Center* South End Press, Boston

———1990 *Yearning: Race, Gender and Cultural Politics* South End Press, Boston

———1992 *Black Looks: Race and Representation* South End Press, Boston

Hooton, J. 1990 *Stories of Herself When Young. Autobiographies of Childhood by Australian Women* Oxford University Press, Melbourne

Horn, P.L. and Pringle, M.B. 1984 *The Image of the Prostitute in Modern Literature* Frederick Ungar, New York

Hughes, R. 1993 in *Time Magazine* June 28

Humphries, J. 1981 'Protective legislation, the capitalist state, and working class men' in *Feminist Review* vol. 7, pp. 1–33

Huws, U. 1985 'Terminal isolation: The atomisation of work and leisure in the wired society' in *Radical Science* no. 16, pp. 9–25

Huyssen, A. 1986 'Mass culture as woman: Modernism's Other' in *Studies in Entertainment* ed. Tania Modleski, Indiana University Press, Bloomington, pp. 188–207

Ihde, D. 1990 'Program One: A phenomenology of technics' in *Technology and the Lifeworld* Indiana University Press, Bloomington, pp. 72–115

Innis, R. 1984 'Technics and the bias of perception' in *Philosophy and Social Criticism* vol. 10, no. 1, pp. 67–89

Irigaray, L. 1985a 'Is the subject of science sexed?' in *Cultural Critique* vol. 1, no. 1, pp. 73–88

———1985b *This Sex Which is Not One* Cornell University Press, Ithaca

Jackson, S. and Otto, D., 1980 'From delicacy to dilemma: A feminist perspective' in *So Much Hard Work* ed. K. Daniels

Jacobs, P. and Landau, S. 1966 *The New Radicals* Penguin, Harmondsworth

Jansen, S.C. 1989 'Gender and the information society: A socially structured silence' in *Journal of Communication* vol. 39, no. 3, pp. 196–215

John, A. 1984 *By the Sweat of their Brows: Women Workers in Victorian Coalmines* Routledge & Kegan Paul, London

Johnson, B. 1980 *The Critical Difference: Essays in the Rhetoric of Contemporary Reading* Johns Hopkins University Press, Baltimore

———1987 *The Oxford Companion to Australian Jazz* Oxford University Press, Melbourne

Johnson, L. 1993 *The Modern Girl* Allen & Unwin, Sydney

Jolly, M. 1991 'The politics of difference: Feminism, colonialism and the decolonisation of Vanuatu' in *Intersexions* eds G. Bottomley et al.

Jones, A. and Guy, C. 1993 'Radical feminism in New Zealand: From Piha to

Newtown' in *Feminist Voices: Women's Studies Texts for Aotearoa/New Zealand* eds P. Bunkle et al. Oxford University Press, Auckland

Kingsolver, B. 1989 *Holding the Line: Women in the Great Arizona Mine Strike of 1983* ILR Press, Ithaca

Kingston, B. 1977 'Rediscovering old women's magazines' *Lip*, no. 2, pp. 27–33

Kirby, V. 1993 "Feminisms, reading, postmodernisms": Rethinking complicity' in *Feminism and the Politics of Difference* eds S. Gunew and A. Yeatman, Allen & Unwin, Sydney

Kirkup, G. and Keller, L.S. eds 1992 *Inventing Women: Science, Technology and Gender* Polity Press/Open University, Cambridge

Kramarae, C., ed. 1988 *Technology and Women's Voices: Keeping in Touch* Routledge & Kegan Paul, London

Kristeva, J. 1991 *Strangers to Ourselves* Columbia University Press, New York

Kuhn, A. and Wolpe, A. eds 1978 *Feminism and Materialism* Routledge & Kegan Paul, London

Laclau, E. and Mouffe, C. 1985 *Hegemony and Socialist Strategy* Verso, London

Landes, J. (1988) *Women and the Public Sphere in the Age of the French Revolution* Cornell University Press, Ithaca and London

Le Doeuff, M. 1989 *The Philosophical Imaginary* Stanford University Press, Stanford

Lees, S. and Senyard, J. 1987 *The 1950s* Hyland House, Melbourne

Lejeune, P. 1971 *L'autobiographie en France* Armand Collin, Paris

——1975 *Le pacte autobiographique* Armand Collin, Paris

Leonard, A. 1991 'Women in struggle: A case study in a Kent mining community' in *Working Women: International Perspectives on Labour and Gender Ideologies* eds N. Redclift and M.T. Sinclair, Routledge, London

LeVay, S. 1993 *The Sexual Brain* MIT Press, Cambridge, Mass.

Lewin, M. 1984 *In the Shadow of the Past: Psychology Portrays the Sexes* Columbia University Press, New York

Lloyd, G. 1984 *The Man of Reason. 'Male' and 'Female' in Western Philosophy* Methuen, London

Locke, J. (reprinted 1960) *Two Treatises of Government* Mentor, New York

Long, P. 1985 'The women of the Colorado fuel and iron strike' in *Women, Work and Protest: A Century of US Women's Labor History* ed. R. Milkman, Routledge and Kegan Paul, Boston

Lorber, J. 1993, 'Why women physicians will never be true equals in the American medical profession' in *Gender, Work and Medicine* eds E. Riska and K. Wegar, Sage, London

Macarthur, S. 1991 'Ripping the beard off analysis: Writing Moya Henderson and Gillian Whitehead into the discourse' in *Sounds Australian* no. 31, Spring

——1992 'Celebrating difference at the gender and music conference' in *Sounds Australian* no. 33, Autumn

——(1993–94) 'Feminism and music: The female energy in Anne Boyd's Cycle of Love' in *Sounds Australian* no. 40

MacCannell, J.F. 1991 *The Regime of the Brother. After the Patriarchy* Routledge, London

McClary, S. 1991 *Feminine Endings: Music, Gender and Sexuality* University of Minnesota Press, Minneapolis

——1993 'Reshaping a discipline: Musicology and feminism in the 1990s' in *Feminist Studies* vol. 19, no. 2

McCracken, E. 1993 *Decoding Women's Magazines* St Martin's Press, New York

McDonough, R. and Harrison, R. 1978 'Patriarchy and relations of production' in *Feminism and Materialism* eds Kuhn and Wolpe

McGuinn, N. 1978 'Eliot and Mary Wollstonecraft' in *The Nineteenth-Century Woman: Her Cultural and Physical World* eds S. Delamont and L. Duffin, Croom Helm, London, pp. 188–205

McIntosh, M. 1978 'The state and the oppression of women' in *Feminism and Materialism* eds Kuhn and Wolpe

McKay, A. 1988 'Speaking up: Voice amplification and women's struggle for public expression' in *Technology and Women's Voices: Keeping in Touch* ed. C. Kramarae, Routledge & Kegan Paul, London, pp. 187–206

McRobbie, A. 1991 *Feminism and Youth Culture* Unwin Hyman, Boston

Mackinnon, C. 1987 *Feminism Unmodified: Discourses on Life and Law* University of Harvard Press, Cambridge, Mass.

Mani, L. 1989 'Multiple mediations: Feminist scholarship in the age of multinational reception' in *Inscriptions* no. 5, pp. 1–25

Marcus, J. 1992 'Fighting bodies, fighting words: A theory and politics of rape prevention' in *Feminists Theorize the Political* eds J. Butler and J.W. Scott, Routledge, New York

Marsden, D. 1912 'The woman movement and the "ablest socialists"' *The Freewoman,* vol. 2, p. 285

Marsh, A. 1993 *Body and Self: Performance Art in Australia* Oxford University Press, Melbourne

Martin, E. 1987 *The Woman in the Body: A Cultural Analysis of Reproduction* Open University Press, Milton Keynes

Martin, J. 1991 'Multiculturalism and feminism' in *Intersexions* eds G. Bottomley et al.

Martineau, H. (1877 repr. 1983) *Autobiography* vol. 1, Virago, London

Matisse et al. 1935 'Testimony against Gertrude Stein' suppl. to *Transition* no. 23, p. 18

Matthews, J.J. 1983 'The proletarian's wife' in *Politics* vol. 18, no. 2, pp. 104–107

Mednick, M.T. & Weissman, H.J. 1975 'The psychology of women: selected topics' in *Annual Review of Psychology* vol. 26, pp. 1–18

Metcalfe, A. 1987 'Manning the mines: Organising women out of class struggle' in *Australian Feminist Studies* vol. 4, Autumn, pp. 73–96

——1988 *For Freedom and Dignity: Historical Agency and Class Structures in the Coalfields of NSW* Allen & Unwin, Sydney

——1994 'Power, knowledge and subjectivity: The making of economic crisis in the Hunter Valley' unpublished manuscript, School of Sociology, University of New South Wales

Middleton, V. 1982 '*Three Guineas*: Subversion and survival in the professions' in *Twentieth Century Literature* vol. 28, pp. 400–21

Miller, C. 1983 *Season of Learning. An Autobiography* Fremantle Arts Centre Press, Fremantle

Miller, J. 1990 *Seductions: Studies in Reading and Culture* Virago, London

Miller, N.K. 1982 'For a dialectics of identification: Women's autobiography in France' in *Women and Language in Literature and Society* eds S. McConnell-Ginet et al., Praeger, New York, pp. 258–273

Millett, K. 1972 *Sexual Politics* Abacus, London

Mitchell, J. 1975 *Psychoanalysis and Feminism* Penguin, Harmondsworth

Mohanty, C. 1984 'Under Western eyes: Feminist scholarship and colonial discourses' in *Boundary 2* vol. 13, no. 1, pp. 333–358

——1989 'On race and voice: Challenges for liberal education in the 1990s' in *Cultural Critique* no. 14, pp. 179–208

Moi, T. 1985 *Sexual/Textual Politics* Feminist Literary Theory Methuen, London

Moir, A. and Jessel, D. 1991 *Brain Sex: The Real Difference Between Men and Women* Carol Publishing Group, New York

Morris, M. 1979 'Aspects of current French feminist literary criticism' in *Hecate* vol. 5, no. 2, pp. 63–72

——1988a 'Things to do with shopping centres' in *Grafts: Feminist Cultural Criticism* ed. S. Sheridan, Verso, London, pp. 193–225

——1988b 'Banality in cultural studies' in *Discourse* vol. 10, no. 2, pp. 3–29

——1990 'A small serve of spaghetti' *Meanjin* vol. 49, no. 3, pp. 470–480

——1992 'Cultural studies' in *Beyond the Disciplines: The New Humanities* ed. K.K. Ruthven, Occasional Paper no. 13, Australian Academy of the Humanities, Canberra, pp. 1–21

——1992 'Afterthoughts on "Australialism"' in *Cultural Studies* vol. 6, no. 3, pp. 468–475

Mouffe, C. 1994 'Post-Marxism, democracy and identity' in *Environment and Planning D: Society and Space* (forthcoming)

Mulvey, L. 1975 'Visual pleasure and narrative cinema' in *Screen* vol. 16, no. 3, pp. 6–18

Mumford, L. 1966 *Technics and Human Development* Harcourt Brace, New York, pp. 63–81

Nead, L. 1992 'Theorizing the female nude' in *The Female Nude: Art, Obscenity and Sexuality* Routledge, London

NSW Women and Arts Festival Research Advisory Group, 1983 *Women in the Arts* Australian Council, Sydney

Nye, A. 1989 *Feminist Theory and the Philosophies of Man* Routledge, New York

O'Leary, J. 1993 'Prostitution as sex work—A step forward or backwards' unpublished paper

Offen, Karen, 1988 'Defining feminism: A comparative historical approach' *Signs* vol. 14, pp. 119–157

Olalquiaga, C. 1992 *Megalopolis: Contemporary Cultural Sensibilities* University of Minnesota Press, Minneapolis

Ong, A. 1988 'Colonialism and modernity: Feminist re-presentations of women in non-Western societies' in *Inscriptions* no. 3–4, pp. 79–93

Overall, C. 1992 'What's wrong with prostitution' in *Signs* vol. 17, no. 4, pp. 705–724

——1994 'Reply to Shrage' in *Signs* vol. 19, no. 2, pp. 571–575

Owens, C. 1983 'The discourse of others: Feminism and postmodernism' in *The Anti-Aesthetic: Essays on Postmodernism* ed. H. Foster, Bay Press, Port Townsend, Wash., pp. 57–82

Parker, R. and Pollock, G. eds 1987 *Framing Feminism: Art and the Women's Movement 1970–1985* Pandora Press, London

Parlee, M.B. 1975 'Psychology: Review essay' in *Signs* vol. 1, no. 1, pp. 119–138

——1979 'Psychology and women: Review essay' in *Signs* vol. 5, no. 1, pp. 121–133

——1991 'Happy birth-day to *Feminism and Psychology*' in *Feminism and Psychology* vol. 1, no. 1, pp. 39–48

Pasquier, M-C. 1981 'Gertrude Stein, l'ecriture et l'exile' in *Les temps modernes* no. 417, pp. 1816–1834

Pateman, C. 1988 *The Sexual Contract* Polity Press Cambridge

Patton, C. 1993 'Embodying subaltern memory: Kinesthesia and the problematics of gender and race' in *The Madonna Connection* ed. C. Schwichtenberg

Peiss, K. 1990 'Commercial leisure and the "Woman Question"' in *For Fun and Profit. The Transformation of Leisure into Consumption* ed. R. Butsch, Temple University Press, Philadelphia

Perkins, R. 1991 *Working Girls: Prostitutes, Their Life and Social Control* Australian Institute of Criminology, Canberra

Pettman, J. 1992 *Living in the Margins* Allen & Unwin, Sydney

Plant, S. 1994 'Cybernetic hookers' paper presented at Adelaide Festival Artists' Week; reprinted in *Australian Network for Art and Technology Newsletter* April–May, pp. 4–8

Poster, M. 1990 *The Mode of Information: Poststructuralism and Social Context* Polity Press, London

Pratt, G. 1993 'Reflections on poststructuralism and feminist empirics, theory and practice' *Antipode* vol. 25, no. 1, pp. 51–63

Pringle, R. 1988 'Socialist feminism in the Eighties' *Australian Feminist Studies* no. 6, pp. 21–32

——1993 'Glittering prizes: Gender and gynaecology' Paper to Women and Technology Seminar, Women's Studies Centre, University of Sydney, May

Pringle, R. and Watson, S. 1992 '"Women's interests" and the poststructural state' in *Destabilising Theory* eds M. Barrett and A. Phillips, Polity Press, Cambridge

Probyn, E. 1993 *Sexing the Subject: Gendered Positions in Cultural Studies* Routledge, London

Resnick, S. and Wolff, R. 1987 *Knowledge and Class: A Marxian Critique of Political Economy* University of Chicago Press, Chicago

Rheingold, H. 1991 *Virtual Reality* Summit Books, New York

Riley, D. 1988 *'Am I that Name?' Feminism and the Category of 'Women' in History* Macmillan, London

Robinson, H. 1989 'Family versus money' in *Newcastle Herald* 18 February, p. 7

Rogers, L. 1988 'Biology, the popular weapon: Sex differences in cognitive function' in *Crossing Boundaries* eds B. Caine et al., Allen & Unwin, Sydney, pp. 43–51

Rogers, V. et al. 1993 *What Difference Does it Make? A Pilot Study of Women in the Performing and Visual Arts in Western Australia* Australia Council and WA Department for the Arts

Roife, K. 1993 *The Morning After* Hamish Hamilton, London

Rose, J. 1986 'Femininity and its discontents' in *Sexuality in the Field of Vision* Verso, London, pp. 83–103

Rose, N. 1993 'Government, authority and expertise in advanced liberalism' in *Economy and Society* vol. 22, no. 3, pp. 283–299

Ross, E. 1970 *A History of the Miners' Federation of Australia* Australasian Coal and Shale Employees' Federation, Sydney

Rowbotham, S. 1972 *Women, Resistance and Revolution* Allen Lane, London

——1981 'The trouble with patriarchy' *No Turning Back, Writings from the Women's Liberation Movement 1975–1980* eds Feminist Anthology Collective, The Women's Press, London

Russell, D. 1925 *Hypatia, or Woman and Knowledge* Kegan Paul, London

Russo, A. 1991 '"We cannot live without our lives": White women, antiracism and feminism' in *Third World Women and the Politics of Feminism* eds C.T. Mohanty et al., Indiana University Press, Bloomington

Schmitz, N. 1978 'Portrait, patriarchy, mythos: The revenge of Gertrude Stein' in *Salmagundi* no. 40, pp. 69–91

Schwichtenberg, C. ed. 1993 *The Madonna Connection: Representational Politics, Subcultural Identities and Cultural Theory* Allen & Unwin, Sydney

Scutt, J. 1979 'The economics of sex: Women in service' in *Australian Quarterly* vol. 51, no. 1, pp. 32–46

Sedgwick, E. 1990 *Epistemology of the Closet* University of California Press, Berkeley

Shields, S. 1975 'Functionalism, Darwinism and the psychology of women: A study in social myth' in *American Psychologist* vol. 30, pp. 739–754

Shrage, L. 1989 'Should feminists oppose prostitution?' in *Ethics* no. 99, pp. 347–361

——1994 'Comment on Overall's "What's wrong with prostitution? Evaluating sex work"' in *Signs* vol. 19, no. 2, pp. 564–570

Silverman, D. 1987 *Communication and Medical Practice* Sage, London

Simon, L. 1977 *The Biography of Alice B. Toklas* Peter Owen, London

Smart, C. 1984 *The Ties That Bind: Law, Marriage and the Reproduction of Patriarchal Relations* Routledge, London

——1989 *Feminism and the Power of Law* Routledge, London

Smiley, M. 1993 'Feminist theory and the question of identity' in *Women and Politics* vol. 13(2), pp. 91–122

Sofia, Z. 1992a 'Virtual corporeality: A feminist perspective' *Australian Feminist Studies* no. 15, pp. 11–24

——1992b 'Hegemonic irrationalities and psychoanalytic cultural critique' in *Cultural Studies* vol. 6, no. 3, pp. 376–394

——1993 *Whose Second Self? Gender and (Ir)Rationality in Computer Culture* Deakin University Press, Geelong

Solie, R.A. 1991 'What do feminists want? A reply to Pieter van den Toorn' in *Journal of Musicology* vol. 9, no. 4

Spellman, E. 1988 *Inessential Woman: Problems of Exclusion in Feminist Thought* Beacon Press, Boston

Squires, P. 1990 *Antisocial Policy* Harvester Wheatsheaf, London

Stead, J. 1987 *Never the Same Again: Women and the Miners' Strike 1984–85* The Women's Press, London

Stein, G. 1966 (reprinted 1983) *The Autobiography of Alice B. Toklas* Penguin, Harmondsworth

——1985 *Everybody's Autobiography* Virago, London

Stimpson, C.R. 1986 'Gertrude Stein and the transposition of gender' in *The Poetics of Gender* ed. N.K. Miller, Columbia University Press, New York, pp. 1–18

Stone, A. 1991 'Will the real body please stand up? Boundary stories about virtual cultures' in *Cyberspace: First Steps* ed. M. Benedikt, MIT Press, Cambridge, Mass., pp. 81–118

Sullivan, B. 1991 'The business of sex: Australian government and the sex industry' in *Australian and New Zealand Journal of Sociology* vol. 27, no. 1, pp. 3–18

Summers, A. 1975 *Damned Whores and God's Police. The Colonization of Women in Australia* Allen Lane, London

The Graphic of Australia 6 May 1920 'Girls' gossip' p. 9
——11 March 1920 'Girls' gossip' p. 9
The Victorian Dancing News various issues 1933–38
Theriot, N. 1993 'Women's voices in nineteenth-century medical discourse: A step toward deconstructing science' in *Signs* vol. 19 no. 1, pp. 1–31
Throsby, D. 1983, *The Artist in Australia Today*, Australia Council, Sydney
——1986 *Occupational and Employment Characteristics of Artists* Australia Council, Sydney
Throsby, D. and Mills, D. 1989, *When Are You Going to get a Real Job?* Australia Council, Sydney
Townsend, H. 1988 *Baby Boomers* Penguin, Ringwood
Townsend, P. 1979 *Poverty in the United Kingdom* Penguin, Harmondsworth
Treichler, P. 1988 'AIDS, homophobia and biomedical discourse: an epidemic of signification' in *AIDS: Cultural Analysis, Cultural Activism* ed. D. Crimp, MIT Press, Cambridge, Mass.
Tucker, M. et al. 1994 *Bad Girls* (exhibition catalogue) The New Museum of Contemporary Art, New York
Turkle, S. 1988 'Computational reticence: Why women fear the intimate machine' in *Technology and Women's Voices: Keeping in Touch* ed. C. Kramarae, Routledge & Kegan Paul, New York, pp. 41–61
Turkle, S. and Papert, S. 1990 'Epistemological pluralism: Styles and voices within the computer culture' in *Signs* vol. 16, no. 1, pp. 128–57
Ussher, J.M. 1989 *The Psychology of the Female Body* Routledge, London
van den Toorn, P.C. 1991 'Politics, feminism, and contemporary music theory' in *Journal of Musicology* vol. 9, no. 3
Vaughter, R.M. 1976 'Psychology: Review essay' in *Signs* vol. 2, no. 1, pp. 120–146
Vicinus, M. 1985 *Independent Women Work and Community for Single Women, 1850–1920* University of Chicago Press, Chicago
Wajcman, J. 1991 *Feminism Confronts Technology* Allen & Unwin, Sydney
Walby, S. 1990 *Theorizing Patriarchy* Blackwell, Oxford
Wallerstein, I. 1974 *The Modern World System* Academic Press, London
Ware, V. 1992 *Beyond the Pale: White Women, Racism and History* Verso, London
Watson, S. 1988 *Accommodating Inequality: Gender and Housing* Allen & Unwin, Sydney
——ed. 1990 *Playing the State* Verso, London
Weisstein, N. 1971 *Psychology Constructs the Female* New England Free Press, Sommerville
Whitford, M. 1991 *Luce Irigaray: Philosophy in the Feminine* Routledge, London
Wilkinson, S. (ed.) 1986 *Feminist Social Psychology: Developing Theory and Practice* Open University Press, Milton Keynes
Williams, C. 1981 *Open Cut: The Working Class in an Australian Mining Town* Allen & Unwin, Sydney
Winship, J. 1983 '"*Options*—For the Way You Want to Live Now", or a magazine for Superwoman' in *Theory, Culture and Society* vol. 1, no. 3
——1990 *Baby Boomers—The Picture Show* Film Australia and ABC
Women in the Arts Committee 1987 *Women in the Arts* Australia Council, Sydney
Wood, E. 1980 'Women and music' in *Signs* vol. 6, no. 2
——1993–94 'Who's calling whose tune? Voice, subjectivity and authority in musicology today' in *Sounds Australian* vol. 40
Woolf, V. 1938 (repr. 1979) *Three Guineas* Penguin, Harmondsworth

Yeatman, A. 1993 'Voice and representation in the politics of difference' in *Feminism and the Politics of Difference* eds S. Gunew and A. Yeatman, Allen & Unwin, Sydney

Yeatman, A. 1994 'Feminism and power' *New Zealand Women's Studies Journal* (forthcoming)

Young, I. 1990 *Justice and the Politics of Difference* Princeton University Press, Princeton

Young, I. 1990 *Throwing Like a Girl and Other Essays in Feminist Philosophy and Social Theory* Indiana University Press, Bloomington

Index